DIARY OF A BECKWATCHER

JOHN FOSTER

 www.trafford.com

North America & international
toll-free: 1 888 232 4444 (USA & Canada)
phone: 250 383 6864 ♦ fax: 812 355 4082

"For the intrepid Salmon and Sea trout, long may they survive"

The persons described in this book are based
on real characters of different name, but are not
definitive descriptions of real personalities and their
actions; although the story is based on true events
it does not in anyway accurately reflect known
individual's actions. Some of the main place names
have been changed to facilitate the storyline

1

THE BEGINNING

It was lunchtime, a July day in the hottest ever summer of 1976. The first fish I ever saw caught by foul means was an ill-fated sea trout squirted through the greedy hands of Jez Bergerac like a bar of soap in a lazy bath, subsequently vanishing in the heat with the villain and his disciples. I had prepared mentally over and over in my mind for this baptism, nevertheless the reality hit me like a bomb. I was alone in the middle of Brockley oblivious to the world and its inhabitants, hopelessly exposed to the situation and witnessing the first such act of many I would encounter over the next thirty years. I stood rooted, watching, sweating, and clutching my binoculars. I was fixed to the spot pondering over what to do next. I was terrified, my heart racing fuelled by adrenaline and powered by fear, however this was a feeling I would learn to accept and even crave. I never saw that fish again, but the lad who caught it that day crossed my path many times during subsequent years.

I was twenty-six years old and learned a huge lesson that day, catching poachers was a serious business and I had just shown a streak of ineffectiveness which asked burning questions over my moral fiber and capability to do the job. I felt very vulnerable to what was the beginning of a very extensive and exciting learning curve.

I suppose I am lucky in a way because I got a second chance or a life change, which ever way you want to look at it. Before I embarked on a life as a water bailiff I had a career in farming that spanned ten years from school leaving age until I was 26. My childhood was always associated with the countryside and especially anything to do with nature and wildlife. I can remember being encouraged by various school teachers in the nineteen fifties, influenced by those wonderful shell (Oil Company) wall charts that adorned the classroom depicting every kind of wild creature to be found in the British Isles. Some depicted woodlands, others portrayed moorland or wetland with all the creatures pictured in close proximity, seemingly living in ridiculous harmony. I even managed to scrounge some tatty copies at the end of term to hang on my bedroom wall. Nature walks were a regular excursion in the school curriculum back then, usually at least once per week. My childhood centered round life in a Cheshire village close to Stockport so I was near to the real world of the town and city but had all the advantages of the countryside to appreciate. I even used to visit local farms and try to help with milking and hay making, I don't suppose that would be allowed today, they regularly still used horses and farm machinery was at a very basic stage. My main interest though was bird watching and I took part in all the associated activities that boys did in those days such as egg collecting, I even hand reared successfully a magpie and then a blackbird chick both recklessly taken from the nest at a very tender age. Surprisingly enough both survived and returned to the wild. They were innocent days when a lad could go out with his mates at nine o clock in the morning and not return until five or six o clock at night. Parents rarely became concerned unless of course you were late for tea, then a clip round the ear was expected and duly received. Everyone was safe baring the usual scrapes and bruises of course. The teenage years were the same except for girls and football of course and my life long love affair with Manchester United. This was fuelled by my Dads enthusiastic guidance and of course the Munich air disaster. I became a regular at Old Trafford nourished by Law, Best, and Charlton.

I never did any fishing surprisingly apart from tickle the odd trout in a Cheshire stream, and then cremate it on a campfire; this was considered pretty cool at the time I can tell you.

In 1965 at the tender vulnerable age of 16 with only two O levels my family moved to Ainstable a village in Cumbria between Penrith and Carlisle, my Fathers Company in Manchester had merged with its sister company in Carlisle, changing my life completely. There was much angst and debate about my future. I was desperately offered a job on a hill farm at Croglin in conjunction with attending the agricultural college at Penrith one day per week. It was there I was taught animal husbandry by Bob Harmer from Brockley who would be a big influence in years to come in a very different way.

I enjoyed my year on the hill farm although the long hours and hard work came as a bit of a shock to a tender young lad from Cheshire. I knew that whatever profession or job I undertook the outdoors would have to be my main environment.

The following year was spent at Newton Rigg Agricultural College; it was there I learnt my trade and also everything going concerning girls, drink, and music. This is how it was in the swinging sixties when just released from home for the very first time. Luckily I was part of this wonderful social revolution when young people broke free, drinking every night in the local pubs around Penrith. I loved playing the Duke boxes filled with on going exuberant music. Little did we know most of those prolific tunes would last for ever.

In 1968 after gaining my certificate I moved to a farm in Brockley and have remained in that part of the world or thereabouts in south Lakeland ever since. I may even now be classed as a local. I was employed on several farms and even worked for a Lord on his estate as herdsman with pedigree Ayrshires. I got my girlfriend into trouble before we married. This situation was quite common back then and my own parents were a bit upset to say the least. I finally married Georgina, we had two sons and my Father in law strangely enough was the Head Water Bailiff in south Lakes. This was the passport to a new career, but of course I didn't know that at the time.

The chance to switch occupations did not materialize until 1976. I had spent ten years in farm work; the opportunities as a career were not brilliant with a sixty to seventy hour week and punishing routine. The prospects were not exactly lined with gold. I wouldn't say I was unhappy because that would be a lie. The skills and experience I gained during those years I would recommend to any young lad leaving school. The diverse range of jobs amongst animals and machinery together with the responsibilities of being in charge at times was unique. Not to mention the improvisation, mend and make do attitude so common amongst farmers then. I would suspect that situation still remains to this day.

The Job as a Water Bailiff I had not considered ever before, because frankly I knew nothing about it until I was married and even considered it a bit of a cushy number, especially from the outside looking in. The Bailiffs including my Father in law often seemed to spend much of their time sat in his house drinking tea. I was not an angler and never had been. I realized listening to my Father in law Joe Marwood relating his various tales of the river bank that my opinion was changing toward what looked like an easier and more diverse job with the bonus of a shorter working week. The whole scenario seemed very appealing considering my young family. There was of course a dangerous side to the job to consider as catching poachers was no picnic; I had even accompanied Joe to see the dreadful aftermath of a "cymagging" incident on the R Leven at Newby Bridge. This had involved the use of cyanide designed to gas rabbits. That particular chemical was easily obtained in those days, but when applied to a watercourse the effects were staggering. The oxygen depletion in the water killed everything, including in this case over one thousand salmon and sea trout ranging from around half a pound up to twenty or even more. The result was Armageddon for the river. The sight of those fish floating dead on the surface over more than a mile of river was a graphic eye opener that had a big influence on my opinion of the poaching fraternity. The perpetrators of this crime would only be capable of taking what they could carry away in a short desperate sortie. This would probably be only about one per cent of the kill; the rest just left to rot. I helped the Bailiffs that day pick and bury all these fish. The river would not recover for many years to come.

Water Bailiff Vacancies did not arrive very often, then when they did everyone and their mothers would apply. The company employing these men was the North West water Authority which had superceded the old Lancashire river authority a few years earlier, this was of course before the world changed and privatisation moved in as we know it today.

The farm I was employed on was okay but I had long since come to the conclusion that the difference between owning a farm and being an employee was vast. The prospects were for very long hard years ahead with the possibility of ownership myself both daunting and financially impossible.

My chance eventually came when a Bailiff covering the River Birley and River Kleen near Burton moved over to the Lune. Georgina and I had been hinting for over twelve months and probably pestered her dad into our way of thinking. He would quiz me over cups of tea in their living room, but I honestly thought he was trying to put me off. I honestly don't really know or care how much my Father in law influenced the interviews for the job, but there comes a time in life when if a chance comes along just go for it even if you have gained a vital trump card. I was sure Joe could influence the powers that be. He must have subtly worked on old Jack Dawson and Brian Bentley the two regional fisheries officers at the time. I therefore applied for this rare opportunity together with three hundred other applicants.

The notification I craved came two weeks later and the date for an interview was set. I was over the moon even if very skeptical about my chances. I kept hearing juicy snippets about other candidates together with Joe's sterling work trying to paint a glowing picture of my character quoting how honest and intelligent I was. Get real I thought, nevertheless I was getting sucked in and my hopes were high.

I had one main rival from Carlisle and he was mightily confident on the day. He more or less told me that as he was already a Bailiff and as a mere farm worker I had no chance! He was a very confident lad strutting about dressed in his plus fours and tweeds, he looked very much down on me and very much the part in waiting. I was therefore not confident which perhaps relaxed me on the day during the interview. Of course Joe was on the panel but agreed only to observe whilst I was interrogated. The rest as they say is history and I never saw Mr. Plus fours ever again.

I started work two weeks later; my patch included the bottom section of the R Stock left bank only. The left and right banks are always calculated by facing downstream, this often proved too difficult for some anglers to understand causing confusion on numerous occasions. I can recall many a conversation over the years when an angler would phone in some state of panic about an ongoing poaching incident or angling violation. I would try and get an accurate location by obtaining a landmark which would always get at cross-purposes concerning which was left or right, upstream or downstream?

The patch started with an area of land that was owned by the Authority and our store was sited here also. This was where all our equipment was kept such as nets, Electric fishing gear, various fish traps and a boat. It was also a bit of a Bailiffs brew cabin I suppose.

The site was an old gunpowder works used in Victorian times still producing up until the nineteen fifties. It was also a garden designed by Isabella Wakefield but this was now overgrown. The site is called "Croftgill".

Downstream two large waterfalls appear dramatically in quick succession plunging through deep limestone troughs much loved by canoeists. This area also has deep lies ideal for accommodating both salmon and sea trout. The fishing in this area was the preserve of the Bailiffs only. Kingfishers, herons and the delightful dipper can all be found here. The now very common Goosander was only just appearing on the river, having spread down from Scotland. This fish eating bird is much maligned by anglers although the effects of predation on the fish population are minimal. Prior to the rise of the Goosander it was the Heron that took all the stick, often taking the blame for a blank days fishing, strangely enough they seem to be tolerated now. I even heard an angler stand up at an association meeting one night and accuse the Kingfisher as a threat to fish stocks. This was duly met with unanimous jeers thank goodness and was almost certainly spouted on the back of a very lively discussion about Fish eating birds, of course the copious amounts of ale flowing didn't help.

The next section is owned by a syndicate and known as the "Long dub" followed by a section of parkland belonging to the local Lord Broxton and aptly named Broxton Park. This is a meandering section of deep pools and riffles and the most expensive length of fishing on the river.

The final section is again controlled by the aristocracy namely Brigadier Weston from Bampton Hall estate. This is entirely influenced by the dramatic tides of Morecambe bay leading into the estuary itself, which then takes the River Stock channel meandering miles down to Morecambe and Heysham. Two smaller rivers join the estuary which was also on my patch namely the lovely R Birley which is fed by Hillingdon reservoir up in the hills close to the M6 and at that time purely a trout stream. Access for migratory fish was blocked by a large weir and paper mill. The R Kleen near to Burton is the final and smallest river on my patch, which did have an excellent sea trout run despite very intensive farming through the small valley.

2

GETTING STARTED

My early years as a Water Bailiff were greatly influenced by Father in law Joe Marwood my first boss or head Bailiff and affectionately known by his family as Jo Jo a nickname closely linked to a certain Beatles song. It was amusing and by pure coincidence he had a land rover with license plate number JJM 453. He was in his fifties when I first met him a very large ruddy-cheeked man with a huge presence about him. He always wore a deerstalker hat, he also smoked a pipe and when it wasn't lit dangled at an acute angle from his mouth. Years of smoking had worn a gap in his false teeth, this was highly visible when he smiled or laughed which was quite often. Joe was deaf too and a hearing aid was visible but I am convinced he was selectively deaf when he wanted to be. He was a keen gardener and grew many prize-winning flowers and veg, many cunning plans and strategies were pondered over in the greenhouse or amongst his flower beds.

Joe liked his fly fishing even more than his garden, especially for sea trout in the nearby R Stock a sport he indulged at its purist on balmy summer nights and he rarely came home empty handed. He would amble down to Long meadow his favorite haunt at around dusk in July as these fine fish began their migration upstream on the long journey to spawn. He would meet some if his pals or even sometimes the Brigadier would come down, which usually meant much merriment and free whisky. The drink driving issue never seemed to crop up on those occasions, and if questioned he'd laugh "it's the night air tha knows it keeps you sober".

His faithful wife Hannah never accompanied him but made sure he was equipped with a flask and gingerbread on each sortie.

Joe was one of those people who had obsessions about whatever took his fancy at the time and his Land rover lasted longer than most, he called it his "auld Mere" which I think meant old mare as in horse although I can't be sure. Joe was a big robust character from a large farming family on the Yorkshire Cumbria border and had also been a cook during the war rising to Sergeant. I think it's fair to say he never cooked again after he married Hannah. He was not a man to tangle with though. He gave the impression and appearance of being a bit thick, rather a country bumpkin almost, but once I had worked with him for a while it was apparent this was a front that belied a cunning and astute mind dedicated to trapping poachers. He could also influence those in power making policy decisions on the river board. Joe could tempt people with his manner to find out what they'd been up to or to reveal vital information.

Joe had some personal habits that singled him out, like he whistled out of tune a la Les Dawson, especially if he was annoyed or things weren't going well. He also had his own unique form of humming which once heard was never forgotten. This was a sign that all was well in the world. He was quite a character and very entertaining to work with.

The Bailiff team consisted of Albert Hankey from Hawkshead who was the second in command or senior Bailiff, as the position was known. He was a stocky character full of his own importance with jet-black hair and a dead ringer for Brian Clough both in appearance and sound. Albert or Hank as we called him didn't really get on with Joe; I was told that when Joe got the Inspectors job Albert thought it should have been his. There would be tension and sparks for years to come. The remaining Bailiffs were Danny O'Hare an ex farm worker and public school boy, Tommy Brown a Methodist who never swore ever, but was obsessed about sex. He was married and totally harmless just had opinions and admired women from the outside as it were. Tommy's patch was the upper Stock which is where all the action occurred. A great deal of time was going to be spent with Tommy once the fish arrived. There were two more Bailiffs but they worked the Duddon and Crake, Martin Dobson who started one year before me and Paul Nugent an ex policeman who lived a strange lonely life up the Duddon Valley.

June 6th 1976 was the day I started as a Water Bailiff and I remember it well, Joe instructed me to make the short journey in my mini van to his home Beechwood in the village of Eastmoor about five miles from his beloved River Stock. Georgina and myself also lived at Eastmoor with our two boy's aged six and two. We had recently embarked onto the mortgage ladder on a small estate not far from Joe's house.

It was 9 am, great my last job started at half six. Once at Beechwood I was greeted by Joe laughing

"Now then Jack Carter how's it feel bein a Becky"

It actually felt very weird and I was more than a bit apprehensive. Tommy Brown was present he had been instructed to show me the ropes and a few sights. Everyone drank at least three cups of tea. Joe answered about ten phone calls, checked his greenhouse twice, also he stoked his pipe too many times to count. Tommy had a Bobby Charlton comb over haircut, which was precisely groomed at all times.

Ten o clock came round and Joe appeared with a plastic bag,

"Here's yur survival kit"

I was handed a pair of second hand 8x40 binoculars, a black pocket book with pencil, a pair of rubber thigh waders, Wellington's, wooden truncheon, handcuffs, a very large Pye radio with shoulder strap, and a torch. That was it go forth and multiply, all training in those days was on the job. The notebook and also a diary would be the most important tools of the trade as a record of events; places visited and people encountered.

I got away from Joe's about eleven-o-clock and went on to Tommy's patch in his mini van. He treated that van better than his wife lecturing me about painting old engine oil under the van and over the sub frame to prolong its life. He told me to buy tyres and keep them in the garage for six months to harden the rubber and consequently get more wear from them. He traveled miles out of his way to get petrol from Lipton's because it was half a pence a gallon cheaper. I wouldn't say Tommy was tight would you?

The day was sunny and uneventful as we toured the upper part of the River Stock and I was shown all the weirs which are a legacy of the forty or so mills that used this river during the industrial revolution plus some of the most poached areas, like a poacher's top twenty. They had evocative and strange names like "cold harbour", Long dub". "Eddies leap", "Church dubs", "sheep dub", "ivy pool", "dynamite dub" "honey pot" and many more.

I returned home at four thirty and that was an easy starter or so I thought.

The phone rang at six-o clock, it was Jo Jo.

"If tha wants tha could have a walk downt Birley and check a few licenses".

When Jo Jo said "if tha wants" he really meant you will go end of story, maybe life wasn't as easy now after all.

I duly had that walk down the River Birley as requested; this river is fairly slow flowing in the lower section with easy meanders wandering on towards Morecambe bay. A kingfisher flashed by in halcyon splendor all was well. I checked several anglers on a warm balmy summers evening religiously recording the details in my diary together with the miles walked as instructed. Information like miles driven, numbers of licenses checked fish caught was all recorded on sight and then entered onto a weekly time sheet.

The first few weeks in June that year I began to adjust to my new life, the shorter working week of forty-eight hours with one day off seemed a really good deal in those days. I started to get to know some of the regular anglers and private Bailiffs on each section of river. I checked quite a few fishing licenses and developed a style and technique of my own that coped well enough with friendly middle aged men out having fun and relaxation. Every person over the age of twelve must have a license to fish with rod and line even if they are in their own garden. I issued tickets to anglers who had left their license at home, they were given seven days grace to produce it to the local Office in Brockley

This all went smoothly but I had yet to encounter anyone fishing without a license, but this would all soon change.

3

FIRST BLOOD

In the first weeks of July things started to hot up, some welcome rain had produced a small lift on the River Stock and both salmon and sea trout were moving upstream out of Morecambe bay to begin the perilous struggle upstream to the spawning grounds. The River Stock is about ten miles from the tidal reaches up to the fells with several tributaries entering above Brockley, the two main ones being the Rivers Brock and Brant. Migratory fish use all three rivers and all three were excessively poached during the nineteen seventies and eighties. Salmon and sea trout had also suffered from a severe fungal disease known as UDN (*Ulcerated Dermal Necrosis*). This disease had been prevalent during the sixties and early seventies. This had significantly reduced the numbers of fish returning to freshwater. This is a disease that attacks without any particular reason and there is absolutely nothing that can be done in the wild to treat it apart from carcass removal.

The numbers of dead fish seen and removed covered in the deadly white fungus ran into thousands. In nineteen seventy six when I started the problem was past the worst period and fish stocks were starting to recover. I still witnessed many such illustrations however well into the eighties.

The concern over fish stocks and species survival was therefore a grave one, my job to protect what we had was vital. I became impassioned about the job as I learned more and more vowing to make this my mission as time would tell.

The first customer to go into my black notebook kept since day one in my new camouflage jacket pocket was a man fishing the River Birley in the company of a small boy.

A fine sunny Saturday morning and I was assigned by Joe to check the entire estuary at low water for poaching activity or "snatching". This is a method of poaching using a conventional rod and line but instead of bait such as a worm or an artificial lure a much deadlier device is attached. It is important to understand that the basic principal of fishing is, a bait or lure to attract fish which quite voluntarily take the device but are then impaled on the hook and vitally only in the mouth, in other words you have fooled it. The skill is there for all to see. The angler can congratulate himself because he has tricked the fish! Well done.

The "snatcher" is much more of a low life, a scroat, cheat, or whatever expletive comes to mind. This method usually entails the lure being modified into what can only be described as a mini weighted grappling hook. The principle here is simple the device is guided toward the fish slowly and stealthily until within striking distance, then a sudden violent jerk and pull on the rod sees the hooks impale the fish usually mid torso somewhere. The hooks have taken the fish as opposed to the fish taking the hook, which is the vital difference between right and wrong. If the fish is large a violent struggle will ensue and it may take considerable strength and effort to land. Sometimes the fish is ripped and torn, it may even get off swimming away to recover or not as the case may be. Usually after many minutes the fight becomes too much until the fish gradually weakens succumbing to its desperate end. It is then furtively removed and dispatched. This method was widespread throughout the south lakes area at the time and for many years to come. This was one of the main types of poaching activity faced by Bailiffs throughout my career.

The same method was also used to catch Flounders in the upper estuary albeit with certain modifications. Flounders, also called Flukes, or more commonly in these parts "Flatties" are as suggests flatfish like plaice or sole. These fish can be tempted with baits usually lugworms. This method is used at high water as the tide is making and attracts many anglers from all over the north of England, indeed they had been there in their dozens that very morning with rods leaning against the railings at Sandside for over a mile. The River Stock tidal channel flows close to the road here making it an ideal place for this type of fishing. Men, women, and boys attended diligently next to an array of vans, cars, and camper vans. Primus stoves, flasks and sandwich boxes were placed randomly along the pavement or on seats. Many were asleep as lack of catch and enthusiasm went hand in hand, others fussing with gear and holding plastic bags aloft to show success, or comparing gear with others, or maybe even just putting the world to rights.

When the tide recedes however these anglers gradually disperse to the local pubs to compare notes or just drift away. There are those that remain nevertheless and these are cause for concern. The Flatties or flukes are left in shoals feeding or resting in certain pools and often fell prey to the infamous "Dragger". This perpetrator of evil is the guy who modifies a fishing lure on his rod and line to foul hook the fish. I have seen some amazing adaptations to a standard treble. The device is weighted often with a piece of lead attached crudely so as to be literally dragged along the sand through shallow water until an unfortunate fish is basically raked or grappled obviously foul hooked in any area of its body. Devices can be custom made with lumps of copper pipe having hooks welded or soldered on. I have seen sink taps modified with a big piercing treble hook fixed to the end. I once confiscated a tackle box with forty-two custom-built pipe adaptations inside. The skill needed to construct some of these devices would have to be admired if wasn't for the intended use. This method is very easy to observe, as the dragging sweeping motion of retrieving the device is pretty blatant. Large bags of fish can be obtained by this method in a relatively short time because these fish don't swim away in frantic fashion like a salmon but just remain waiting to be ruthlessly dragged out. It's a similar act to seal culling for want of a comparison. I have confiscated bags of fifty or sixty fish on more than one occasion. This is nothing less than ruthless cruelty and above all it's just cheating, no skill involved! The fish are a sorry sight when tipped out, most being still alive and badly mutilated or wounded. Excuses given by the anglers are usually pretty pathetic,......

"I didn't know it was illegal",

"mi mate said everyone does it",

I thought it were all right",

"Everyone's at it why shouldn't I have a go".

There are many more together with those full of remorse of course especially if they get fined. A good fine has focused many a mind.

This morning was uneventful however; all the "flatty bashers" as we call them had drifted away except for a few die hards or families just on days out sticking around on low water to idly enjoy what was a lovely summer's weekend. There were no snatchers to worry about, which was just as well bearing in mind my naivety at this stage. I was parked openly at the roadside enjoying a packed lunch and planning my route back upstream. I was able to examine all the bird life feeding busily on the sands. After my lunch I decided to call in at Birley foot an area on the River Birley about quarter of a mile downstream from Bampton Hall. This section was still tidal the main centre of attraction being a six-foot high weir known aptly enough as Birley foot weir, which indeed did just about define the foot of this lovely river. I had been told by Joe that morning that sea trout congregate under the weir. I was detailed to spend some time observing the pool and make an assessment. I was also given advice on what indications may have been left in the area to suggest signs of recent poaching activity. This was a reference to the field craft that would have to be acquired to recognise signs of activity such as netting, which apparently was the most probable method of poaching suited to this long deep section of river. Further signs to look out for might be flattened grass, footprints, or even fish scales and accompanying blue bottles in the undergrowth.

I duly parked up nearby and set off towards the river, then immediately noticed a small boy of about nine or ten trying to sort out a fishing rod and line that was obviously tangled. Close by was a man probably his father sat on a deck chair lazily holding a conventional spinning rod baited with garden worms, he casually cast into the water unperturbed by my impending approach. They were both on my side of the river and about thirty yards downstream from the weir. This to all intents and purposes looked just like the other situations I was getting comfortably used to in my short career. If anything even more harmless, just a man and boy enjoying a day out fishing. What could possibly go wrong?

I duly approached in the casual friendly manner that I had applied thus far with relative success. Nearer and nearer, very relaxed, I had my warrant card in my hand ready to produce, this is a golden rule, always produce your warrant, in fact It's a legal requirement, just show it that's all is required. Don't let anyone get hold of it, that is not necessary and a definite no no!

Why? Because if they want it they will probably keep it, rip it up, or more likely chuck it in the beck. Without a warrant a Bailiff is basically undressed as far as the job goes. I was almost there!

"Afternoon, is he in a tangle then"

The guy didn't reply in fact he didn't even acknowledge me,

I was puzzled but not alarmed!

"I'm a Water Bailiff"

I flashed my warrant confidently only to be surprised by his sarcastic retort

"Bully for you"

The small boy was timid and indifferent to the events unfolding; he busied himself face down trying to sort his tangled line. I was in new territory here. This was the first angler who hadn't been friendly; in fact he was the first person on the job that had not greeted me with a smiling face.

Right then, try again,

"Have you had any luck?"

"No"

This was all he said he didn't move or even look my way. He was a small insignificant middle aged man in a woolly jumper on a hot day with an attitude problem.

I tried again,

"What you after then?"

"Anything that's going, trout actually"

Hallelujah he spoke, I was getting somewhere, but he still didn't make eye contact.

The next question would change everything,

"Have you got a fishing license Sir?"

"No don't need one mate",

Great that's all I wanted to hear this was it, the guy hasn't got one. I was close to panic but trying to look cool. I tried explaining the facts that fishing for trout required a North West water Authority license. He still didn't look at me but started to fidget and look very annoyed. I pulled my black pocket book out and went for it.

"I'll have to report you for fishing without a license"

This got a reaction all right; he turned and glared at me,

"Jesus Christ have you nothing better to do I'm just out with my son for a quiet days fishing why don't you fuck off and leave us alone".

I would gladly have done just that if I could have got away with it. The seeds were being sown here however for situations to come. This state of affairs needed sorting out, but was unfortunately about to get much worse.

I opened my notebook with pen in hand, a slight adrenaline tremble occurred as I asked him what his name and address were.

"Fuck you I'm telling you nothing Go and harass some other poor bugger".

Christ this was serious, what am I supposed to do; he won't say who he is! He didn't move at all, he just sat there arms folded and looking down. The young lad kept his head down and looked as though he wished the world would swallow him up. I knew just how he felt.

Several minutes passed in heated argument but the guy just retreated into his shell; sometimes there was silence as I tried to think of where to go next. The saving grace although I didn't realise it at the time was the fact that he didn't do a runner which, in similar future situations would be quite often.

We were getting nowhere and I remembered Joe's words, " If tha needs to, gan and fetcht Bobbies".

This had to be my next move, but would this Pratt still be here when I got help.

I warned the guy that he left me no option than to call the police. He wasn't fazed he was turning out to be the most stubborn man I had ever met.

"I've got rights I am just here minding my own business fishing with my lad"

The lad was still acting as if both of us didn't exist, head down solemn face.

I tried one last time to extract a name and address and warned him that failing to give his details was an offence. The powers of water Bailiff at this time only allowed an arrest to be carried out during the hours of darkness. The legislation comes from the *Salmon and fresh water fisheries act 1975;* my copy was to be my bible and still is today. The exact definition says "between the end of the first hour after sunset and the beginning of the last hour before sunrise". A Water Bailiff is also deemed as a Constable for the purpose of the Act. The present day powers now include the *Police and criminal evidence act 1984* which gives us much wider powers including arrest under such a situation as faced me that day in 1976.

I left the scene and drove the short distance to Sandside where I found a phone box. I dialed the police Station at Birley and explained my predicament. I was told if a constable was available he would come and assist, so I gave them the location and returned. The man was still there thank God .I waited in my car. Time went by, it seemed like hours, but it was only about fifteen minutes. I was getting doubts perhaps there was no Bobby available after all.

Then, at last there it was slowly approaching, the cavalry… a panda car.

A very tall young copper emerged, somehow the sight of his uniform made me feel worse, I had never had to call the Police ever before in my life. The gravity of it all hit me and I felt very small.

"PC Turner what's the problem"

He was a bit on the sarcastic side but I gave him the low-down.

"Right then lets go and sort yon bugger out"

I followed like a dog.

The outcome was fantastic, the man saw the Policeman and was immediately affected by the power of a uniform just as I had been, he suddenly became very timid and co-operative. He was instructed to cough up his identity details, which I greedily wrote down in my pocket book. I managed to issue "the caution" for the first time ever. He was in the bag; I took great pleasure in saying

"You will be reported for fishing without a licence and failing to state your name and address"

I was up and running.

I triumphantly watched him packing up his gear to leave. I thanked PC Turner and felt ten feet tall. The guy was from Stoke-on Trent, up here on holiday, never mind not my problem any more.

I thanked PC Turner a second time and we both left.

I arrived home and phoned Joe, I couldn't tell him fast enough. To this day after having dealt with hundreds of rod anglers I have still never met one so stubborn over a simple license case as that guy was back in 1976. My confidence had been boosted big style by the previous days events, but as we all know life can hit back when least expected. The very next morning when I arrived at Joe's I could see all was not well.

"Paul Nugents bin bloody well attacked,"

Joe was sat with head in hands, his cup of tea untouched.

"He's been stabbed with a spear, come across some frogmen poachin int Duddon"

I had to sit down myself, this was bad news indeed. Joe left soon after to sort things out. The perpetrators of the attack were never seen or heard of ever again, which was a good thing in many respects. It was a few weeks before patrols got back to normal and Paul returned to work. I questioned Paul on several occasions in the next few years, but he always declined to elaborate, instead preferring to change the subject. There was a scar on Paul's left cheek attributed to the attack although apart from shock he had not been badly hurt. Paul's story has never rung true in my eyes, I have always felt that something mysterious happened on that day. I don't suppose the exact truth will ever be known.

4

HANK

Albert Hankey was exactly twenty years older than me to the day, I found him a bit intimidating at first and it was obvious from day one that he held some kind of resentment towards me. This I'm sure was due partly because I was Joe's son in law and partly because of the means by which I had acquired the job.

Hank was an imposing character who knew it all. What ever anyone achieved or mastered he would belittle, he'd done it better or years ago before it was invented, he was as Joe put it "the great I am". The chemistry between Hank and Joe was hot, they just about tolerated each other and that was all. The day to day running of the team simmered with jealousy and subterfuge, but of course crucially Joe had the upper hand simply because he was the boss. I would often get sucked into situations of being pig in the middle as tension mounted.

It was during my third or fourth week that I was detailed to patrol with Hank, again it was a red-hot day during that phenomenal summer.

Reports had been coming in from Tommy that some lads from Burndale were seen poaching the R Brock near its confluence with the Stock.

I was summoned to Beechwood as per usual to await the arrival of Hank.

On this initial day he was clad in tweed suit with shirt and tie. This was always how he would be, even when turning out at three-o-clock in the morning. Of course he smoked a pipe as seemed to be the requirement of a well-heeled Bailiff. In all the time I knew him he was ultra clean-shaven, he just didn't do stubble.

Hanks heart was always elsewhere usually on the R Leven near Newby Bridge, which was his patch. He would always have a dozen reasons why that's where he should be and never had much time for the River Stock. This particular morning was no exception.

"There's a big shoal of sea trout int Honey pot Joe, Peter Teasdale says he could do with me of a night"

Joe listened distantly and didn't even reply. The decision was non negotiable for Hank and he knew it as always.

Hank rattled the loose change in his baggy pockets in a sigh of frustration and inevitability. Joe peered over his glasses his eyes glinting with a hint of mischief.

"Tha can take Jack tut gravel trap; tha might just drop on yon buggers".

Hank had a blue mini van that he amply filled. It was sparkly clean and looked as if country lanes had been avoided at all costs. The journey was made in silence taking us slowly to Brockley where Hank made a diversion to by some paint for his kitchen a task that seemed to cheer him up no end.

"Jane likes egg shell blue emulsion"

He mumbled a snigger

"Thwole house is bloody blue near as damn it"

I laughed with him.

We checked the town water in Brockley an opportunity for Hank to strut around with his conspicuous white shirt and green tie, hardly covert I thought, still who was I to question? I could see why Joe called him "the big I am".

It was around two-o clock when we reached a point above Holme houses, a set of terraced cottages mid way between Brockley and Burndale. Hank stopped his van and rather than get out surveying the alleged felons he broke off on another tangent electing instead to give me a lecture on pumps and bearings, he showed me a small pump that he had been working on and obviously hoped I would be on the same wavelength. I wasn't of course so no bonding on that day. He fussed about at the back of his van and strode about the pavement without once glancing towards the river. He was obviously playing for time and manifestly wanted to be somewhere else. I was becoming bemused by the whole scenario, whilst Hank ignored my description of the scene around us.

The mood changed however when I observed three men on the bank of a large gravel trap just above the confluence of the two rivers. These turned out to be the first actual poachers I had seen. Hank at last gave me his attention.

"Put your glasses on em Jack"

His remark was made with vague indifference.

I could see a large fat guy wearing a denim cap, sunglasses and holding a fishing rod. Two further men, one medium build and one very small were pacing about peering into the water also in sunglasses. Further instructions ensued.

"What they on with Jack? keep your eye on em"

Hank continued messing about with his damn pump and was showing no great interest in the activities, nor did he make any attempt to keep out of sight.

My feelings were mixed at this point. On the one hand I wasn't in any danger, but on the other hand neither were they.

I then noticed some snatching actions by the big fat guy, which I immediately relayed to Hank, he produced his own binoculars at this point and to my relief showed some level of concern at what was happening before us.

"Yon buggers snatching you know, write it down in your book Jack"

I clumsily pulled out my book, picked up the pen that had just spilled across the road and hurriedly wrote details down relayed by Hank.

"Man wearing blue cap brown shirt, Polaroid's, and has rod in right hand"

"Eh up his mates pointing int watter, Yon buggers sin a fish Jack, and… yes He's had a bloody strike, put the time down Jack"

It was ten past three.

I was writing as instructed and could easily see the action as well.

This continued for some time until inevitably all the three men became aware of our presence, not helped by Hank's white shirt flying like a flag.

They obviously became very nervous, but carried on never the less. Eventually they hooked a fish and even though they were about two hundred and fifty yards away it was obvious what was happening. The rod was bending and flashing in the sunlight and the men were now running, pointing in between anxious glances across to where we stood.

Hank never lost his cool, but did become very animated strutting his stuff all around the van. Then the unavoidable happened the fish was caught landed and knocked on the head.

"Fish taken at 15.20 Jack, have you written it down?"

Needless to say the fish was now bundled unceremoniously into a bag and all three men ran off upstream glancing furtively back, then finally to add insult to injury the fat guy gave us the V sign before disappearing.

I was sweating profusely, rather stressed and looking for guidance, but Hank was lighting his damn pipe.

After what seemed like an eternity he eventually spoke.

"Lets gan round and cut em off at Brock Bridge"

It was another fifteen minutes before we reached the bridge, Hanks van never exceeded twenty five miles per hour and consequently our men were history for that day.

Hank lit up again without a care in the world fondling his large silver pocket watch extracted elegantly from his waistcoat pocket.

"Yon buggers could be anywhere bi now Jack mun as well bugger off"

How right he was, but their paths and mine would cross again, hopefully without old Hank.

5

TOMMY AND THE EARLY YEARS

I was very lucky during my first two years of Bailiffing because I worked for the most part with Tommy Brown; he proved to be my main mentor. Tom's patch was the upper Stock including the notorious Brockley town stretch and the upper reaches including both the smaller Rivers Brock and Brant. The poaching activity was rife mostly from locals who embarked on a life of state benefits supplemented by an income from the sale of salmon and sea trout. The main employers in Brockley were a shoe manufacturer and a big insurance company. The seeds of decline for these industries were already germinating and the years ahead would see them both disappear completely like an endangered species. The national unemployment figure was high enough in any case during the seventies even significantly affecting a Lakeland town like Brockley.

I was sent out on patrols with Tom most days from July onwards where we encountered numerous different types of poaching activity. The really big time gangs who netted or poisoned rivers tended to poach the mid and lower reaches in areas such as Broxton park or below, indeed my first ever night patrol was actually with Joe who as ever was more than keen to initiate me into the nitty gritty of Bailiffing.

I was summoned down to Beechwood as pre arranged one night at about ten thirty, I was all dressed up and ready to go with warm protective gear resembling a commando rather than a Water Bailiff. When I arrived Joe wasn't ready of course,

"I'll just watch news Jack, my missus can mek thee a cuppa"

Joe would have to have his nightly fix of Jan Leeming or Anna Ford.

I was getting used to this routine by now of course, but also more importantly getting paid into the bargain. I always reckoned on adding an hour on to a patrol with Joe before we even set off.

Eventually he appeared after much twoing, froing, and tuneless humming, with his deerstalker in position he would declare himself ready. Ten minutes pipe lighting in the land rover still had to be endured outside the house before we actually got moving.

It was nearly midnight when we finally arrived at the river, fifteen minutes further delay occurred as we checked the pool in Croftgill for sea trout numbers.

Joe mused and puffed his pipe as this secret fish compromised itself with gentle head and tail swirls in the warm smooth current. A mirad of flying insects and bats lustily picked their way across the misty pool indulging in frenzied feasts abounding on such a warm night.

Joe quietly hummed one of his non-tunes contentedly as we turned to leave.

"Might just ave a do tomorrow night Jack".

We met a regular angler called Johnny Jones as he arrived at the "Long Dub", a large robust man engrossed in his knowledge and predictions of the river. He was standing in the doorway of the fishing hut, his face ghost like in the reflection of his Tilly lamp. He donned chest waders ready to enter the deep runs and outwit his quarry. Various fly types were discussed, casting techniques mimicked, the weather was thoroughly analysed, the world was briefly put to rights, and another twenty minutes went by.

Eventually we did arrive at the top entrance to Broxton Park, which is basically a parking area surrounded by dense sycamore trees and at the time looked exceedingly foreboding and dark. The park is about a mile long and during daylight hours a very lovely place containing many mature native trees, some of which are three hundred or more years old. A long avenue of oaks is a particular feature.

Joe took great pleasure in reminding me of how haunted it was, explaining how a grey lady and dog walked the avenue at night; she had apparently died of consumption whilst in service in the hall. After that the dog had to be shot because it never left her side whilst protecting her. They were by all accounts buried together somewhere in the grounds. He then started to tell me about a coach and horses also, but I managed to change the subject before he got going and the mischievous glee on his face was beginning to unnerve me.

The River Stock meanders its way through the park and contains many deep pools providing ideal cover for both salmon and sea trout. The fishing at this time was upper class old school type, the preserve of the rich only. Magistrates, Doctors, Lawyers, that type of individual. The wildlife was excellent too; red squirrels could often be seen tip toeing nimbly in the grass between the bigger trees, together with deer and assorted birdlife.

Joe lit his pipe of course and turned radio 2 on, he turned the volume down low as Simon and Garfunkels Bridge over troubled water played somewhat appropriately it seemed.

"Now then Jack thas got tha torch has tu"

I nodded, not that he could see me in the dark clouds of St Bruno.

"Tha could gan Throught Park and Ill pick you up at tuther end Jack"

This was it! I was to be dumped there in the pitch black and made to walk the path complete with ghost and all downstream to Broxton Bridge, where Joe would be waiting.

No problem?

"Don't shine thee light Jack whatever, someone might si thee"

Those were his parting words

The land rover slowly growled away like an Old Faithful Labrador until silence was my companion, I was alone!

The gangs of poachers that had poached this area mainly during the nineteen sixties hailed mostly from Burnley which for some reason seemed to have dynasties of such individuals and families. Joe told tales about the Notorious Garners and Whittams that terrorised these parts and had me quaking in my boots.

All this of course didn't help when left alone to walk the walk. I set off gingerly along the path, my eyes soon became accustomed to the conditions and I wasn't even concerned when a tawny owl gave an eerie hoot as it ghosted past, he was probably wondering who this idiot was on his patch. Walking in the dark down many such paths would become second nature as time went on, it becomes a skill and I can't ever remember any Bailiff actually falling and hurting himself on this type of maneuver, even Danny O'Hare was sure footed at night. The secret is not to shine a light as this affects the eyes for a while and can cause a type of night blindness, also I tried whenever possible to walk the area in daylight hours to familiarise myself with any obstacles and get a general lie of the land, but generally its just a skill that's acquired like riding a bike.

I walked cautiously on that night even starting to feel quite confident. The sound of the river gently washing across gravel shoals was soothing enough. No lights flickered and I was now approaching roughly the half way mark, every so often I paused to breath it all in.

I continued slowly for another hundred yards until suddenly the rhythm was violated with the sound of splashing on a huge scale. I was instantly frozen to the spot completely baffled, what the hells going on? At that point my brain was in overdrive I soon came to the conclusion the sound was actually men crossing the river, a dissonance, twenty or more at least, an army. My heart was pounding, the sound was like something from a John Wayne film, I felt very alone. I gripped my torch greatly tempted to switch it on or even better turn round and make rapid steps from whence I came.

I listened intently until just as suddenly as it had started the sound changed.

Even more confusing I thought? This was now cause for concern, I had no radio and mobile phones hadn't been invented, I could just picture Joe chuckling to himself in his nice warm land rover.

What followed next was also startling, but my mood changed from panic to shear relief as a herd of resident deer in the park hurtled passed me like Wildebeest in the Serengeti.

I felt like such a fool although much relieved, I sat down on a stone seat strategically placed for panicky rookie Bailiffs and started to laugh. I started talking to myself like some sort of loony

"They're deer, fucking deer you Pratt"

It was some minutes before I composed myself and continued to the bridge.

Joe greeted me with a smoky smile and whispered

"Did tu see out Jack?"

"No all quiet Joe"

I climbed calmly into the haven of his land rover.

I would go to Tommy's house most days probably about lunchtime; his wife Lena a woman of large size and equally large heart would make me the customary tea and biscuits. Tommy and Lena were of country stock from the Yorkshire dales and like myself had been in farming. They hailed from a family farm handed down over several generations. Tom had got out of farming about ten years previously as the living to be made on a hill farm was in decline. He had done a variety of jobs even selling insurance door to door. The last four years however he had patrolled the River Stock and had a reputation for being firm but fair with everyone he dealt with. Tom was very religious without ramming it down your throat. He was your archetypal do gooder but sincere with it, he was also a serial hospital visitor. When Joe went in for his hernia operation Tom was the first there which was typical of this caring man.

A characteristic patrol would be, leave in his mini van and maybe check some of the River Stock angling association waters at Haig Bridge, this was just down the road from Toms home. This bridge was notorious for certain anglers in the association that foul hooked fish despite using legitimate spinning or worming tackle. They would greet me or any Bailiff all smiles and be your best friend and then as soon as I left they would be bang at it, my ears burning into the bargain. This was a significant problem on the river for many years and certainly the hardest type of offence to detect. The moral issue alone was very significant and caused a lot of ill feeling amongst club members.

In those early years however it couldn't be a priority as the much more blatant acts of poaching took up the majority of our time and these quick visits to places like Haig bridge were just a deterrent, just to remind them we were still around.

Tom introduced me to the covert side of the job, which I had to learn quickly. He would suggest certain hot spots that could be likely to get a visit from one or more of the many poachers that lived in and around Brockley and Burndale. He would then show me a secret place to park his van. A Bailiffs vehicle was well known so keeping it out of sight was paramount. This usually meant quite a long walk to the area of river selected. Essential tools included a trusty pair of small binoculars, the small black pocket book, a pen knife, Polaroid sunglasses, and of course the trusty thermos flask.

We would approach the scene like Indian trackers straight out of a western; the actual terrain would influence the method of approach. If it was in the town we would nip between cars, bushes, putting huts, houses, anything available. I am sure Benny Hill would have been proud of some of the maneuvers. The element of surprise was always the trump card, a person apprehended without prior knowledge of your pending arrival was nine times out of ten bang to rights. Of course in the town stretch ordinary Joe public was going about his daily life even as we crept about amongst them. I found this very strange at first and was conscious of some very funny looks especially if we had to duck down or crawl on hands and and knees. As time went on I learned to focus on the job in hand and became oblivious to the rest of the world.

Tommy and I became a useful team with some notable successes, characters like Jez Bergerac the lad I saw take that first fish in Brockley were just starting out on careers in poaching; he was only fifteen, as was Lesley Gaunt, and Sam Mcgowan. Many more would cross my path as the seventies passed through to the eighties when poaching was rife.

I went on patrols alone sometimes when Tommy was on his days off or on leave. I gradually developed the skills needed to track down poachers. I learnt to pick up the faintest smell of a cigarette drifting by on the wind betraying someone's approach. I learnt to observe the wildlife, a Heron may be alarmed by an intruder on his space and meet me coming downstream. Of course it worked both ways. If I got to a pool and Mr. Heron stood peacefully it was fair to say nobody was present or had recently passed that way. I always tried to walk with the sun behind me whenever possible, that was a useful screen against anyone approaching or operating ahead. The most effective method I developed that brought me much success was to find a position of concealment close to a pool or stretch that contained fish. This was usually somewhere close by in a bush or tree, or actually up a tree. One can see out through foliage from within, but can't be seen looking in from the outside. Providing I was still and had the patience to sit in one place for hours at a time a good vantage point with cover was the platform to many a good prosecution. The actual poaching incident unfolded in front of my eyes frequently providing the vital evidence required.

Of course many such occasions produced nothing; indeed ninety per cent of stakeouts drew a blank. Patience was the name of the game and would every so often be rewarded. Of course luck was necessary too, but like a lot of things if I was prepared to put myself out or go the extra yard I could create my own luck.

6

DANNY O'HARE

Danny O'Hare was the second longest serving member of the team, the son of an aristocrat from a large country estate near Hawkshead. He was definitely the non-achiever of the family with a brother practicing physiology in Harley Street and a sister who excelled in the NHS hierarchy. His father was of dubious military background and all a bit mysterious. Danny carried that military air he had inherited despite failing disastrously with his public school education in Sedbergh.

He nevertheless outwardly played a good game coming across as relatively authoritative with a decidedly educated appearance. The flaw was his condescending manner, which didn't endear him to many people, although in truth he was actually very kind, with a flawless honesty. Of course appearances as we all know can be deceptive and believe me in Danny's case very definitely so.

A typical outfit for Danny would be plus fours over tweed socks and military shined walking boots, however driving whilst wearing these was not permitted under any circumstances, that was left to brogue's or even trainers.

The upper torso would be immaculately donned with tweed shirt, faithful red cravat and the "coup-de-gras" was his green military beret. He also had a red one for special occasions such as court appearances or church. Danny would spend ages just getting the thing perched at the right angle free of any crease or flaw.

Danny's physique was boxeresque without exaggeration because in his former life he had been a farm labourer much as myself on various hill farms. The life was forced upon him due to his educational failings not to mention the failings towards him by his family. Farm work in the sixties was hard and developed a man's physique without compromise, Danny being no exception. Long hard days of humping bales, sacks, calves, muck, anything really from here to there and back again. Bob Harmer a college tutor of mine at Newton Rigg once said

"Farming is entirely the moving of one thing from a place and putting it down somewhere else" and if you think about it the argument is sound.

Danny also smoked a pipe and in fact was never without it, even when asleep, which was very often. He was never lacking some bizarre walking stick also. He had several specially honed with badgers, pheasants, or ducks head handles, you name it he had one. When I first met Danny he would be about forty going on sixty and a confirmed bachelor, he even claimed to have owned an MG roadster but this was never verified and the thought of Danny whisking some blonde off to the flix was a bit far fetched to be honest.

Danny's Achilles heel was his inability to stay awake for more than an hour or two at any given time, which in our job was at times disastrous. Danny would often be seen at various favourite parking spots well out of it, usually in some physically challenged position in his Austin 1300. He would sleep through anything and I think he actually invented the power nap, his pipe would be either still in his mouth or his hand or even somewhere in between and hence the frequent burn marks on his jumper or shirt. In hot weather he would even sleep out on the grass verge or riverbank and usually where everyone could see him. Joe used to get many a sarcastic phone call from chuckling anglers,

"Tha needs to give yon Becky more time off Joe every time tha sees im he's flaked out ont grass"

This would lead to a blood curdling bollocking the next morning, however it all went over Danny's head; he'd just sit there sup his tea and stoke up the old pipe.

Jo would rant,

"If Tha needs a nap do it where there's nay one about not where tha can be sin. Why dist ya need a sleep any way? tha does nowt all day"

When driving with Danny one had to be very alert because his sleep button was always delicately poised, consequently I never took my eyes off him; in fact being a passenger with Danny was harder work than actually driving. Many times he would suddenly dramatically swerve into a lay-by and say in his public school hoity toity voice

"You drive"

It was like a pit stop in the grand prix, he was an erratic fast driver anyway without all those extra hazards. I would then quietly drive his car home; Danny was asleep even before we left the pits.

Danny had another string to his bow in the form of Zara his German shepherd. This dog was his own although he took it out to work on an unofficial basis. There seemed an unwritten rule amongst Bailiffs back then that a big hairy Alsatian was a useful tool in the fight against poachers. This was true in a few cases Joe even had one on the job before I started. Joe's dog was bigger and meaner than Zara and quite a formidable force, indeed throughout the North West there was probably half a dozen such animals. Officially of course if anybody had been savaged the owner of such a dog would be hung out to dry. It wasn't till the nineties that official dogs were taken on with authorised and proper training from Home office trainers. Back then though Danny and Zara were all we had in south Lakes. Danny had other dogs as well over the years including a cocker spaniel and a Cavalier King Charles. These dogs all had two things in common; they stank, and were uncontrolled free spirits that totally ignored any form of instruction from their master. When David's Austin 1300 set off laden with dogs the noise and commotion they made could be heard for miles. He seemed oblivious to it all as he serenely drove off, his upper class chin pointed skyward under his immaculately poised beret and shiny cravat clad neck.

The first real problem with Danny I was involved in came when we had concerns about a character called Michael Macadam from the notorious fishing village of Flixton-over-sands, he was brother of Stan "fish" Macadam a fairly respectable and licensed netsman. He was almost certainly the sale outlet for Michael's fish although this would never be proved. The fishermen of Morecambe bay were spread evenly from Morecambe itself up to Barrow, however the small villages in between had there own little cliques. Nine times out of ten they were related in some close or distant way. This of course provided very close ties but, intriguingly also quite often betrayal based purely on family jealousy and one upmanship.

The crack in this instance established that Michael worked away on North Sea rigs and became out of sight out of mind in the poaching world. He did however return about every three months and in this particular case it was July 1978. Michael was poaching migratory fish on a regular basis from the River Stock channel probably with a gill net, according to the bush telegraph he was leaving them hidden by the railway line for Mr. Unknown to pick up at a later date.

Danny was the Bailiff on the Stock estuary and was soon on the case. Several days of observation brought no results so Joe hauled Danny in for a progress report one Friday teatime.

"Has tu sin out yet Dan"

Joe asked casually in his jovial style, I was positioned near the window to escape the two pipes now stoking on full power, they reminded me of the sidings at steam town. Hannah plied us all with gingerbread and tea, testing my metabolism to its limit. We discussed the case in hand at some length, it became obvious that Danny had put some time in hidden on the Marsh and had actually seen Michael Macadam and his dog. Regrettably nothing incriminating had been discovered. It was obvious he must have slept a fair bit on the job and this was testing Joe's patience.

"I hope thou hasn't bin asleep Dan, and don't take yon daft dog wid yu neither"

Danny shuffled sheepishly before departing leaving me to watch Joe pacing round the room

"Useless bugger whets he bin on with".

Joe looked my way, he was a scary character in this mode and I could swear some pipe smoke emitted from his ears and red inflamed face.

"Lets gan down and have a butchers Jack"

He scowled as we headed for the land rover.

We traveled down that evening and parked up at the gas substation close to the railway at Myretop it was a balmy summer's night and a joy to be out, oyster catchers and redshanks were complaining a bit too much was my first observation. A face at the window of the first Myretop cottage ducked out of sight as I looked round, something wasn't right. I gingerly moved up the embankment binnocs at the ready, Joe was behind stoking up as usual and humming one of his silly non-tunes. We hit the top of the embankment when it was dead on low water; the sands were glistening in the evening sun like polished leather. I was still taking in the surroundings some five minutes later when all of a sudden out of the blue Macadam himself appeared larger than life walking along the railway line. He caught us totally by surprise that's for sure, There stood a tall daft looking lad around mid twenties curly black hair sporting a denim cap of some vintage. He also wore a blue denim bib and brace overall, which was wet up to the waist, a significant fact of incrimination. He carried nothing except a very confident and cocky grin; his shabby lurcher sniffed us indifferently as he stopped to weigh us up. Joe was right on him,

"Now mi lad what yu on with"

The reply was cocky and had the sound of you wont catch me written all over it,

"Just out for a walk Boss, no harm there is there?"

"That depends lad, on what you're up to, how comes you're so wet"?

"Bin paddlin mate"

His counter was extremely flippant, Joe was not amused.

The verbal sparring continued as it usually did in these situations for several tense minutes, Macadam giving nothing away except his obvious guilty as hell attitude indicating "you wont catch me tonight because I saw you coming you thick bastards".

Joe used his thick as pig shit tone with cunning undertones to give the required signals,

 "Game on lad It's only a matter of time".

I watched as Macadam slouched away like a guilty Hyena complete with laugh.

A search of the immediate area proved fruitless or should I say fishless, a nice bag of salmon hidden in the undergrowth would certainly have put the cat amongst the pigeons but it wasn't to be.

Joe whistled out of tune all the way home which was typical of him when a bit rattled.

"Will av yon cocky bastard Jack, see if we don't"

That was all he muttered before heading for the sanctuary of his greenhouse as we parted company.

Several more days went by until Joe got a tip off by Mr. X that Macadam was going again that very night. All the troops were summoned to Beechwood, Joe, Big Don, Albert Hankey, Danny and myself. This propelled Hannah into domestic overdrive serving the assembled Bailiff huddle amid clanky china and St Bruno fog. Scones, gingerbread, ginger nuts, and the trusty rock cake were all on display; she served us diligently as eager mouths devoured all.

The plan was to arrive at low water around 23.30, then hide in flixton golf club car park and wait for an illegal rendezvous.

We duly assembled on site in good time huddled in the car park. Danny volunteered to go out on the marsh and observe the poaching as it happened or at least see anyone coming off. He could then direct us to our man hopefully with the incriminating evidence.

Joe paced around whilst Radios were tested and everything was set.

Danny marched purposely away into the gloom. He called fifteen minutes later on the Radio to let us know he was tucked away on the marsh hidden in a gully. Suddenly to our horror just as we were about to hide from view in the car park, headlights appeared from nowhere sweeping an arc like wartime searchlights, instinctively I dived into the nearest long grass commando style. This just had to be done, being compromised wasn't an option. The whole job could so easily be scuppered. My heart was racing as I peered out of the grass, what I managed to make out was a police car circling the car park, something that obviously happened routinely every night. This was performed without great purpose or enthusiasm fortunately, they didn't even bother going round the back of the clubhouse where our vehicles were discreetly parked. In someway it was disappointing; I hoped maybe our target had already arrived. Never mind our position was safe, we congratulated ourselves emerging unscathed even Joe had managed to hide successfully

Paul Nugent was the only casualty, his dive for cover landed him in a pile of dog shit, I had to laugh watching his efforts, anxiously trying to clean himself up, a task that was accompanied by some very choice language, needless to say we gave him a wide berth!

We sat for an hour when all was quiet, Hank tried to raise Danny but the airwaves were dead. He tried and tried.

"Romeo 4 come in do you read?"

No reply! The silence was deathly.

Two hours went by until Joe called it off, the tide was making therefore any chance to net the channel would have gone. We were all stood ready for the off, except for the inevitable, where was Danny?

I knew in my own mind what had probably happened and I guess everyone else did too.

Old Hank didn't mince his words in these situations.

"Yon buggers asleep, bet yur life on it"

Joe growled in frustration,

Hank and I were quickly tasked to conduct the search gingerly heading off along the railway line. Eventually after some ten minutes I heard the faint steps of a figure approaching in the gloom; it was Dan thankfully crunching along on the stone ballast. I gave one flash on my torch for reassurance, poor old Danny stood defiantly in the darkness

"Never saw a thing chaps"

That was the best he could come up with, Hank was shaking his head and we both laughed quietly to ourselves.

Everybody slowly departed from the scene, all affected by the sombre calm that follows such an operation when things don't go to plan.

The following day I got a phone call, Joe solemnly informed me that Mr. X had phoned with the news that Macadam was bragging to the whole world. It appears that his dog had sniffed out yon Becky asleep on the marsh, apparently he had just about tripped over poor Danny in a hole, shame really we so nearly had him. Macadam as expected went back to the rigs in the North Sea so we could forget about him for another three months. Fate however intervened in a dramatic and tragic manner. News filtered through that Michael had been killed in an accident on the rigs whilst repairing some drilling gear. Alas he would not tread the sands of Morecambe bay again.

This event gave me no satisfaction at all despite the fact he was never caught obviously, big brother Stan would ensure the family name figured in future events out in the bay, of that I had no doubt.

Danny and I worked together many times during what I called the Sergio years, that man was causing me no end of bother. Sergio Ferraria was a thorn in my side all through the eighties. He worked the River Stock a little, but much preferred the Brock his favourite out of the three rivers, probably due to its close proximity to his home allowing easy access to Elmbank. He would visit this area sometimes up to three times in any one day. He would skulk along with his short spinning rod or a stick, and always wearing Polaroid's, then he would dab in at all his favourite lies for poaching a fish, he was a human weasel and sly as a fox. Sergio nearly always had an accomplice usually just some young lad tagging along but very useful as a lookout.

Poachers however could develop bad habits that could bring their downfall on occasions and Sergio was no exception. Getting careless and cocky was usually down to not getting caught. Sergio was on a good run, I needed to change that. He had been visiting Elmbank at about two-o-clock most afternoons. I had observed him on several occasions as he retreated. Routine was a flaw in a poacher's make up and indeed in a Bailiff too.

I decided a stake out the area in close proximity to the weir; this consists of a long bend covering a distance of about one hundred metres. My plan was to hide on the south side and good old Danny would take the north side, this would allow a view of the whole section between our positions. I parked up a good mile away for safety and walked quietly in. I instructed Danny where I wanted him to hide; I had previously selected a place behind a thick blackthorn tree allowing a reasonably clear view of the right bank. I took up my own regular hide on a raised bank opposite the left bank.

Romeo 6 and Romeo 4, in position 13.00 hours!

I waited patiently; my red squirrel friend paid a visit to scold me passionately.

I checked the radio with Danny.

"Come in Romeo 4 do you read?"

The reply was crisp and instant in that unmistakable public school twang

"Romeo 4 receiving loud and clear, nothing to report"

Excellent so far so good!

Another half-hour went past but nothing untoward was seen apart from a heron landing on the weir. His presence helped our anonymity providing a reassurance to any interlopers.

I checked with Danny again, worryingly the response was delayed this time and the reply less precise.

I sat another thirty minutes, as all stayed calm.

I tried Danny once again but this time all I got was silence.

"Romeo 4 do you read? Come in Romeo 4"

More Silence! Come on Danny where are you? I couldn't help but whisper to myself,

"Oh no wherefore art thou Romeo"

I was expecting Sergio to appear any second, sods law would surely dictate this of that I was certain.

Strangely however nothing happened, I repeatedly tried to raise Danny but to no avail, luckily there was no sign of Sergio either. I just needed to pace around and swear, but circumstances prevailed unfortunately.

I sat back and waited, until finally at half past three out of the silence came a voice, a weary hesitant but oh so familiar voice.

"Romeo 6 are they still on the weir?"

What the hells he saying?

"Romeo 6 are they still there?"

I was perplexed at this dreamlike utterance

"Romeo 4 is who still there"?

"Sergio is he still on the weir?"

I had a mini panic attack as I scanned the weir with my binoculars, but no sign of Sergio or anyone actually, except of course our friend the Heron.

The fact he was still happily standing on the weir made me finally realise what had happened, Danny had actually fallen asleep, yes nothing new there I had already worked that bit out, but what I didn't realise until it dawned on me was the fact that he had actually dreamt Sergio's appearance.

Danny had been dreaming the whole thing. I was starting to get very annoyed by this time.

I called him

"Come in Romeo 4, there's nobody bloody well there"

A short pause followed before Danny replied again

"Has he gone Romeo 6?"

I took deep breaths

"He was never bloody there"!

I'd had enough by now, I shouted down the radio,

"Romeo 4 I'm standing down"

I left at once my moral was down just a tad! We never spoke a word on the journey home. Danny was conveniently oblivious, so what's the point I thought, any way later I calmed down enough to relate the tale to Georgina and the kids, we had a right laugh.

Danny got married to a school teacher from Sedbergh a few months after I joined the team. She was very formidable and ruled the roost from day one. The feature I remember most about Delia was her voice; she had one of those high pitched school Mam tones which certainly kept Danny in line. Delia had a Citroen CV which she drove like Nigel Mansell, how she never killed anyone I'll never know. The marriage came out of the blue taking us all by surprise, the last of the confirmed bachelors had finally been tamed. They were chalk and cheese!

7

TOWN WATER AND A DEADLY DUO

In August 1977 I was looking after Tommy's patch whilst he was on holiday in Scotland. Fish had moved well up the river and were in all the usual hot spots in and above Brockley. I had become quite familiar with Jez Bergerac who was regularly making a nuisance of himself on the town stretch. This information was passed on to me by one or two anglers and general busy bodies who observed this youth in action on a number of occasions. The content was usually exaggerated, several days old or both, which was no use to anyone apart from making me aware of the problem. This I had already deduced for myself anyway, of course information from the public could be vital at times and my golden rule was never to rule anything out, always go that bit further to be absolutely sure.

One man who walked the town every day was Timmy Dunne a well-known figure in Brockley, unmistakable in deerstalker and sunglasses. He was disabled from birth due to a deformed left arm on which he wore a rather sinister looking black leather glove giving him the appearance of some sort of Hitchcock character. He was a member of Brockley AA but very rarely actually fished himself, he was single and his personal hygiene left a lot to be desired. This was not helped by his avid use of snuff, a habit which was quite common amongst many middle-aged men in Brockley. The habit regrettably involved some disgusting nasal sounds coupled with a tell tale brown residue that found its way down his shirt and jacket. Snuff manufacturing was world famous in Brockley and still exists today so this may account for its popularity.

I saw Timmy most days whilst patrolling the town. He would without fail fill me in on all the devious crimes that had been committed on the river in my undeserved absence. Jez Bergerac was one of his pet hates because Jez lived on Cinderbarrow a notorious council estate. Several of my adversaries lived there, and so did Timmy unfortunately. Jez would take great delight in winding him up bragging of all the fish he had caught, sold, or got away with.

Jez was an expert in catching fish with a wire rabbit snare either fixed to a stick or wrapped around his wrist and tied with string. This was the most common method used that didn't involve a fishing rod.

When a salmon or trout is laid low waiting for the next lift in the river to trigger another dash upstream it will often lie with its tail poking out. This behaviour is akin to an ostrich burying its head in the sand, in other words the fish puts its head under a tree root, rock ledge, or grass banking leaving just the tail exposed tailor made for the likes of Jez to carefully slide the wire noose over. It was finally violently yanked tight before being unceremoniously flung ashore. The fish was dispatched by a sudden blow to the head and then concealed in someway followed by a sharp exit. There were those who poached in Brockley who could catch sea trout with just their bare hands alone. Jez had already learned this skill very quickly as I had witnessed on that July day the previous year. He liked nothing more than to stalk fish lying low in the forests of green ranunculus weed that wafted and waved so typically within the currents of the River Stock during the summer months.

I experienced numerous chance encounters with Timmy, who always talked a good game bragging how he sorted our Jez out.

"I chessed him tha knows, only this morning and the day afore, where's tu bin hiding, He wont do out if Ize aboot. Av telt him, I'll scop him int beck next time"

Timmy was always full of his own bravado, until one significant day. I was cautiously watching two young lads at Jubilee Bridge at the south end of Brockley. They were not regulars I knew but one was wearing a facemask and the other was sat on top of a rock holding his mate's legs enabling a submerged look under the rock to see if there was a sea trout or salmon to plunder. I hid directly above them watching for the inevitable snare. I was poised for several minutes ready to move in, until suddenly they stopped what they were doing looked up and across to the wall at the opposite bank.

Lo and behold there was our Timmy walking serenely past, he never glanced down at the boys or at me once. He was wearing his Polaroid's with which he usually scanned every inch of this pool, but not today he just kept right on going, he wasn't having any of it. Not so brave now Timmy I thought as he kept on walking, he never even looked back, true colours nailed to the flag there that's for sure. The lads concerned got a deserved ticking off; they were only about thirteen and quickly ditched all incriminating evidence. Inexperience and ignorance was typical of many such youngsters, I could only hope they wouldn't be back. I always preferred to warn young lads whenever possible providing they took heed. Some would be at an age when determining their actual progression from snotty nosed kid to obnoxious adult proved quite a challenge. The required age to purchase a fishing license is twelve, at times this is nigh impossible. You wouldn't believe how many would be twelve year olds there was in Brockley sporting moustaches or wispy pubic beards.

Jez was often knocking about through the town water; he had one of those annoying cocky faces painted with a permanent grin. He would sometimes fish legally just to wind me up, not surprisingly Danny O'Hare was the most susceptible to this practice. Danny nicknamed him "Smiler", which fit the bill very well.

Jez and many others like him also loved to snatch salmon out of a stretch called "railway dub" so named by its obvious close proximity to the railway situated at the north end of town. The Right Bank featured iron railings along the full length restricting anglers by means of a bylaw that allowed fly-fishing only. This was in place to protect stocks of fish from illegal snatchers operating in the late sixties and early seventies. The byelaw meant that catching offenders proved easier because it was an absolute offence.

I had visited several times both on my own and with Tommy or Danny; apart from some badly timed near misses Jez was still very much at large. I had good information that Jez was coming off the estate via the railway line then checking the river by the viaduct just above railway dub itself. In the river at this point were some tangled tree roots where sea trout had been lying prior to removal by foul means?

I decided one day in August to stake out this area making use of some sycamore bushes about fifteen yards back from the river. I consequently got in a nice position after lunch at about one o clock; it was a nice warm sunny day absolutely ideal. Two hours went slowly by as I sat tight, the odd rabbit passed blissfully by, then a woman with a dog that looked my way briefly but was too much of a pet to follow it up. I was beginning to waver mentally before eventually telling myself

"Give it till four o clock Jack, then bugger off".

I sat transfixed by the sound of running water for another thirty minutes, by this time I was low on concentration and ready for a move. Then without warning out of the blue a man slowly appeared walking upstream on my side of the river. I was alerted at once not least to his manner because he was moving warily and looking round in an odd guilty sort of way. He was about thirty something, scruffy wearing bib and brace denim overalls, he had a newspaper poking out of his side pocket. He moved closer, not Jez unfortunately, but who cares he looked up for it was my quick assessment.

Nearer and nearer, "oh yes we're definitely in here"

He got ever closer; my heart was thumping so loud I feared he might hear it.

Eventually he looked directly at me or so it seemed, although the leaf canopy screened me. He was now no more than six feet from my lair, I held my breath for what seemed an eternity, "has he sussed me out, does he know about my hide-hole? Surely not"!

He was now so close I almost said, "how do mate" when he peered around, however my anxiety was abruptly switched to his new and impending purpose, he turned his back on me once again before dramatically dropping his overalls in a heap on the ground, then to my shock horror he had a crap right there in front of me, he was surely very desperate. I became paralysed and unmoved as this appalling event unfolded before me. The Daily mirror finally reappeared for a sanitorial finale; I couldn't quite see the date on it despite such close proximity. I was tempted again to converse, maybe something on the lines of "nice crap pal", but I decided the shock could prompt a nasty accident. He quickly dressed before departing into the afternoon sun leaving his steamy deposit for me to saver. He left none the wiser of my presence to this day. I also left immediately heading straight home, that was quite enough for one day. Needless to say I didn't use that hideout ever again.

In 1977 I honed my skills amongst the up and coming poachers of Brockley becoming acquainted with some of the regular offenders such as Robert "Rusty" Bentley and Len Dixon. The pair mainly worked together specialising in face mask and snare type work. They were the first of my adversaries to show any signs of violence. I discovered this one day out on patrol with Tommy at Stoneybase pool about half a mile above Brockley. This was an area that consisted of a large pool designed to accumulate gravel as it swept downstream in the fast spates typical of that particular river. What followed was a long weedy glide that held many a fine sea trout. These two characters were both in their early twenties. Bentley was a very placid guy and would never offer any resistance whatsoever; in fact he was almost likeable. His appearance didn't match his personality. He was in fact big and rather wild looking, with wispy stubble and Afro hair. Dixon however was a lean mean farm worker from a farm at Burndale. He was never away from the river, a fact that eventually cost him his job. He was much livelier than his pal though, as I found out that very day.

Tommy and I had patrolled the town water earlier that day with no real problem apart from an introduction to one angler namely Les Paltrow. This man was a bit of a low life who suffered badly from gout and a weird sexual deviance that centered on small boys and teenagers. We had checked his license and left him fishing in peace. I thought at the time there was something odd about him and time would prove me right.

Following that we moved up to Stonybase and hid in the trees directly overlooking the long weedy glide running downstream from the big pool. Tommy combed over his hair for the tenth and final time then we sat it out. Before very long Bentley and Dixon came into view walking down the left bank towards our position on the opposite bank. Len Dixon wasted little time before wading into the weed directly opposite our position, whereas Bentley lit a roll up and kept nicks, if a bit casually. Tommy gave me a dig in the ribs and I saw Dixon don the facemask before bending down to commence peering under water. He was looking very furtive as he performed, carefully feeling and fingering his way through the weed. It wasn't long before he had a fish. I clearly saw it break the surface very briefly. On his return to the bank Dixon skillfully held the fish underwater. The fish was finally and triumphantly placed at Rusty's feet. Dixon grinned confidently at his accomplice before he set off again retracing his steps into the main flow for a repeat performance. It was barely a couple of minutes before he obliged us with another fish. This was poaching at the height of efficiency, the fish was gently grasped with fingers inserted into its gills then its head brought back with the other hand in a smooth deadly force to brake its now vulnerable neck.

I felt a sharp prod from Tommy, he gave the nod and we sprang into action, always make a beeline for your prey. This of course meant wading directly across the river. No other thought crossed my mind as I dashed straight in, even in summer the cold rush of water makes you gasp, good footwear was in danger of ruin here. The two miscreants were quickly on the move already heading downstream by the time I reached the safety of the left bank. In no time at all they were fifty yards in front, this was hot pursuit on foot yet dripping wet into the bargain. Tom started to run so we eventually caught them up and got them stopped. Tom did the honours with Dixon and I was left with Rusty Bentley. They both denied everything of course.

"We're just out for a walk"

and

"Just looking to see if owts about"

These I soon realised were standard bluffing replies for such a situation.

Bentley was blank and as co-operative as ever and nothing incriminating was found, he even voluntarily emptied his sodden pockets.

Dixon however still had the facemask that Tommy badly wanted to seize.

Dixon started to get rather annoyed to say the least,

"Thas not tekin that mate It's not mine to give up".

Tommy tried to reason with him but didn't get very far, all his persuasive powers were tested to the limit. Len Dixon dug in and stuck to his guns resulting in both men clutching the face mask resolutely. A tug of war ensued; it would have been funny in any other context.

"Give it up Len your obstructing me"

Len tugged even harder as he responded

"No It's a matter of principle we're not in America you know".

Next thing even Bentley was telling Ken to give it up, but he was having non-of it.

I had never come across anything like this and wasn't sure how to help.

The two men then went to ground in the continuing now bitter tug of war, a religious mild mannered Bailiff and a local thug in broad daylight.

This was serious, if anyone had ventured down this normally popular path God knows what they would think. As luck would have it no one materialised.

I couldn't let things get any worse and felt I had to intervene.

"Let him have the damn mask Tom, we can do him for obstruction"

Eventually after what seemed like an age Tom reluctantly got up and brushed himself down. He attempted to bring some sort of order to bear on proceedings whilst at the same time adjust his bedraggled comb over. He eventually recovered his composure enough to question the two men about the fish they had caught.

"Where are the two fish? And don't try and deny it, we both saw you catch them"

Rusty Bentley went pale on hearing this but a now very irate Len Dixon denied any knowledge with invincible certainty.

"What fucking fish are these then, have you made them up".

Tom had had enough and proceeded to book Dixon for obstruction as well as taking the fish. Dixon argued some more before leaving still firing a tirade of abuse waving his face mask triumphantly. I was left to book the compliant mild mannered Rusty Bentley before he slid away after his accomplice like a lingy dog.

We now had to work quickly returning to the crime scene where thankfully the two Dead Sea trout lay hidden under a nearby tree root, both were bloody with cleanly broken necks, fresh as daisies. We again pursued the two men who by this time were approaching the outskirts of Brockley.

Tom intercepted them and triumphantly displayed the two fish, Bentley said nothing and Dixon grinned sarcastically.

"Nice fish eh! But I've never seen em afore"

Tom was also smiling.

"Well you're being reported for taken em laddie whether you like it or not".

These situations often developed when everything didn't go according to plan, sods law or just plain bad luck would always apply. Prosecutions usually followed nevertheless despite total denial from most offenders. Now in this case we didn't come away with any confessions of guilt and we hadn't managed to secure the facemask. Tommy had always drummed in to me that you should never back down, so I could see why he was disappointed; however under the circumstances at least only pride had been hurt.

In cases like these we would each make out a report and submit it to the legal department for our day in court a few months down the line. The fish were secured in freezers at the office in Brockley.

During the summer the same two men poached relentlessly, several sightings and near misses were recorded. Circumstances like these could get a bit disheartening if they eluded any meaningful capture. On occasions when the beck was in flood I would sometimes come across one or both of them by chance at the big weir in Brockley. This weir was a magnet at such times, both salmon and sea trout could be observed trying to ascend this pointless structure. The weir was built to protect a sewer pipe apparently. If the rivers were in spate it was generally accepted that poaching was not possible, so some respite was experienced. Joe would be able to tend to his greenhouse or indulge in golf. Golf was his latest whim. He would talk of nothing else, at times annoying everybody by practicing his putting in the living room. Getting his attention was more or less impossible; occasionally he'd acknowledge my presence,

"Spates the best Becky there is Jack, Why dunt thee take tha day off?"

Joe would often award days off when the river was in flood, this caused some ill feeling especially for Hank who would be left seething and refusing to comply at such short notice, complaining bitterly to anyone in earshot.

"If yon man thinks I'm havin my day off to suit him, when ave already put mi bait up an everything. What good's a day off arranged at nine-o-clock that same morning?

If I was privileged enough to be working on such days I would be sent to various weirs to observe fish movement and discovered the joys of seeing all your eggs in one basket.

Regulars would appear in turn, poachers licking their lips as fish moved upstream, anglers like wise swapping tales of bigguns that got away. All the accusations insinuating anglers exaggerate the size of fish are completely true believe me I've heard them all. On days like these at the weir a five-pound salmon caught could easily be fifteen pounds before the day's out. Naturally fish that got away could reach unlimited record size, with fifty and sixty pound fish quoted with regularity. These then became legendary monsters of the deep that never actually got landed just regularly hooked played in dramatic fashion and then tragically lost to fight another day. Witnesses to these events were very rare of course.

The weir could be host to twenty or more assorted spectators on days when fish were running.

I encountered Jez, Rusty Bentley, and Len Dixon plus many more on such days at the weir, oddly a strange sort of truce would evolve. Both parties were interested in the ascending fish, but no action was possible from either party. It was a bit like Christmas day in the trenches with both sides sharing a drink. We would even admire the fish as they appeared from time to time. I would also try and humour them hoping to sift snippets of information out of them, who was running with who and what area was in favour? They in turn would quiz me about where I lived or when was I going on holiday, or which was my car. This was generally friendly sparring only to return to hostilities as soon as we met on the river at a later date. The exchanges were generally good humored providing you didn't get too clever or authoritative, then much respect was gained. There were the exceptions of course, some people never get over being nicked and these individuals had to be treated very carefully or ideally given a wide berth.

Bentley and Dixon eventually came unstuck again later that year on the R Brock; once again it was Tommy and I that struck lucky.

We had just left Brockley during one of Tommy's petrol runs and parked up about half a mile from the river. We crept covertly and calmly across footpaths and fields making detours around flocks of timorous sheep or nervy rabbits. Eventually we reached our destination stopping at a vantage point on a high banking above Elmbank weir. This continued to be the most poached section of river on the whole catchment. The banking by the weir itself and the deep section above were paddled to death with the constant traffic of expert and novice poachers. Well worn pathways were the most obvious way of knowing if fish and those that persecuted them had recently been active. Many sections of river were affected this way. In low water conditions it seemed just about every fish would be taken despite our best efforts, but you just couldn't be there all of the time.

We stood motionless here for up to five minutes, all was quiet, too quiet maybe.

We then made use of a long spinney of silver birch and alders running above the course of an old disused millrace. The race stretched like an old wound leading to the disused Brock mill, a further kilometer downstream.

We continued stealthily down like Indian scouts stopping frequently to sniff the air or listen for any human sound, after that I watched in anticipation for our human prey. Hunting men, that was the ultimate game and I was definitely warming to it, I fed from the flow of adrenaline slowly released as we progressed. Excitement and fear walk hand in hand, sometimes I wasn't sure which one I was operating under, I think both would be an accurate analogy.

We passed the actual mill to access the mill pool itself, a popular venue for our friends. I accidentally snapped a twig underfoot, which at the time sounded to me like a gun going off, consequently that stopped us in our tracks automatically. I instinctively felt the first sign of intrusion.

The faint yet unmistakable whiff of Rusty Bentleys roll up touched my senses; just enough for me to put a hand on Toms shoulder and alert him. He nodded calmly and gave the familiar faint grin. We both went down on all fours and gradually crept towards the pool.

The way was barred by holly and brambles, not a good combination so progress was slow and a bit painful to say the least.

Eventually I reached a vantage point about twenty yards from the waters edge with Tom along side. Great care was now needed the last thing we wanted was Rusty to look our way. We needn't have worried he was keeping nicks in his usual manner, nonchalantly smoking and watching Len Dixon untangle a small net, I could just about make it out to be a gate net often used for catching rabbits .

Motionless I watched carefully raising my binoculars to get a really good view. Len was now putting on his trusty facemask almost certainly the very same one he had refused to give up on the previous encounter. I hope we don't have to go through all that again I reminded myself.

In the middle of this pool was a large rock on which Len Dixon was about to use for a platform to examine the irresistible cool deep water home to several innocent sea trout now lying there.

He equipped himself to lie across the rock prompting Rusty to glance around looking as guilty as hell.

Len put his face beneath the water for what seemed an eternity before eventually surfacing for breath with a quick shake of his dripping head. Next he adjusted the net before sliding in the water; he fixed it somehow on a sharp section of the rock. Finally he stretched it across the pool and repeated the process at the far bank. Time stood still as a gentle breeze waved inoffensively across my face. The peace was suddenly shattered as Len struck violently; inevitably the net gyrated upwards from the water. The entangled desperate fish glinted in the sun amidst a shower of spray as it made its final journey onto the stony shore at Rusty's feet. Len Dixon fell backwards violently into the water amidst the confusion, only to emerge again smiling wickedly. Rusty wasted little time in giving the gasping victim a sickening blow from a rock clutched in his right hand. A second blow soon followed to make sure of a kill.

Tom was up like a gazelle waking me instantly from my concentration. I quickly recovered to pounce along side him. We had them in an instant; they hadn't a clue what hit them.

Dixon faced me chin to chin his mouth open with shock and anger, eyes bulging, his fist was clenched, I guess it was touch and go at that point. He didn't breathe as his brain fought desperately with the predicament he now found himself in. He finally let out a long deep breath, then his body shrank back falling limp and defeated with the realisation he was well and truly bang to rights. The fish gasped pitifully one last time on the slimy gravel, a few streaks of blood painted the wet stones; Rusty just shrugged his shoulders trying to appear unconcerned.

"What happens now then Mr. Brown?"

Tom smiled in victory

"We take the fish, snare, and mask as well this time.......Mr. Bentley"

Len Dixon appeared even more subdued at this point he didn't mention America or his human rights once.

"Fair enough I suppose".

That was the best he could come up with.

We walked away with all the necessary evidence feeling very pleased with ourselves, barring a bureaucratic disaster it was see you in court lads!

Results like this boosted my moral and confidence no end, rather like scoring a winning goal. All the vital elements of effort, timing, and good luck played their part.

8

COURT

Court was something I had personally dreaded during the early stages of my on the job education. A day out at Carlisle Crown court to watch and learn at one of Tommy's poaching cases was arranged to broaden my experience.

I had not needed to give evidence as yet, all the fishing without license cases had been guilty pleas, dealt with in the absence of the offender. In such cases our legal department produced a written statement of facts which I then had to read out to the magistrates. The first actual attendance at Brockley Magistrates court eventually arrived due entirely to the rod and line cases I had accumulated. Thankfully I was shepherded by Tommy sent specifically to hold my hand. I soon learned that Joe never attended court unless absolutely necessary due to his poor hearing, the possible embarrassment was too much for him apparently. Danny wasn't considered reliable enough as a guide on the day so it fell to Tom.

I was terrified of course never having been inside a witness box in my life. Dressing up smart was another requirement I had never really gone in for either. On the day I picked a good tweed jacket with white shirt and tie. I felt very uncomfortable as the three magistrates entered the court in all their pomp and majesty, I watched as the usher took control,

"All stand"

This command was strictly obeyed by everyone in the room. Silence and shuffle quietly followed allowing the clerk to sort the correct order of events.

I then had to listen whilst several Landlords applied for extensions to drinking hours followed by a rather amusing domestic dispute over a dog fouling the neighbour's garden. This did not prevent some nervous tension whilst awaiting my turn. I tried to remember what Tom had told me. Always look at the magistrates whilst reading the oath, always start your statement of facts by saying,

"This case is as follows your worships"

And then finish with,

"That is the case your worships"

Hopefully and usually an application for costs followed, which in those days was £3 to £5, emphasis was put toward administration fees as a reason. I mulled over all that had been drummed into me until suddenly the clerk looked across towards me, this was it!

"Can we deal with case seven on your sheet your worships, that of Philip Talbot, 26 Green lane, Platt bridge, Wigan. The defendant is accused of fishing by means of an unlicensed instrument"

The clerk sat down and outlined the fact that the defendant had pleaded guilty by letter. He addressed the Magistrates pointing at me in the process,

"The Water Bailiff concerned is present in court to deal with the matter your Worships"

He looked in disdain over his bifocals in my direction.

"Have you got a statement of facts Mr. Carter?"

Tom gave me a dig in the ribs, I stood to attention, then he pushed me forward, I could feel all eyes on me.

I successfully baptised my court career if rather nervously.

My victim got a £15 fine plus £3 for costs; I finally sat down with a sigh of relief.

I had proved quite successful in those early days nabbing a succession of offenders on the River. I had comparative success on lakes and tarns also, especially at weekends. Windermere and Coniston were heavily fished in those days, but my most prolific hunting ground was Hillingdon reservoir. Hillingdon is a man made lake designed to supply the Lancaster canal with a steady water supply.

Weekends often brought an influx of anglers, ninety percent predictably from Wigan. I have never known exactly why Wigan has so many anglers but it did then big style and even now to this day many Wiganers as we love to call them still fish in this part of the world. Many are your typical scroat, but there are plenty of bona fida anglers also. I have made many good friends amongst them over the years; however there are also many I would gladly never meet again.

Hillingdon was a productive venue at weekends although I don't know why because catches of trout were generally poor. Pike and roach were also present and occasionally good accounts of these fish would boost enthusiasm and numbers. One April Saturday morning in 1977 I booked twenty-five anglers without licenses on that lake alone, followed by another fifteen the day after. This proved to be a record never to be beaten. The down side of this materialised several months later at Sedbergh court. I had thirty-five of these anglers in court on the same day. Yes imagine thirty-five statements of facts to read out, but read them I did. It took nearly four hours, quite a marathon. The bench heard all of them before retiring. I waited half an hour in limbo, so I knew they must have been arguing about something.

Finally the clerk stood up at the reappearance of the bench.

"All stand"

The chairman looked me up and down; he was a big robust Farmer with ruddy outdoor features and just the hint of a dewdrop threatening to make an untimely appearance. His co jurors were both women of W.I. ilk and obviously under his spell.

"Mr. Carter we have been wondering why so many anglers have been fishing without licenses on Hilllingdon, are there any signs up stating a license is necessary?"

What! I was caught right off guard, not what you want in court I can tell you.

I was desperately thinking on my feet.

"With all due respect your worship that is not a requirement"

This fact is very true everybody has a driving license but there aren't signs on the road every few yards reminding us all, get real I thought to myself. They put their heads together mumbling and murmuring. After a short while he looked at me rather contemptuously.

"Well we think there should be signs up so could you please recommend to your employers that this be carried out"

I promised to relay this request; one doesn't. argue with a bench, I learned that soon enough. They went back into a huddle before glaring at me again.

"All the defendants will be fined five pounds each."

The very smug clerk sprang from his chair,

"Any costs your worship"

Another quick huddle immediately followed before the Chairman once again looked up.

"We have decided not to award any costs in any of these cases"

This statement was followed by a triumphant take that lad! gaze by all three magistrates.

I bowed before executing a swift exit.

I couldn't relay the news fast enough and needless to say Joe wasn't amused, the legal department dismissed it as plain bad luck on the day. The number of cases presented was obviously too many, a mistake never to be repeated I made sure of that.

The first actual trial I attended was none other than Len and Rusty involving the slow but thorough process of our legal department. I had completed the offence reports very soon after each offence ably guided by Tom and Joe. The facts of course had been recorded in my notebook in the form of contemporaneous notes as soon as possible after the actual poaching incident. These reports were then sent to our administration department and into the very capable hands of Miss Dorothy Squires. She would formerly lay the information before summons could be delivered by traditional mail to the defendant's home address. This process usually took several months, which was a bit frustrating to say the least. Time could play tricks with your memory as regards what actually happened at an incident.

The trial day eventually arrived; Tom and I met at the Town hall in Brockley which was the courts venue in those days. I was very nervous; this was not Colombo after all, it was me giving sworn evidence in court. I had learned all the facts off by heart as instructed, I repeated them back to myself over and over again, any where would do during the night, on the loo, and lastly in the car journey on the way to court.

I duly met Tom who had collected a bag of frozen sea trout, the net, a snare, and of course the infamous face mask. The Usher greeted us, a very jolly chap whose eyes always lit up at the sight of a bag of fish. I would get to know him well over the coming years.

"What happens to those then?"

He grinned mischievously opening the sack containing the sea trout seized from Dixon and Bentley his eyes widened again. Tom grabbed the bag before he got too carried away.

Miss Squires arrived; all we needed now was a Solicitor.

Miss Squires informed us we had acquired a new solicitor called Victor Bailey. He was an unknown factor at this point, his reputation however labeled him as very good at least and even a circuit judge in his other life at Manchester. The down side was he new nothing about fish.

Len Dixon arrived followed in the usual hangdog manner by Rusty Bentley. Dixon came straight over quite forcibly, so much so that I was startled. I thought for one moment he was going to grab Tom, thankfully he subsided on the last of his heavy strides.

"Am gonna plead not guilty" He was in our faces, his chin pushed out with his own importance.

Miss Squires ignored him completely causing him to visibly wilt on the spot. All part of this wonderful new game I concluded. Tom stayed pretty calm generally, so I tried my best to do likewise, Len recovered enough and grinned at me probably due to my uncertain body language. Rusty just shrugged his shoulders, rolled a fag and sat down.

Court convened at 10.00 so it was a relief when Vic Bailey finally arrived.

Vic was a short bald man with glasses and a moustache, a bit spitfire pilot in appearance. Formal introductions were made before we were ushered into a private room for pre trial talks. Len and Rusty also had a brief, how can they afford it?

Vic was a very smart cookie that was my first impression. He soon had both the usher and clerk eating out of his hand. Victor fired instructions and demands at them with his confident demeanor, trial time wasn't until 11.00. He smiled as we opened up the files to review the case. He had done his homework, although he needed us to guide him on the finer points of practicality and fishing jargon.

The two defendants were called at 11.10, Tom and myself were in court waiting for the pleas. If they pleaded guilty we could heave a sigh of relief sit down, relax and watch the show. With that scenario life would be easy as we could stay in the room without having to give evidence, however if they plead not guilty we had to leave and then be called as witnesses.

It was a three man bench that was the norm except in this case the chairman was a woman. A formidable woman at that, namely Mrs Olivia Briggs. She stamped her authority on proceedings right away weighing up our two bedraggled poacher's shuffling defiantly into the dock. Neither had smartened themselves up one bit. Len Dixon was wearing an unironed yellow T-shirt with jeans and very mucky black shoes; Bentley donned all denims with white tatty trainers, but a great deal worse he was chewing gum, he also had his hands in his pockets. They were the perfect picture of non-conformity. Mrs Briggs looked them up and down from the lofty position of the bench, she didn't say anything for about twenty seconds, and then she let them have it.

"You get those hands out of your pockets now young man, AND! Are you actually chewing gum?"

Rusty immediately stood to attention and almost looked alert,

"Remove that chewing gum now young man, I will not have this in my court do you hear"

Her voice seemed too loud to be emitting from such a small frame.

Both men were now at full attention, Rusty nervously removed the chewing gum, which I think found its way clumsily into his pocket.

She glared at them again with another long cold silence.

"Right, now you both listen very carefully to the clerk, do you understand?"

They both nodded tamely. The two remaining Magistrates were both men, one was a big farmer type, the other a small insignificant little man wearing a green velvet jacket with purple cravat. Both glared at the two wilting defendants so hard I almost felt sorry for them.

The allegations were put to both men, both timidly pleaded not guilty, the usher signaled for witnesses to leave the court. Tom and I were duly ordered out.

I was very nervous during the long wait outside.

Inside Victor Bailey was painting a picture of events as to what happened on those two occasions we had watched the two scroats at work. He emphasised the deliberate and callous acts that had occurred in the removal of those unfortunate fish. I could imagine how he would look pacing slowly around the court as his audience was sucked in. He would have them all enthralled as the sequence of events was spelled out, how the two men had set out prepared for a poaching sortie, specifically equipped with the tools of the trade. He would be explaining how Tom and I lay in wait, how it was calculated with criminal, financial, and self-gain uppermost in their minds. I could just about hear his voice from outside as I awaited my call,

Then unavoidably it came. The usher emerged donning his mischievous grin.

"Mr. Carter please come this way"

This was it I walked apprehensively into the witness box, heart bumping twenty to the dozen.

"Please face the Magistrates then read the oath from the card Mr. Carter"

I cleared my very dry throat before reading the oath. This done everybody in the room settled back with a shuffle of papers and synchronised coughing. Vic Bailey purposefully and confidently stalked across the courtroom.

He was excellent, leading me through my evidence allowing me to relate events as I had seen them, the clear view of each man, how I observed the swift even skilful removal of the fish, the way they were quickly hidden, where the snare went, and of course the face mask plus all their other incriminating actions. I was starting to enjoy myself, after all I wasn't on trial here they were. I identified the fish to the court together with actually parading them round the room demonstrating how the fish was killed and the black net marks from the second incident.

I was finally thanked and instructed to stand down after what seemed like an eternity although was in actual fact only about fifteen minutes. I then sat just behind Miss Squires; she circumspectly gave me the thumbs up. Tom was ushered in and the whole process was repeated although more emphasis was made of the wrestling match with the facemask, now sitting inoffensively on a table in court.

Next it was their turn

Robert Rusty Bentley gave evidence first; he stood typically hang dog in the Dock about to put hands in pockets but correctly thought better of it at the last moment instead they hung at sort of half mast by his sides, he was obviously very uncomfortable. Vic Bailey tore into him from the word go. He hadn't really a leg to stand on. Rusty gave some lame tale about going out for a walk to hunt a few rabbits using the net, but couldn't really explain how it ended up in the water with a sea trout entangled in it. I think left to his own devices and not heavily pressured by his pal he would almost certainly have pleaded guilty. The tale dragged on and on as he described the route they had taken, how they changed there plans and ended up by the river. It soon became rather boring, people were in danger of nodding off. Everyone positively bucked up when he stepped down.

Len Dixon followed immediately very alert and ready for battle, obviously well practiced in court procedure and not at all phased. He argued every point trying to imply that we had made the whole thing up and acting like Americans, now where have I heard that before? He was no match for Vic Bailey though, that was plain to see, and his body language faltered with each blow Vic landed. Just like Rusty Len was on a hiding to nothing, but obviously thought it was worth giving it a go.

Eventually he was allowed to sit down in the row in front of me, the bench retiring to try and reach a verdict. Once through the doors everyone relaxed and began to chat. Vic and Miss Squires had their heads together whilst Tom and I sat tight.

Rusty sat with head in hands, the epitome of a condemned man.

Len Dixon stared impassively across towards Vic Bailey........ If looks could kill!

A few silent minutes later he turned to me and spoke profoundly,

"Where the hell did you find him? He's like Perry Bloody Mason"

Len became humble and friendly at this point as the realisation of events sunk in; he even quizzed me about the possible outcome.

"How much do yu reckon then Mr. Carter?"

I shrugged my shoulders

"Who knows Len?"

Well I certainly didn't I had never been here before but Len didn't know that of course, so I tried to look knowledgeable I even stuck my neck out.

"Fifty quid happen Len"

I was positively enjoying myself by now.

His face creased to weigh up my guess,

"Aye maybe, I could cope with that I suppose, do yu think al get mi mask back"

Rusty gave a half smile in a faint look of hope,

"Not if we can help it Len"

He switched off following that comment.

Generally as time went on I learned that the longer a bench was retired over a verdict the closer a decision must be, which is not rocket science I know, but as with all courts this wasn't always the case.

This day however they were back after fifteen minutes, a mere nothing, just enough time for a cup of tea or coffee. The usher was up once more,

"All stand"

In they marched with faces a picture of neutrality, what would happen? Silence and tension gripped the room especially me. We all sat down except of course for Len and Rusty who stood acquiescently awaiting their fate.

The chairman blew her formidable nose and glanced at the sheets of paper before her, finally peering over her glasses ready to deliver.

"Mr. Dixon, Mr. Bentley, we have listened to the evidence put to us by the North West water authority and of course the water Bailiffs. We all consider these offences very serious and find you both guilty on all charges".

All three magistrates glared at the two men with further contempt, both visibly shrunk in shame. I of course wanted to shout hallelujah but restrained myself with a wink at Tom instead.

Vic Bailey shot up like a cork, puffed out his little chest ready to pronounce his coup de gras.

"Madam the water authority has spent much time and money preparing these cases, they are genuinely very concerned about dwindling salmon and seat trout stocks in the south lakes and indeed nationally. These fish are subject to persecution at sea where multi-national fishing fleets, predation by seals and other wildlife exploit them. They are also removed by legal angling, and subject to pollution in some rivers. I would therefore like to emphasize the seriousness of incidents like these before you today and their direct impact on fish numbers caused by poaching. I am therefore making an application for £100 in relation to costs for this prosecution".

Victor sat down triumphantly, Len and Rusty went a whiter shade of pale wilting even more. The bench scrutinised social reports and the clerk enquired as to the financial means of each man.

Rusty tried to emphasize the existence of his wife and four kids, how he was out of work with a bad back and on income support, a right hard luck story if ever there was one. This was obviously hopefully going to influence the court. He even stood with a slight hunched back for effect, and slyly casting a culpable glance my way in to the bargain.

Len was much more open and simply relayed the fact that he was a farm labourer on thirty pounds a week. He was clearly now resigned to his fate. The Clerk stood to move proceedings forward

"All stand"

The bench retired yet again.

We waited another thirty minutes during which time Len and Rusty sat down looking very anxious and concerned, good I thought sensing a victory.

Vic and Miss Squires talked about gardening with Len and Rusty's solicitor who had done very little for them except emphasize their meagre means and lifestyle. Both men had acquired legal aid which explained my earlier reservations.

The four sea trout they had plundered were typical of those found in the R Stock system. The smallest was a respectable 2lbs weight, whereas the best fish was a hen about 5lbs. In total all the fish weighed about 14lbs, the going rate on the black market in the late seventies was anywhere from £3 to £8 per pound depending on the outlets available. This haul therefore was worth anything up to £80 if sold to a dealer or restaurant. The amount would be less if hawked around from door to door as was often the case. Back came the Bench

"All stand"

They were soon seated. I was rubbing my hands. The chairman spoke in a sober tone emphasizing again the seriousness of all the facts.

"Mr. Bentley, Mr. Dixon for these offences we have decided that you will each be fined the same amount on each charge".

"For the first incident using an illegal instrument to remove fish you will each be fined £10

For unlicensed fishing you will each a further £10 and the same fines shall apply to the same offences committed on the second occasion, making a total of forty pounds each".

"Mr. Dixon for the offence of obstructing a Water Bailiff in carrying out his lawful duty you will be fined a further £20 and you will both pay a contribution of the Water Authorities costs of £25 each".

"Mr. Bentley that is a total of £65, Mr. Dixon in your case that is a total of £85".

There was an uneasy silence as the information was digested by all present, whilst Mrs Briggs stared unerringly at the two men before speaking again,

"How can this be paid?"

Rusty looked to the heavens, however Len replied at once

"Very slowly your Honour"

A hint of muffled tittering almost broke free, but Mrs Briggs intensified her stare totally unfazed by Lens flippant appraisal.

The clerk intervened to commence bargaining between the two convicted men. A deal was set and put to the bench. £5 per week was agreed although Rusty begged for less, however common sense prevailed fortunately and that was that.

The clerk shuffled his papers and requested the next victim. I stood to attention and bowed, before leaving, I loitered somewhat allowing Len and Rusty to leave licking their wounds. That was my first trial successfully completed. Tom and I treated ourselves to a coffee in Toggnarellis café to savor our victory.

9

GOODBYE TOM AND HELLO BIG DON

By May1978 I was coming up for two years in my career on the river, I was grateful for all the skills I had gained working with Tom. Tom had shown me the ropes more than anyone else on the team. I considered myself well on the way to becoming a half-decent Bailiff becoming familiar with all the methods and tricks of the trade required. The main field craft skills took in activities such as crouching behind walls, crawling along on your belly or hiding in bushes for hours on end. Understanding wildlife behaviour was vital plus the ability to distinguish fresh foot prints from those several days old be they human or otherwise. It often went wrong of course as was the case of the three poachers I had seen on that first eye opening day out with Hank, luck played a big part also as it does in all facets of life.

The three men in question on that fateful day with Hank all lived in Burndale and worked at the paper mill. If they worked the night shift they would invariably surface after lunch to go fishing on the River Brock in their own customised manner. Their style was rod and line with the inevitable snatching device fixed on the end. I had come across them several times just walking into or returning from their little sorties. Each occasion had been embarrassing and nerve racking from my point of view as I was still learning the job. They also favoured elm bank and it was there I almost caught them. I had been in a hide about fifty yards away from the fish pass located at the corner of the weir. This pass was an old wooden structure that frequently became blocked with debris, however salmon and sea trout could be observed ascending during high water. I had sat for about an hour; the only human intrusion was a woman passing leisurely by with a Jack Russell. Dogs are pretty good at finding Water Bailiffs as a rule, but I was far enough away so as not to be detected in this case. Luckily there wasn't any nose pointing or sniffing to upset the job, maybe this old mutt was too mollycoddled to worry. I had also been examined by a very irritable red squirrel that scolded me from the tree above my head. This was a performance I witnessed quite often in such situations. These delightful creatures were still quite common in the area at that time, indeed throughout south Lakeland. I had regular close encounters which made being there worth while even if no poachers turned up. I was obviously invading his space and he certainly let me know it. The much-maligned grey squirrel has now regrettably all but replaced the red in south lakes making the world a much poorer place that's for sure.

Eventually the three musketeers as I had nicknamed them came skulking up the footpath like three hobgoblins. The big fat guy was a nasty piece of work and what brains there was appeared to be all his. The other two never seemed to use a rod, although they were pretty good lookouts. Fatty began assembling the rod with what was almost certainly a large treble hook or some similar fiendish device. I soon came to the conclusion that I was too far away to spot anything meaningful from my present position. I decided to sneak in a bit closer, unfortunately the cover was a bit sparse, only comprising of flimsy Hazel saplings and the odd Holly. A dry stone wall stretched about thirty yards to my right but unfortunately a short piece of open ground lay between it and me. If I could just get to the wall I could then sneak along and come up ten or fifteen yards behind them. I waited till fatty was about to make his first cast before crawling on all fours through the dry grass to the mossy clad stone sanctuary. I made it with ease gaining a better vantage point, a process that took about five minutes, no problem. I crawled stealthily further along the wall until I reached a gap once occupied by a coping stone now dislodged and lying in the grass. I paused for breath, waiting to confirm my anonymity before slowly peering through the breach. The three men were examining the pool all wearing Polaroid's and pointing at fish swimming nervously in the beck. Grunts of exclamation at fish sightings were now within my earshot. Fatty then picked up the rod, regrettably in my enthusiasm I stretched my head up just a little higher straining for a better view. This alas was a fatal move, fatty himself scanning round alert as ever spotted yours truly, all I heard was one word "BECKY!" instantly all three were on the move, I have never seen such a speedy exit as was executed by the three musketeers that day. I only had myself to blame for overstepping the mark and allowing my position to be compromised. Needless to say I was very annoyed with myself. Nevertheless it's a very fine line I crossed that day between success or egg on the face; in this instance most definitely the latter.

The three musketeers never did get caught because fatty moved to Lancaster leaving the remaining brain dead duo to fade away forever amongst common law wives, young kids, and government handouts.

My confidence was a bit bruised after that experience; however a similar situation arose a few days later, except on this occasion on the River Brant between Brockley and Mill Bridge.

I was gently returning home one Lunchtime prior to doing an estuary patrol with Danny O'Hare. I was beck watching from the car as I usually did when the river ran close to the road, Georgina my wife regularly told me off for veering off course whilst craning my neck to see over a wall or along the banking.

On this occasion I unexpectedly spotted Rusty Bentley quite by chance skulking along the path by the river in his own familiar hang dog style. I kept on driving so as not to alert him to my presence. I performed a hasty circular tour of about three miles bringing me around and ahead of Rusty. Eventually I parked up in the small industrial estate at Millside. Hurriedly I grabbed the essentials and set off back downstream. I anticipated Rusty's pace and found a hide in a small hazel thicket close to the road. My vantage point was clear and looked towards a bend in the river. Situated there was a deep pool intertwined with the roots of large alder trees towering overhead.

Needless to say I didn't have to wait very long until Rusty appeared. He was alone except for a large placid looking lurcher loping along just behind, the dog comically carried the same gait as its master. Rusty inevitably stopped by the pool and lit his customary roll up, after which he sat and quietly smoked in his usual laid back style. Five minutes went by before anything happened, typical Rusty! Until eventually he started fiddling about in a white carrier bag, the dog sat down and yawned lazily, they were a perfect match. Five minutes later Rusty was down in the water to commence systematically working the pool; he managed a further five minutes or more before returning to the bank to sit down again. I put my binoculars on him and watched patiently as he ratched about inside the carrier bag again. This time however he pulled something out, I strained to see, it was a pair of binoculars which he put round his neck. I couldn't believe my eyes, worse was to follow, I watched him turn my way; consequently it was quite a shock when he looked through the glasses right back at me. There followed a frozen moment in time as I looked at him looking back at me, it felt surreal, we both just looked at each other. Rusty's next action was as cool as you like, he actually waved at me, even the dogs ears pricked up as it to looked nonchalantly in my direction. The next thing I new Rusty was on the move downstream with a shake of his head leaving me stranded. I sat for a few irritating minutes trying to absorb what had happened.

Finally I regained a little composure before deciding on an examination of the area just in case I could find something incriminating, although this was clutching at straws to be fair. I eased out of my hide before walking gingerly across. I spotted his fag end in the grass close to the waters edge and it was clear where he had flattened the grass under some brambles. Above was a hole in the banking probably the vacated lair of some bygone mink. I convinced myself for some reason this was a likely hiding place for a pilfered fish, so in I went with my arm up to my elbow. I was immediately confronted by a swarm of very angry wasps. They of course showed enthusiastic appreciation by stinging me once on the arm and twice on top of my head, as if I hadn't had ample pain for one day. Enough was enough so I retreated wounded and well pissed off. The tale I relayed to Joe and Danny on my return, was needless to say not received with any degree of sympathy and none was expected.

In November of 1978 at Beechwood one wet miserable morning I was discussing the next night patrol with Joe and Danny, when Tom arrived with a very satisfied look on his face.

Joe peered over the top of his specs and puffed triumphantly on his pipe

"Has tu got it then Thomas?"

"I'm afraid so Joe"

Tom emitted his goody goody holier than thou Methodist laugh,

I was sure someone would let me in on the secret in a minute.

Joe glanced my way and gave a low chuckle,

"Yon fella's ganin up int world Jack"

"What do you mean?"

I met Toms gaze but Joe spoke again

"He's gittan a promotion tha knows; he's bin tekan on as Inspector for the R Eden at Carlisle"

I was shocked, I never really imagined Tom moving away. How would we cope?

Or even how would I cope?

I sat supping my tea and rock cake mulling over the news, Joe and Tom discussed the finer points of the R Eden. It didn't take long to get my head round the present scenario, the team was now or about to go a man down and new blood would be introduced, a rare event indeed. It was at this point a certain penny dropped. I realised this could be an opportunity for me also. I knew within minutes I wanted Tom's patch, the more I thought about it the more I wanted it, the street credential associated with the upper Brock was very desirable if a bit daunting. I certainly had the hunger and was now sufficiently experienced or at least in my own eyes I was. The seeds had been sown that first day when Jez Bergerac took that initial fish from under my untrained nose. The very same day Tom was successfully rounding up Ben "fingers" Jackson half a mile upstream with the help of Brockley police. Jackson had netted ten sea trout before being nicked. I had sat in Carlisle court as an observer fascinated by the new experience and the satisfaction as Fingers got twelve months. I remembered very clearly the drama as they took the oath and the frozen exhibits of fish displayed across the courtroom. The guilty plea given that day sent a feeling of relief throughout the prosecution so we could sit back and watch the Barrister graphically describe the sequence of events of the unfolding tale. Jackson came across as a very lazy man on the dole, spending his days working the river. A vivid and drawn out blow by blow account was relayed to the magistrates, how this man stripped off, strung a short net across Stoneybase pool in the R Brock on a hot summers day. He then removed ten unfortunate fish efficiently and ruthlessly into his sack. Unbeknown to him however all this right in front of the watchful gaze of Tommy Brown. I will always remember the look of hate on his face as they led him away.

So yes I wanted Toms patch; I was hooked and very keen, now all I had to do was convince the powers that be. Tom left a month later to become a very successful and well-liked Fisheries Inspector, surprisingly I hardly saw him ever again in the ensuing years.

Joe was keen enough for me to fill the breach Tom had left, so after the winter of Seventy eight seventy nine I took over the upper Stock together with all the associated delinquents.

Joe and Hannah had my successor lined up in a very short space of time. Don Parker was a butcher in Tesco's apparently he'd been pushing for a career change for sometime and because Hannah worked in the same supermarket he had obviously used the situation well, he also lived close to the bottom reaches of the R Stock. Don was a big bloke of six foot two with large torso to match, he started in the spring of seventy-nine and we soon became good friends. He was young at twenty-four with wife and three kids already; he had a great sense of humour, which is crucial in our job.

He began much as I had, learning as he went along, although I was now in the lofty position of being able to pass on a lot of the knowledge I had picked up from Tom and Joe. Big Don as he became known in the team liked the estuary work quickly gaining a good knowledge of all that went on in that mysterious environment. He took the east or left bank side whilst Danny looked after the west bank. In reality they did both at times especially when covering for each other.

Don came on to my new patch in the early summer to help me just as I had done with Tom, he soon adapted whilst I showed him all the hot spots. I introduced him to the likes of Jez Bergerac, Timmy Dunne, and of course Len and Rusty plus many more. The situation was as bad as ever when on any given day from July onwards to Christmas we could have stayed in Brockley alone just to chase down poachers, never mind going into the upper reaches.

Thankfully Don was keener than most so we soon became a deadly force and cases mounted up. Jez Bergerac was caught using a snare. The Hodgkinson brothers likewise, Jez was caught again using a rod in the town stretch without a license. There was another duo operating namely Sid Cooper and Chris Collins, they were becoming quite a problem that summer. We chased them for weeks resulting in a few near misses mostly on the R Stock but it was at night when we finally made a breakthrough.

Don was up for some night work, so as the late summer blended towards autumn we trailed the evenings and nights both by vehicle and on foot. We covered every inch of all three rivers in the dark looking for our quarry without too much success throughout the season. One night in September we decided to walk from Burndale up to Grubbins Bridge on the R Stock a distance of about two miles there and two miles back. It was a dark starless sky bereft of any wind, sound traveled well as we moved cautiously upstream stopping every hundred yards or so to assess each sound and shadow. The odd splash of a restless sea trout, or plop of an eager mink together with the familiar hypnotic gurgling of fast flowing water. These familiar sounds were about as much as had happened until we approached the old bridge. Oddly as we neared I heard an unfamiliar noise, Don who was slightly ahead stopped dead in his tracks and pulled me back.

"Listen what's that"

It was weird, not a noise I could associate with straight away, all I could hear was this thumping sound which materialised into none other than a horse galloping round the field.

"We must have spooked him Don"

The horse was white and eerily visible.

There was more to come, Don at this point was creased up stifling uncontrollable laughter as best he could.

Not only was this white ghostly beast prancing round the field, but a round of thunderous amplified farts accompanied each landing of thudding hooves. This was to become the farting horse of Cumbria;

I too was doubled up by now, both of us collapsed in a heap trying to come to terms with the situation, listening to a bizarre symphony played on the night air whilst the horse circumnavigated a five-acre field continuously. The purpose of our mission proved futile as we fought back tears and retreated.

The horse remained in that field for several years. Needless to say even to this day it is the field of the immortal farting horse!

Obviously we didn't see anything of Collins and Cooper, or anything else for that matter. Later that backend in November however something remarkable happened. Following the first spell of frosty weather Big Don and I embarked on another short evening patrol commencing just after tea following what had been a glorious autumn day. It was just nicely dark ideal time to cruise around by vehicle looking for poacher pick ups. It often proved to be the case after daytime poaching expeditions that fish were hidden or carried to a place of concealment near a road to be picked up in a vehicle later that evening under the protection of darkness. The risk of carrying the fish home in daylight was obviously too great so we aimed at maybe dropping on to something. This particular evening would turn into our lucky night; I accompanied Don in his blue Vauxhall Viva van checking everything carefully through Brockley, then following the river up to Burndale. The trip so far had been uneventful. Unimpressed by events so far we called in at Barkers paper mill for a brew with the night watchman. Half an hour later we resumed the journey further upstream on to the R Brock past Brock Bridge then up the valley, it was 19.00 by this time. The road was a typical country lane flanked by traditional hedgerows laden with sloes and blackberries. Don drove slowly but purposely in silence until a strange occurrence took us both by surprise. The van rounded a bend to almost collide with a lad who suddenly jumped out waving his arms about. Don swore immediately, hit the brakes, and then pulled up abruptly. Don wound down his window to reveal a sight well worth seeing. To our bewilderment who should be stood there shivering and bedraggled but the one and only Christopher Collins, his face a picture of shared amazement and horror.

A brief silence followed before the poor lad managed to speak

"Oh….uh, its you lads is it?"

Don was nearest to him illuminating his face by maglite, Collins froze like a rabbit.

"What you on with then Chris?"

Collins recovered some vague coherence,

"Nowt much as just waitin on a lift like"

I sprung out of the van grabbing my own torch in the process. Cooper was just behind his accomplice hemmed against the hedge looking hugely embarrassed. I could see Don now peering behind Cooper

"What's on the ground behind you then Sidney?"

I too had spotted it by now dumped on the roadside, a large white plastic carrier bag wedged between Sid Cooper and the hedge, a fish tail was just visible protruding. Poor old Sidney made a desperate even comical attempt at concealing the booty. It wasn't their lucky night he soon realised we had both clocked it.

I moved round shining my torch in the area of his legs supposedly hiding the offending article

Sid burst into full voice at this point,

"Its nowt to do wid us like, we just appened on it, honest to God"

I took the bag whilst Don got out of his van, Collins was about to walk off only to be collared at once by Don.

"You just hang on there a minute or two mate"

I gave Don the nod to shine his light on the bag as I opened it. It wasn't any surprise as by now not one but two large fish tales protruded. I tipped them on to the tarmac still warm from the day's sun. Two fish lay before for all to see, one was a cock sea trout about 5lbs, complete with deep snare mark around its tail obviously fresh, the second fish was a hen salmon of at least 7lbs weight. This fish also had a snare mark round its midriff so would have given them quite a tussle. Fresh caught fish such as these don't show signs of rigamortis for several hours after capture. I looked further into the depths of the bag where I also discovered two wet face masks, a soaking wet shirt and two wire snares… Bingo!

I challenged both men who by now were becoming resigned to their fate. The pair stood before me wet, cold, and filthy. Collins gave a shrug of the shoulders, took a deep breath and spoke first,

"We was waiting for our lift, thought you were it"

Sid Cooper couldn't contain himself as he questioned Don

"How long you had yon van like?"

"Why?"

"Cause its bloody well same as the yan was supposed to pick us up like"

The poor sods had apparently been waiting for a blue Viva van just Like Dons so no wonder they were sick. Unprofessional as it was spontaneous laughter broke out.

"Not your lucky day lads"

Collins even managed a sickly smile of his own,

"You're not fucking joking, took us all day to catch them buggers"

They graphically relived the day's events for our benefit, detailing how the fish had been taken from Cold harbour pool. It wasn't unusual for poachers to describe exploits in this manner once the game was up. Fantastic tails of survival in freezing water, or how they had stayed under for five minutes until bursting lungs forced a retreat. I often had to walk away from exaggerated tales embroiled in the verbal diarrhea fuelled by over active egos.

I put the two men successfully in my book before seizing the booty. To spoil their night completely I left them to walk home. I don't know if another blue Viva van ever turned up or not but I bet they didn't try it again.

The next day I was relaying the previous night's success to Georgina, but she obviously had something else on her mind. I was then given a bit of news about Danny and Delia, which took my mind away from our success completely. The pair had only gone and adopted a child. I was flabbergasted at this piece of news. If ever a couple were unsuitable to have children then it was those two. I felt almost like telling them to send it back, Georgina put me firmly in my place, so that was that, a done deal apparently. The young lad concerned was from a broken home in Workington. Indeed later that day whilst down at Beechwood this was confirmed when Danny was seen with a spotty faced ten year old kid in his garden.

Cooper and Collins pleaded guilty some months later at Brockley Magistrates court. The exploits of that autumn afternoon cost them £100 each in fines together with £50 costs.

10

DON GETS TO GRIPS WITH THE BAY

The main problem months out in the bay are July and August especially in a dry summer when salmon and sea trout build up in huge numbers. The fish wait in the tides to run up into fresh water, unable to progress if flows are inadequate. Joe also had a keen eye for the estuary except he was more a people watcher trying to keep one step ahead of the Flixton fishermen. A typical estuary patrol with Joe would involve parking in Flixton at a place where the bay could be observed without actually getting out of the Land rover. Surprisingly there are several such venues, sometimes he would use more than one depending on tides or net positions. Tractors used by the fishermen could be observed in comparative comfort with the aid of binoculars and a good supply of St Bruno. Joe was however one of those thick skinned individuals who thought nothing of knocking on someone's door, then inviting himself in for a cup of tea. This method was very productive as it took advantage of any family fall outs that had occurred in Flixtons close knit community. Joe was very adept at persuading certain individuals to spill the beans when it concerned a bit of illegal fishing. He used flattery, bribery or subtle threats to get information. Quite often though the best information arrived without any prompting at all, usually in the form of a phone call grassing up a cousin, Uncle, mate or even ex mate.

Just such a scenario occurred in July 1979 not long after Don started work. Joe got us together at Beechwood armed with information gained about a certain individual in Flixton. This guy was a full time fisherman out of the village who had obviously upset the applecart somewhere along the line.

Jack Dixon or "Mad Jack", as he was known was one of the many Dixons in Flixton, quite a few of whom fished either part or fulltime. Jack however was not licensed to catch salmon or sea trout, instead he earned his fulltime living quite nicely trawling for shrimps, beach netting for flukes, or cockling. The number of fishermen licensed in Flixton to catch salmon was only eight. The method used is an ancient tradition by way of a lave net; this net is rather like a large landing net with a wooden handle. The net has a frame to which is attached a single sheet of netting forming a bag or purse. It is V shaped and about two metres across. This method still continues today, each license costs £100 per annum and is not transferable.

Jack so it seemed was working outside his remit, coming off the sands with more than just a few salmon, which would no doubt be considerably boosting his income. He had an accomplice as well according to Joe's source, a scroaty little man called Willie Bland alias the "Flixton weasel". He was well known for latching on to anyone who wanted help with anything a bit dodgy. In fact it seemed to me just being in his company sent out all the wrong signals to anybody unfortunate to cross his path, especially those in authority.

So it came to be Don and I were sat in Joe's living room amongst tea and slab cake, Joe sat pensively sucking hard on his faithful pipe. We sat waiting in anticipation for the inevitable words of wisdom.

"We'll gan down tomorrow at first light, tide should be just reet. We'll catch em coming off wi a bit a luck".

It materialised that Mad Jack and the weasel had some beach nets about half a mile out from Flixton Promenade, The scam involved sneaking the catch off close to the golf club in the same area that poor old Michael Macadam had used.

Beach nets were used extensively in the bay mainly for catching flukes and the occasional Bass or Mullet. Wooden stakes were pushed into the sand on a slightly raised or dipped area of beach, and then a wall of netting was attached in a way that allowed the incoming or making tide to lift the netting. The site was carefully selected and could easily be up to a hundred and fifty yards in length, success would come with years of experience and a trained eye. The net fished as the tide ebbed off catching the fish as they dropped back into the main channels. If the net was set too close to a main channel the risk of intercepting salmon and sea trout would be increased, it was this very scenario that Mad Jack was exploiting.

The three of us arranged to meet at Croftgill stores at three thirty the following morning, which was in fact a Friday.

It was a fine clear summer dawn when we set off in Joe's Land rover; he didn't even light his pipe. Joe anticipated they would visit the net at first light when the tide was about one and a half hours ebb, this would mean that fish would be already drawn back to the net but not exposed long enough for gulls to plunder.

Our plan of attack was simple Joe and I would wait by the golf clubhouse near to the railway crossing, meanwhile Don was sent on to the marsh edge to hide in the bushes on the seaward side of the railway. From here he would have a clear view across the open sands and hopefully see them coming off. In this case they hadn't been using a vehicle at all, opting instead to operate solely on foot necessitating a mile walk out from Flixton followed by a further mile round trip out to the net. The duo obviously didn't want a vehicle discovered on site as a give away. We waited about half an hour aided by the old and bulky first generation of Pye hand radios, so when Big Don excitedly chirped up it was 04.30.

"Romeo seven to Romeo one, they're coming off Joe, walking right this way"

Joe was whispering and whistling quietly in anticipation as we waited. I in turn was ordered to operate the radio, Joe didn't do radios!

"Romeo seven to Romeo one they have a bag each"

This was brilliant news, two men coming off carrying bags of what could only be fish. I wished and hoped that at the very least some salmon would be in one of the sacks. Ten, fifteen minutes went by it seemed like forever. Joe signaled we move up to the railway by the road, I thought we were a bit exposed but all seemed quiet.

"Romeo seven to Romeo One, they're on the railway now."

My heart was doing its usual drumbeat; I could hear the sound of footsteps on the gravel track. Almost at once they arrived, Mad Jack had yellow oilskins smeared in sand for his efforts, he was tall, about fifty but looked more like sixty he was also carrying a heavy Hessian sack. The weasel aptly named with toothless dribbling mouth hanging ajar, donned an old slimy parka over similar waterproof leggings that had seen better days. Joe intercepted the two men with a friendly smile

"Now then lads what we got here then?"

Mad Jack looked ready to explode, but Joe ignored him and instead looked directly at me,

"Grab the sack Jack"

That was my prompt, I took it gingerly under the impression that Mad Jack might just kick off by putting me on the deck, fortunately however he seemed to calm down at this point before he spoke.

"They're na but fleukes tha knows"

He was right, he watched intently whilst I eagerly delved in the bag to find twenty plus fine flukes and nothing else. One nil to Mad Jack and the weasel.

Joe was stoking up the old pipe at this stage and didn't seem overly concerned, whereas I assumed we'd drawn a blank, but what about the other sack?, I needn't have worried.

Right on cue Don appeared like the cavalry over the railway embankment

"They hid this sack Joe"

Don had a similar hessian sack to the first one looking even heavier, Mad Jacks face fell to the floor, his eyes went red followed by some serious trembling, he appeared apocalyptic. The weasel was obviously of the same ilk as Rusty Bentley, he seemed to shrink into acceptance mode compliant that their little scam was about to be laid bare, he was right!

Don was on a high at this point,

"The bags got seven salmon in Joe",

One all or even two one to us, what a result!

They were bang to rights and Joe let them have it with both barrels, he was a formidable force with such damning evidence at hand. The two men were booked for unlicensed fishing and the fish confiscated. We could have gone and seized the net but the practicalities of doing this were too great, so Dixon was instructed to remove it after the next tide to prevent any further chance of catching salmon. They eventually left with their tails well and truly between their legs and victory to us. I went with Don out to the net to measure and locate it whilst Joe sat in his land rover supping tea listening to the farming programme on Radio four.

That should have been that but Mad Jackie Dixon wasn't quite done yet.

Joe instructed Don and I to go out again the following morning to double check that the net was removed and our duo were not still performing.

I met Don at Croftgill again the following Saturday morning at 04.00. We traveled in his van. We even checked some of the bottom pools on the Stock showing face amongst the die hard sea trout anglers still on the river. It didn't do any harm to be seen and give the impression that Bailiffs were out and about twenty four seven. I managed to create this illusion for thirty years, even though either as an individual or as a team despite many long hard weeks it was impossible to be on duty all of the time, after all we did have a life outside work as well. Sometimes what with holidays and days off it was impossible to have any body on duty at night for long periods even weeks in extreme cases. I can think of many anglers and landowners who just assumed we were around all the time, when in fact this was seldom the case at all.

Don and I followed a similar pattern that morning as we had done the previous day excepting we both went to Dons special place of concealment, a nice friendly sycamore on the railway embankment. We waited and waited but no sign of our men. Finally I concluded that catching them had done the trick so at six thirty we left our position and returned to the van for a quick brew and a rethink.

I suggested a run to Flixton prom, so a few minutes later saw us proceeding slowly along the coast for about a mile until we reached the railway station in Flixton. The van was ditched in the car park before we walked out on to the promenade. The promenade at Flixton stretches about two miles adjacent to the sands providing an excellent if rather open place for observations. It was now 07.00, Flixton folk were out getting newspapers and walking dogs, so our presence on the prom was not out of place. I scanned the sands with my binocs and couldn't believe my eyes.

"Don do you see what I see?"

He nodded

"Cheeky bastards"

It was none other than our two culprits walking calmly home across the sands laden down yet again. Don was laughing away to himself,

"Are they all like this?"

I replied reluctantly.

"Often"

We returned to the Van to quickly head further west for about half a mile, here a small level crossing was situated not far from Mad Jacks home. It was a fair guess this was the point of intended egress and we were not to be disappointed.

The two men clocked us about three hundred yards from shore, surprisingly no panic set in, they just kept coming looking unconcerned. I was puzzled enough to consider maybe they did only have flukes on this occasion.

I was very apprehensive watching as they approached, especially when I saw what Dixon had in his grubby right hand. It was a rod, an actual fishing rod. Don looked across to me and swore,

"What the fuck are they playing at?"

On arrival we were greeted with all guns firing Mad Jack thrust his considerable chest forward and grinned roguishly.

"We av three salmon, caught em wit rod...... ha ha"

I was not amused, they were just taking the piss, and I had to think quickly. The job often had a tendency to throw up a situation totally unexpected, resulting hesitation being a recipe for confusion. If I was sat at home able to mull things over, plan, look at maps and get all possible offences into perspective then the way ahead would be straight forward usually. If however, when out on the job something like this situation occurred offences had to be identified at the time and very quickly. Of course as time went on I learned from experience so it happened less often, but never be off your guard, life could kick you in the nuts at times.

After a bit of small talk I was able to think long enough to wipe the smile off Mad Jacks face.

"Have you got a license Mr. Dixon?"

"Aye, I have that laddie"

He proudly showed me a full rod license for salmon purchased the previous day together with a very smartarse grin.

"Can I inspect the fish then Mr. Dixon? "

"cus yu can laddie be my guest"

Don tipped the fish on the deck, my eyes lit up.

"They're net marked Mr. Dixon"

He wasn't fazed,

"So what like"

I replied head on

"I don't believe you caught them with that rod"

He stepped back indignantly

"Callin me a liar now is tu"

"I am taking these fish for forensic examination"

Mad Jack stepped back to scratch his frowning head

"Tha can't do that laddie I gitten em fair and square"

I took hold of the bag, refilling it with the salmon, Mad Jack lurched forward to make a grab for it, and luckily for me big Don made a timely intervention.

"I wouldn't do that if I was you mate"

Mad Jack was trembly red by now and salivating, however Don's formidable frame stood between him and his booty. I took the bag and stepped back. The weasel stood huddled as usual probably wishing he'd stayed in bed.

"I am reporting you for taking these fish with an unlicensed instrument namely a net, the marks are clear for all to see.

"Nay nay lad them marks must of happened before I gitten em"

I stood my ground

"We'll see about that".

I cautioned him as we had done the previous day then I issued a receipt for the fish, it was now 07.30

"Tha can stick that up your arse pal I ain't signin nowt, and I'll be gittin a Solicitor fust thing".

All this went down in my book of course as said verbatim. We then made a timely sharp exit, Mad Jack did not look amused, and I didn't want to give him the chance to argue further.

The next job was to revisit the net, which we did as soon as the fish were locked safely in Dons van. Half an hour"s walk across the sands warmed me up considerably. We found the net still positioned as per the previous day, only this time Don fixed a waterproof label to it stating a direct instruction to remove it.

It came to our knowledge after these events that as word got round the fishermen's grapevine Mad Jack was telling everyone that he had been caught by a young lad, an old man, and a Pakistani. The Pakistani was me apparently due I think to my suntan and good looks?

I presented the bag of fish to Brian Holloway our resident biologist at the area office first thing Monday morning. He phoned me later the same afternoon confirming net marks on all the fish consistent with the mesh size on Mad Jacks type of net. The most telling fact however was the lack of any hook marks in the mouths of any of the three salmon. If a fish is caught by rod and line the hook obviously leaves a puncture mark somewhere in the mouth, but these had none giving valuable weight to our case. My only concern would be whether our legal department would buy it, fortunately they considered it worth a shot, and bearing in mind we had the previous day's offences as well. This also lead to an extra charge of taking salmon during the weekly close season, that commenced at 06.00 on Saturday morning until 06.00 on Monday morning, this rule allows free passage of migratory fish at weekends thus increasing the stock in the river and also appeasing the rod anglers.

This case eventually came to court the following January and I was a bit worried to say the least. The two men appeared on the day looking half decent, very subdued, unrepresented and extremely nervous.

They were called to the witness box just after lunch after we had waited all morning held up by an assault case featuring non other than Len Dixon would you believe. Len apparently had attacked a man in one of the many pubs in Brockley because he was chatting up his wife. This did make the morning a bit more entertaining as I watched poor old Len get six months, which was great news for the salmon in the R Stock. He would not be back in the river till at least July. It's a pity they couldn't have started his sentence then, when the fish would just be arriving in the river.

Our two men eventually appeared standing in the dock side by side. The weasel was first to hear the charges read out, now Willie Bland had never said much on any of our numerous encounters always preferring to let Mad Jack do the talking. There was a very good reason for this apart from the fact he was a naturally quiet sort of guy at the best of times, it turned out Willie had an unfortunate speech impediment in the form of a stammer which was obviously exacerbated when he became stressed.

The clerk read out the charges,

"Mr. Bland on the 15th of July 1979 at the R Stock estuary near to Flixton-on- sands in the company of John Dixon you did fish for salmon or trout with an unlicensed instrument, how do you plead Guilty or not guilty?"

The weasel took his time and an awkward silence filled the court "n-n-nuuuuuuu not g-g-guilty"

It was embarrassing, I felt almost sorry for him, then as each charge was read out he became more stressed each answer taking longer and longer. Then after the final charge of taking fish during the weekly close season was read out he once more attempted to speak.

"n-n-nu-nuu"

a long pause followed, we all held our breath until, Willie finally gripped the witness box tightly with both hands shaking his head in frustration, it had all become too much. Suddenly swiveling round he looked the magistrates straight in the eye, his face red with embarrassment through utter defeat, he spoke dramatically.

…. "Oh bollocks to it I'm guilty, I done it all"

The look of relief on his face was supreme he slumped forward across the dock, all this despite the laughter that erupted from everyone except the magistrates and of course a now furious Mad Jack.

If Jack Dixon could have got hold of the weasel at this point I think he would be on a murder charge.

The whole defence was now in pieces leaving poor old Jack with little choice but to enter a guilty plea as well.

The end result was total fines of £250 each with £65 costs, quite a good fine in those days. Jack Dixon left the court in a blaze of defeat and never spoke to me again until one more encounter yet to come!

11

INTO THE EIGHTIES

The nineteen eighties turned out to be a significant decade for Jack Carter and the world of fisheries in south lakes. Important changes were taking place both socially and environmentally and the poaching situation was still dire despite good prosecutions during the two previous years. I had acquired a growing knowledge with the help of the team especially Tom and Joe. Big Don and I forged a good partnership, Don had also made good inroads in the Bay resulting in several successful prosecutions.

The summer of 1980 was Joe's last before he retired after reaching the full distance of sixty-five. The estuary was very active in July and August that year, whatsmore Joe's snitch was also productive.

Mad Jackie Dixon was supposedly busy yet again, reportedly up to his old tricks bringing off fish from his stake nets, so the rumors indicated.

I was as usual summoned to Beechwood along with Danny to discuss a new plan of action; Danny was well up for it, mainly because they had run rings round him for weeks. Joe peered menacingly at Danny over his specs

"What's tha bin doin down yonder Dan, yon buggers coming off all owert spot"

Danny stuck out his chin and adjusted his beret.

"Oh no Joe I've been watching from the Nunnery, I haven't seen anything suspicious"

Joe glared back at him,

"Well Danny boy my sources tells me thas wrong so tha needs to shape up and stop yon bugger coming off,…. or the Nunnery is where yull be permanent like!"

I knew what was coming next, as soon as Danny looked my way,

"We could go down this afternoon Jack if you like the tides just right"

So that was that I was lumbered, Danny spent half an hour getting organised running backwards and forwards from his house and garage like a nebulous poodle. Joe had really wound him up to the point where panic wasn't quite set in, but close. Joe could soon wind Danny up like this and the fact that they lived almost next door to each other didn't do Danny any favours.

Eventually he was in my van together with pipe, tobacco, walking boots, gaiters, flask, various apples, pears, and an assortment of notebooks and diaries. We had only done half a mile before Danny discovered he had left his faithful walking stick in his garage, so back we went for it, he even wanted to bring Zara, but there I definitely drew the line. I only had that mutt in the van once and the stink of German shepherd lasted a week, much to the disgust of Georgina and the kids. Danny's adopted lad watched the whole performance in silence. I always felt uneasy in young Andrews's presence; he was a bit odd to say the least, always on his own. If he played with other kids they were always girls for some reason. Maybe he just preferred their company?

We arrived at Flixton beach at low water about 13.00. I parked the car behind an old barn whilst Danny began to arrange his assortment of boots, cravat, and general paraphernalia before we got set off across the marsh. Danny was in charge and seemingly had a cunning plan; this was in actual fact very simple. We walk out to the point where the marsh turns to sand and wait in a hole or gully until Mad Jack obligingly comes off on his tractor.

We finally got settled side by side in a dry hole ideally placed for letting the sun beat down nicely on us both, the wait would be anything up to two hours, they had to come off when the tide was making.

Half an hour went by during which time Danny advertised our position with frequent pipe smokings, otherwise all was quiet. It was at this time however Danny announced an unanticipated change of plan,

"You wait here while I go further across the marsh"

He got himself up in readiness to commence plan B and leave our comparative comfort zone.

This was typical of Danny, a brainwave was born from god knows where.

"What for, for Christ's sake Danny, he's bound to come along the track"

"Ah but what if he drops some fish off"

I had a bad feeling about this unexpected course of action,

"What if he comes before you get back Dan?"

"Hold your warrant up and tell him to stop then check his catch, but don't worry I won't be far away"

I wasn't too concerned at this point, I assumed Danny would return to my position as and when required… how wrong I was.

Danny duly disappeared across the marsh, I was alone. The marsh was very warm that day, extremely peaceful and any other time would have been idyllic, but the thought of Mad Jack out there somewhere dispelled all pleasure from the moment. I sat and waited, curlews gurgled, their song blending amongst pernickety redshanks and gulls in the distance. I sat and waited until at least 15.00 I was almost convinced he must have gone off somewhere else. I even tried telling myself perhaps he didn't actually exist at all, just lie back in the warm sun and fall asleep. A nice idea but reality kicked back in. It was possible he may leave by a different route? Gillys head maybe? another of several egress points off the sands he could have chosen. Mad Jack would probably not be expecting any hassle therefore I expected him to come via the main track into Flixton.

Eventually after turning all these possibilities over in my mind to pass the time a noise interrupted my thoughts, waking me from the world of speculation. I heard it again! A very faint drone, a distant aeroplane maybe. Then no perhaps not, then yes there it was again. It definitely got louder it was like waiting for an air raid, a Lancaster bomber perhaps. Louder and deeper, nearer and nearer.

Where the hell was Danny? We had no radios; Dan had forgotten his as usual.

Louder, louder, my heart was racing true to form. I got my warrant ready just in case and clutched it in my sweating right hand. I checked with the binoculars and for sure on the horizon I could see the speck that was unmistakably Mad Jack steaming off the sands ahead of the racing tide. I saw puffs of black smoke resembling dragons breath bellowing from the red vintage Nuffield, coughing and barking across the sands.

Where the hell was Dan?

Gradually the shape grew bigger and much more menacing. I could make out the yellow oilskins. He was heading my way at full throttle like an iron dinosaur. Ten more minutes, it seemed like an age. Sweating profusely I waited until the tractor was 500 yards away, still not a bloody sign of Danny. I now had no choice but to leave the comfort of my sunny den, this was time for action. I stood up positioning myself slap-bang in the middle of the track. I could see his boiling face gaping straight ahead.

Mad Jack was now bearing down on me at what seemed like 60 miles an hour, but was probably only 20. I watched him wrench the throttle lever down to the limit closing down on me like a fighter pilot spitting and snarling, I saw the whites of his eyes thundering towards me until only yards separated us. No way was Jack going to stop for me or any one else. If I ever wondered why he was called mad Jack now was the moment of truth.

The tractor was almost upon me by now so I tentatively held up my warrant whilst attempting to pronounce,

"Bailiff Stop!"

My parched lips barely moved whilst the picture unfolded, I dived off the track to save myself. Mad Jack flew past dust and smoke swirling from his machine like an angry dragon. Finally he turned and shook his fist in rage disappearing over the dyke in seconds. I was left like a lemon splattered with mudded debris propelled from Jacks machine. All I could think of was bloody Danny, I cursed and stamped round in circles.

"That's another fine mess you've got me into".

After about ten long minutes I was calming down. Danny eventually did wander into view a few minutes later enquiring in his usual pompous manner,

"What had happened?"

I just listened in bewilderment.

"Did you stop him Jack?"

I couldn't believe this man; I was not amused despite regaining some composure since my near death experience, I glared intolerantly.

"He almost killed me Dan, wouldn't stop you know, where the hell were you?"

He replied as if he'd just been to Sunday school,

"Covering the back door old chap"

I had to walk away before doing something rash, I'm not a violent man, but Danny was fairly close to getting a fat lip. I mumbled and turned away totally deflated.

"C, mon lets report back"

I wasn't looking forward to Joe's reaction on our return, Dan and I sheepishly assembled in Joe's dining room, Hannah as usual put the kettle on.

Joe ambled in from his greenhouse humming a non tune then glanced across the kitchen.

"Cup a tea our Mother"

I relayed the afternoon's events without trying to drop Dan in the brown stuff,

Joe wasn't impressed, that I could clearly see.

"Yon buggers becoming quite a pain in the backside Danny, what's to do about him?"

Danny was mid pipe refuel while Joe fixed an iron stare on him, then growled

"I know what to do, Ill send Hank with thee, ista fit for tomorrow you lads"

I was gutted tomorrow was Saturday and I was hoping for my day off, but arguing didn't seem an option at the time so I nodded obediently.

Joe was straight on the phone barking instructions to Hank who as usual wanted nothing to do with any of Joe's plans. There was no doubt about the outcome of course all Joe had to do was pull rank and arrangements where made. The plan was for Hank to lead Danny, Big Don, and myself on a mission to successfully stop Mad Jack as he returned off the sands at Low water the next morning.

Hank picked me up on Saturday at 05.00 to rendezvous with Don and Danny at Cliff head just outside Flixton.

Hank went into masterful mode as soon as we were all assembled. He instructed the three of us to cross the marsh in a repeat exercise similar to the previous day's debacle. This time however it was thankfully emphasised that nobody went walkabout.

Hank typically informed us that he would wait on the road in case Jack didn't stop.

So here I was again waiting and wondering secreted in this desert. I didn't have to wait too long however before the hair raising growl of Mad Jacks tractor could be faintly heard in the distance. All the wildlife went silent with anticipation; they knew what was coming all right. I was glad Don was there this time; at least we had half a chance, Dan sucked on his pipe, and didn't seem in any way concerned.

Mad Jack finally came into view at about seven-o-clock, the feeling of de-ja-vous was very apparent, the big red Nuffield bellowed smoke and fumes across the sands once more. Don was a big lad but not suicidal enough to stand his ground when Mad Jackie Dixon flew past yet again like a wild dinosaur and out of sight before we new what hit us. Don swore profusely,

"Jesus Christ Jack yon fuckers barmy"

"Tell me about it"

This time we made chase running swiftly back up to the road, Don and Danny got into the Viva van whereas I was plucked off the shore by a very animated Hank. I don't know whether Hank had had a row with his wife or he'd just got out the wrong side that day, because I never saw him before or since as worked up as he was that morning hastily pursuing Mad Jack towards Flixton. We reached the main street just as Jack was slowing down outside his terraced home; Hank put his foot down then screeched to a halt in the middle of the road next to the tractor, this was pure Starsky and Hutch comes to Flixton. The old Nuffield was ticking over faithfully despite being laden with nets, ropes, buckets, and bags of fish. Jack tried to ignore us by casually dismounting, but he hadn't bargained for a hot fuming Hank whose face by this point was redder than the setting sun and on the point of implosion. Hank amazed me that summer's morning, the way he dived out of his van and went for Mad Jack; he literally launched himself on to the Nuffield's footplate grabbing a loose bull strut as he landed. A bull strut is a piece of wood about a metre long bound in this case with lead at one end. A pair can be used to hold a wall of netting upright at either end, especially in shallow water or in this case a useful and formidable weapon.

Hank bellowed at Jack, I just watched in awe,

"Stop right now yu bastard, you know who we are and what we want"

The bull strut crashed on to the Nuffield's bonnet lead end first causing the engine covers to jump up at least a foot in the air sending a cloud of dust skywards. How the tractor survived the second harder blow as well I"ll never know, but the effect on Mad Jack was astonishing. He froze in a mixture of fear and anger. He descended from the tractor, Hank steadfastly eyeballed him from six inches face to face, all seemingly to be enacted in slow motion. Jack was utterly livid, and actually foaming at the mouth, I have never seen a human being do that either before or since that day. I am certain if Jack had been in possession of a Kalashnikov he would have wiped us all out and half the village too. Every resident was out in the street at this point. Not a doorway was empty; the entire village watched the spectacle. Hank barked out a command jolting me back to reality,

"Search his bags Jack"

I snapped out of my temporary trance tipping out three bags of fish expectantly, ironically the entire catch was sea fish consisting of mainly flukes plus a few mullet and one bass. We didn't leave with a case against Mad Jack, but Hank certainly brought him down to earth with a bang.

Hank went way up in my estimation that day. The small town of Flixton was well entertained that morning when the Becky's rode in ably lead by Albert "Wyatt Earp" Hankey.

Joe wasn't impressed of course but that was down entirely to The Hank element, I never saw Mad Jack again after that day although I know he did fish for several more seasons if a bit more low key. I think he learned his lesson that day and knew maybe in his own heart that he'd had a lucky escape.

1980 continued to be an eventful year, not with standing because of my own personal problems adding to the long list of people getting divorced in that period. It was agreed that for the sake of our two lads I would move out leaving Georgina in the family home. Joe and Hannah took it pretty well under the circumstances, probably as I was not the cause of the break up. Georgina had been working behind the bar at the Commercial Inn in Brockley where she took a fancy to the guy working alongside her, the rest as they say is history. Eventually after the divorce they married, but most importantly I kept in close touch with my kids.

I moved into a flat forming part of a large house in the country about ten miles from Brockley and the River Stock. It was known as Moss end and in actual fact owned by Father Moses a Dutch priest of all people. I had been put in touch with him by a land agent I knew living close to the R Brant. Obviously I was curious as to why a Dutch priest would own such an establishment. I think it was probably some sort of tax evasion. The agent was a devious and mischievous looking guy called Dick Longhorn, but as needs must at the time I was steered down this particular path. Longhorn lived on a farm adjoining the river, his land coveted an area known as Briar woods which from late summer until Christmas held large numbers of salmon and sea trout waiting to move on to the spawning grounds. Dick Longhorn was one of those guys who didn't like anybody on his land that wasn't there without his say so. He was nice to me however, arousing suspicions of an ulterior motive at a very early stage in our acquaintance. I was reaching the stage in my career when everybody at all connected to a riverbank became suspicious. I never knew whether he actually owned his farm or it was the property of the mysterious Father Moses, I suspect the latter. It was often the case amongst Cumbrian farmers who had rivers running through their land that a certain taste for salmon might be acquired. A character called John Sutcliffe who farmed in the valley of Stockdale graphically explained this to me one day. He was of the same breed as Longhorn, defending his land with whatever force was necessary. In conversation he was inquiring into the numbers of fish up the river prompting me to explain that anyone and I meant if anyone took a fish they must face the consequences. He stood and pondered this for a minute before making his reply.

"Them fish is on my land, so if I want yan I"ll gan and git yan laddie"

I had to laugh, I knew this went on and let's face it if he got the odd fish and only the odd fish his chances of detection were pretty low. Poaching is very much governed by the law of averages, its simple, the greedier a poacher gets and the more often he operates the more likely he is to be caught. The guy that goes occasionally with a modicum of skill may never be caught and of course more importantly isn't a big threat to fish stocks.

So my friendship with Dick Longhorn was based on my need to patrol his riverbanks and his need to have me onside for his respect and credibility. Time would deal a wild card of course.

I moved out of the family home into the big house on the night of Halloween following a nights heavy drinking in the Plough Inn. I will always remember that night because not only was it Halloween, but thundering and lightning as well. Add to this the belief that the tower section I moved into was supposedly haunted. The alcohol kept me calm and no ghosts materialised on the night or ever after for that matter. It was a great conversation piece though at social events.

I lived in Moss end for one year after my divorce, during that difficult period of adjustment and bitterness I threw myself into the job with great gusto. I had a very productive year apprehending more poachers both in the estuary, through the town, and up the dales, I was a man on a mission.

I also acquired my new best friend in the form of a Lakeland terrier named Ben. Dick Langhorn had shown me a litter from his menagerie of dogs and animals kept mostly for the amusement of his ever-extending family. He had a fascinating collection of poultry including turkeys, bantams, and even a couple of peacocks. His most recent arrivals though were Llamas of which he had three. Llamas had become quite trendy for those few farmers around the south lakes prepared to give them a go. I think the wool was rather sought after. Dick showed his off to me, he liked to show off most things.

"Don't go too near em Jack cos they spit at yu"

I was alarmed at this remark; the look on my face must have been highly amusing,

"Aye tha knows, they chew balls of grass and food tha knows and if yu upsets em they fire em at yu like a gun, straight out the mouth, yan just missed us tuther day, so as a bit wary"

Consequently I eyed them warily too and definitely saw an evil glint in the eye of those beasts. I couldn't resist his terrier pups though so Ben came back with me for the princely sum of £10, an eight-week-old ball of ginger fluff.

Joe of course was in his last summer and craved one last stab at an old adversary called Freddie Blencarn, another and probably the longest serving of the Flixton fishermen. His track record was mixed consisting of periods fed by greed followed by a year or two of inactivity, probably relating to the abundance of salmon at the time.

This particular summer salmon and sea trout were hold up in parts of the channel below Sandside off whitecross point. This is a large wooded promontory where Big Don and I had recently seen Blencarn operating with his lave net. The temptation to put a gill net through the channel was proving too much for Freddie, this method would net large numbers of fish in a short time, he could then bring them off under the umbrella of claiming he caught them with the very same legal lave net. Our plan was to wait in the woods on the rocky point during the dead of night to observe our man using the said gill net, and then jump him.

Joe was like a coiled spring primed by anticipation. His enthusiasm for a man in his last working year was amazing. He was nothing like some of the fifty or sixty plus employees around in Northwest water who just put in an appearance counting off the days until gold clock time. I convinced myself that night I wanted to be just like Joe. Even Hank was winding down and he was only just over fifty, whatsmore he was quite open about it,

"am peddling mi bike very softly, but not too softly as to fall off tha knows".

This was his catch phrase used as some sort of excuse I suppose, but we all saw through him, knowing full well he had just lost the will.

The full team turned out that night with the exception of Danny who was visiting his sister in Hawkshead.

It was a fantastic night, clear very warm and dead calm. We all stayed together in a proposed show of force hiding within the deep wood. The trees were mainly alder and silver birch; unfortunately the stony ground could be very noisy. In fact noise across the water or sands on such a calm night is quite remarkable, voices especially carry for miles and any one in a boat can be even more audible. Even the slightest knock of an oar on the side of a boat can be heard two miles away.

We crouched in silence not even a pipe was smoked, only the constant chatter of birdlife. There was banter as ever of course when we all got together like this. Joe kept pulling us up if laughter threatened. Big Don was the main culprit, although it helped pass the time waiting for the tide to ebb quietly back revealing the pools full of vulnerable fish. The wonderful sounds of redshanks, oystercatchers, curlews and gulls played their strange haunting tunes as dawn broke, patiently we stood our ground. The sounds of salmon jumping were frequent, yet strangely I never recalled such abundance in that same place ever again.

By 04.00 Joe had finally convinced us to be completely silent so we listened patiently and intently for the familiar drone of an old Nuffield. It was ironically at this point of complete order that Joe himself broke ranks, he emitted the most enormous fart I have ever heard booming across the whole of Morecambe bay like a fog horn, had Freddie or anyone else been out there I am sure they would have dived for cover.

Joe's follow up remark tipped us over the edge,

"You didn't hear that did you lads"

I was choking with laughter by now as was everyone else, fortunately we were still alone.

Freddie finally turned up about twenty minutes post fart and order was thankfully just about regained by this time. The sight of his tractor circling slowly and steadily around held us all in suspense, I watched him standing upright, staring down in absolute concentration carefully scrutinising every inch of the channel for the most suitable location to pay his net. He towed a small boat and trailer behind.

Finally he came to a stop, the old Nuffield ticked over reliably like a mantle clock. Freddie slowly dismounted and moved to the back where he lifted down a large sack. My heart was away again pounding with anticipation. Freddie duly obliged, I could see him casually tip out a monofilament gill net, then load it into the boat. He remounted the tractor to maneuver the trailer and boat into a deep section of the channel. He calmly dismounted a second time then easily launched the boat; the net was anchored at one end in the sand. The task was simple and deadly, just row quietly across to the other side, then anchor the other end in identical fashion. The result was a wall of virtually invisible netting right across the channel. This was going well; Joe allowed himself a faint chuckle.

Freddie remounted the tractor and drove off downstream leaving the net to do its worst. I breathed out heavily when he disappeared around the point. Joe farted again but no body laughed this time. Joe looked disappointed so briefly outlined our strategy instead.

"Soon as he cuz back and starts to fish yon net we jump him, oreet lads?"

We all nodded, I treated myself to a sandwich and cracked open a flask of tea. I like everyone else waited patiently in comparative silence.

Freddie eventually returned out of the gloom, cool as a cucumber at 05.50, he sat completely motionless on his stationery tractor peering down at the net for several minutes, he reminded me of a crafty Heron. Even from our vantage point I could see the corks were down, a sure sign of captured fish. There was a splash near the surface prompting Freddie to stand up.

"Yes" he said it out loud to himself; he was counting his chickens with glee.

Soon after that he was in the boat rowing purposefully to the far side; Joe held up his hand, and then turned to whisper,

"Wait till he's pulled her all in"

Freddie started to haul the net laboriously working his way back across by pulling the net towards him into the boat. I could see round fish were involved as he slowly reached our side of the channel.

Joe dropped his hand sharply to signal the advance, I legged it the two hundred yards arriving there just ahead of Don to issue the command,

"Stop Bailiffs"

Hank and Joe just walked across of course, leaving any aggro to the younger end and why not. Freddie was gob smacked and immediately went into victim mode.

"Hell thas frittened mi near to death young fella"

Don was into the boat by now, no less than fifteen salmon and two sea trout lay gasping their last breath in the tangled mass that was Freddie's net.

Joe waded in to Freddie big style.

"Thas in big bother now Freddie Blencarn and thas had it coming, thas just a greedy bugger, just a greedy bastard."

Freddie stood defeated,

"Aye well thas got me allreet no need to rub it in"

By the time we got Freddie booked, seized all his fish, his net, and the boat towed away it was after 08.00. He took it pretty well all things considered, that is the seizure of the boat apart, this he protested against almost but not quite violently.

Joe whistled non tunes and hummed continuously with delight as we left.

"I needed to catch yon bugger one last time tha knows"

I returned to my van to find little Ben waiting, he greeted me as only dogs can and had even managed to keep a clean bed. It was time for a well earned breakfast. Joe was like a dog with two dicks for weeks after.

12

PROPAGATION

1980 was fading out when Joe provided an amusing finale to a distinguished career. In the backend each year the need for propagating salmon and seat trout was considered vital after all the years of UDN that threatened the survival of both species. The method adopted at the time involved all the team working closely together obtaining brood stock or breeding fish from the upland streams just prior to the actual physical act of spawning. Both salmon and sea trout spawn in loose gravel by digging a nest using their tail, this forms a nest known as a redd. All the upper reaches of the R Stock contain feeder streams ideally suited to accommodating both species, generally the smaller streams are used primarily by sea trout. Smaller pound size fish commonly spawn away up in the fells and a very long way from the sea. A good majority of the salmon however spawn in the main rivers, which of course can better accommodate bigger fish; in fact spawning is spread from just above the tidal limit in Broxton park right in to the fells. On all three rivers a large waterfall or natural barrier stops the fish ascending any higher. This wide distribution of spawning ensures a better chance of survival allowing for any disasters that may occur, such as drought, flood, or pollution.

A general idea of population numbers could be assessed by physically counting each redd as soon as possible after conception, ideally before a rise in water levels flattened them out. I took to this job like a fish to water if you'll pardon the pun. Tom Brown had enlightened me on the skills needed to recognize redds in situe. I can't think of a better sensation at work than waking up on a fine, sunny, and frosty autumn morning knowing that redd counting was the order of the day. We often worked in pairs traveling to a selected section of river. One member of the team would be dropped off whilst the other would begin a few miles further downstream. The vehicle was parked up for the first person to collect once he had finished his section, thus leap frogging the beck. Large distances could be covered in one day using this method. I would also work alone many days which meant walking back along each section counted, this didn't bother me one bit, I loved just being out there and able to watch fish thrashing about on the redds. Cock fish frantically chase each other around vying for females and territory before running out of life, left moribund or dead. I took great satisfaction in observing fish on redds. I had protected them all year from their early days out in the bay dodging mad Jack or Freddie Blencarn, then up into the lower reaches in the hands of the aristocrats of Broxton Park. Next on past long dub and its snatchers. They might lie low all summer in Scroggs resisting a fly or lure before swimming on up through Brockley to face the town poachers and more anglers. If they survived all that, it was head on further upstream past the farting horse or the mischievous Dick Longhorn. Let's not forget the perils of the Burndale crew and all associated snatches and snares. Lastly into the fells and dales where an opportunistic calculating farmer may be waiting or a deadly lamper and his dogs. Consequently I have always greatly admired these tenacious fish determined enough to reach the climax of spawning. I still feel very fulfilled when the stage is reached, where I can't do anything more to help them, that's it, the whole purpose of there torrid life is fulfilled and together we've beaten the odds.

Rusty Bentley once said to me whilst chatting at the weir in Brockley,

"If it wunt for you Becky's tha wouldn't be any fish left"

I took this as a great compliment spurring me on to make sure he was right.

Our breeding fish were obtained by a method of capture known as Electro-fishing. This involved a small but heavy portable petrol generator producing an electric current fed directly into the stream via a 50-metre cable. This was connected to a hand held electrode or anode made up of a wooden pole with a circular steel ring at the end, a wire cathode completed the electric field. The task was both clumsy and laborious but very exciting and good fun to be part of. Each Bailiff had his own task; Joe would direct operations from the bank and carry any captured fish back to Hank who now had a land rover and trailer with which to transport the fish. Tom of course had the honored position of using the electrode until he moved on to Carlisle. I was entrusted with this vital task after his departure and considered it to be a kind of promotion. In actual fact it was probably a bit of nepotism creeping in rather than favoritism as had been the case with Tom. Of course Hank should really have been doing it but in all honesty it would have been too much like hard work, he was much happier messing with fish transportation. Nobody questioned this it just seemed to be understood and needless to say I was chuffed to bits. The generator was set up on the bankside with the cable played out downstream the whole fifty yards; Danny had the job of keeping the cable untangled before being laboriously reeled in after each section. Each length was fished back upstream to the generator followed by another fifty yards upstream after that and so on. The cable was then reeled in and the whole process repeated. Big Don was chief netsman showing great skill and determination to bag each fish sent into muscle spasm by the electric current, however competition with

Martin Dobson and Paul Nugent was fierce. Paul took up the rear on most occasions to try and nab any fish bolting downstream eluding Don or Martin. He was christened "backstop". In truth Paul was not a fit lad so by mid afternoon he was often lagging behind somewhat. It came to light in the next few years that Paul who was an ex policeman had a bit of a drink problem, that would eventually be his undoing.

This process was ideal for catching and propagating sea trout although less effective with salmon. Back in those days we collected fish from all over the area keeping them all together in wooden keep boxes tied up in the river at Croftgill. The only concession was to separate salmon from sea trout. This meant that a male fish from the River leven may be used to fertilise eggs from a female fish out of the River Stock or Brant for instance. This would certainly mess up the genetic integrity of the species because normally if left alone they would home back to the stream of birth with unerring accuracy. This process was wisely changed some years later so as to ensure that for example a Leven hen fish would only be fertilised with a Leven cock fish. The genetic damage done in the seventies and eighties will never be known, however we did plant many thousands of extra fry into a vast area, it is an age old debate, right or wrong nobody is quite sure.

The general feeling within the angling community about our policy was of course mixed and contentious, as was nearly always the case with any subject amongst anglers. Some said propagation was vital to increase fish stocks whilst others accused us of robbing the becks of all the fish that would spawn naturally anyway. What was certain however was the fact that we the Bailiffs were on hiding to nothing, the argument was never proven either way. In time we stopped all propagation attempts, leaving nature to run its own course. This policy has since been vindicated by increased fish stocks in most rivers especially the Stock, the only exception being the River Leven, which has a mysterious lack of salmon for no recognized reason despite much scientific study.

The final electro fishing season for Joe was a busy one with around a hundred hen sea trout boxed up with a supporting number of about thirty cocks. One healthy cock fish could be used on the collective eggs of several hens; thus the need to keep a lot of cocks was unnecessary. The salmon usually numbered only about twenty fish of which six or seven would be cocks. I was very much against keeping salmon as they soon became much stressed in the wooden keep boxes sometimes resulting in the loss of up to half of all salmon captured. Salmon just didn't seem to like being cooped up, soon sickening, or become badly diseased. Joe wouldn't have this at all, he just seemed programmed to catch as many fish as possible to produce as many eggs as we could. It was soul destroying and pitiful to open a box and see several corpses floating, cruelly denied the final sacrifice in their native stream. Sea trout proved much more resilient however and it wasn't unusual to have losses of only single figures, why this was I am not sure but it may have some relation to the fact that many sea trout don't die after spawning in the way that salmon do. In fact sea trout can return back and forth from sea to river for several years with up to six spawnings not uncommon. So it was for these reasons that we concentrated our efforts mostly on sea trout.

After a day out on the beck's collecting fish we would sort them out back at Croftgill, fish that weren't ready to spawn were known as unripe and transferred straight away into keep boxes for another day. We often had good numbers of fish ready on the day luckily, these were classed as ripe fish. The job of milking the eggs out of the hen fish was another task I inherited from Tommy Brown. This process is known as "stripping". Sea trout are the easiest to deal with, the size factor makes for better handling, each hen fish is held by the tail pointing downwards into a plastic washing up bowl. The eggs are then gently squeezed or milked into the bowl. If a large fish is handled the tail would be held by a second person, it was vital that the hen fish totally relaxed otherwise the eggs would not be shed. This process was very rewarding with no finer sight than fresh orange eggs tumbling liberally into a clean plastic bowl.

The eggs were then fertilised by holding a ripe cock fish in the same manner then squeezing the abdomen to ejaculate the sperm known as milt. A teaspoon of milt can easily fertilise five to ten thousand eggs. I then stirred the mixture with my finger prior to finally adding some water producing a milky solution. This was then washed clean with river water after which the plastic bowl and precious contents were put to one side allowing the eggs to swell before measuring.

It was on one of these busy November days back at Croftgill following a successful exercise collecting both salmon and sea trout that Joe became concerned about the large amounts of ova collected.

"Put yur salmon eggs in yon yella bowls Jack, and sea trout int reduns"

"Aye okay Joe"

This was a simple but very necessary plan we put into practice as instructed to finally end up with three yellow bowls laden with salmon eggs and five redd bowls containing sea trout eggs… not a problem? 17.00 passed and all the remaining fish were boxed up. Don and I washed off all the eggs carefully making sure we didn't mix the two species up before carrying them up to the gates where my mini van was waiting. Joe watched this procedure like a hawk

"divent mix em up now willst yu"

This didn't help of course and I don't recall ever knowingly getting it wrong.

Finally we all gathered together up at the hut to sup the remaining stale remnants of flasks and suffer a mass pipe smoking event. I could see Joe becoming more fidgety and uneasy.

"Thou hasn't mixed em Jack has Tu"

He was making me nervous by now, so I assured him all was well glancing assuredly at Don and Danny standing in a circle over the precious cargo,

"No Joe don't worry"

Joe shuffled again his weathered red cheeks contracted like bellows as he dragged on his faithful pipe. I could see him studying each plastic bowl intently, but I could never have anticipated his next profound remark.

"Anyway tha knows what's what Jack It's easy; just remember the reds in the yella!"

I shot a glance at Don and Danny immediately whereupon we all cracked up and poor old Joe never did realise what he'd said.

I ignored all Joe's protestations, together with any remaining small talk from Big Don who was now milking the situation to its limit. He kept repeating Joe's remark under his breath and in my earshot. I manfully concentrated on loading my cargo securely before departing to the hatchery post haste.

Once at the hatchery the eggs were measured courtesy of a homemade scale, which is simply a piece of aluminum curtain rail on which the eggs are placed in a single row and counted off. The amount was then calibrated on a chart. Finally the eggs were transferred to wire baskets in troughs fed by pure spring water off the fells. It was paramount to have a constant supply of unpolluted water which never freezes in winter or dries out in spring. The hatchery was about twenty miles away close to the River Lune and it was there that the eggs remained until hatching after about ninety days. Once hatched the eggs would be either kept on or planted out in March or April. Sometimes the eggs were actually planted prior to hatching in a state known as eyed ova, this means that the embryo is visible in the egg and close to hatching. These could be transported to a feeder stream up in the fells or above a natural barrier such as a waterfall inaccessible to adult fish. The ova were then planted into the gravel in the form of a man made redd. This process required locating suitable deep gravel in to which a hole could be excavated using an ordinary garden rake. The eggs were poured down a rubber tube held in place by hand allowing the gravel to be raked back into the hole.

Lastly the tube was slowly and carefully retracted. If all went well the eggs would be nicely nestled within, amply fed by the turbulent fresh current high in precious oxygen.

This is another task that gave me a feeling of well being because we were actually putting something back into the environment, hopefully helping to save the species in the process. Occasionally however the redd making process didn't go well and there was no sight more annoying than the eggs bubbling up out of the gravel due to careless work or unsuitable substrata, too shallow perhaps? Generally though I mastered the skill needed in making redds and spent many happy days involving this work. It was vital to have a good man with you on the day as well of course, Big Don was my favoured choice but the other lads were probably just as good. The exceptions were Joe and Hank who would willingly drive on such expeditions but when it came to the nitty gritty of raking gravel or walking long distances carrying rakes and buckets, well that was left to whoever got the short straw on the day.

If the fry were kept in the hatchery until just about feeding stage they would be planted as "unfed fry" again in small beck's high up a fell somewhere. This process was equally rewarding especially if the fry had developed well and looked fit to cope with life in the wild. The job entailed a vehicle and trailer with tank or tanks of water into which the fry were placed fed by oxygen. This usually involved Hank, but providing Don or Danny came too the work load could be spread evenly enough, of course Hank stayed with the vehicle whilst everyone else walked off with the fry. Fry were planted one every square yard in theory, this generally meant a handful for every few yards of beck walked. Ideally a crisp, dry, cool spring day was perfect together with medium to low water levels. Hopefully these conditions would prevail allowing the fry to acclimatise in their new home and start feeding before a fresh or spate could wash them away. The last thing we wanted was our precious fry delivered straight into the mouth of a hungry trout or propelled swiftly into Morecambe Bay.

I have walked many miles carrying buckets of fry spreading them as evenly as possible, refreshing each batch regularly with new oxygen rich water. Of course the personnel concerned varied, reflecting directly the standard of work produced, in other words, by the length of time a man was away with his bucket. Joe maintained that Hank would have all his fry planted before lunch. Hank would usually tip a bucket full out at each bridge rather than set off and walk. I would have to say from my own observations that this was probably an accurate inference.

The exception to the rule was a Bailiff from the River Lune namely Glen Bracken. Glen was another one off character, probably born in the wrong time; he was a medieval thinker, he sincerely believed that poachers should be birched there and then on the spot at the point of apprehension. He was a formidable force patrolling the Lune valleys, a short very heavy built pocket battleship with rustic Cumbrian features and body odor to match. If he hadn't seen me for some time he liked nothing better than to greet me with a lusty bout of play fighting. This would either be a right hook into the solar plexus or a bear hug of grizzlian proportions leaving me reeling or gasping for air. He would laugh wickedly at my obvious discomfort. He too had a dog; a black working terrier called Max which He used as a hunting aid. Max loved to hunt mink, Glen could never control his dogs and Max was no exception, going near Glens van was not a good idea if Max was aboard. That dog guarded his van like Conan the barbarian and would bark hysterically biting the windscreen with such force in the process that it actually left teeth marks in the glass. Once whilst Electro fishing on the Lune Max had excavated and devoured a whole family of mink whose only crime was just being alive.

I only experienced one day out with Glen and Max and that was to plant salmon fry in Weasdale beck. This appeared no big deal despite Joe warning me that Glen took this job extremely seriously.

I met Glen at the hatchery at nine o clock on a Monday morning fully expecting to be done shortly after lunch; we only had about twenty thousand fry to plant. I was greeted by a big smile followed by a hands on demonstration in Cumberland and Westmoreland wrestling. Luckily this only left me with a sprained wrist and disheveled clothing. Glen's enthusiasm for the job in hand was admirable at this stage and indeed quite infectious. The fry were meticulously transferred into two plastic tanks in the back of his mini van.

Glen's mini van was a testament to British Leyland engineering having one careful owner from new in 1964. Glen was a bit tight to say the least he never took it to a garage but did all his own service and maintenance work making sure he got the best use of his employers generous allowance. In fact together with Tommy Brown they probably made a profit. Regular visits to the local scrap yard were a way of life to Glen, he would dismantle discarded old minis collecting CV joints, wheel bearings, sub frames, wiper blades, plugs, head light bulbs, the list was endless, in fact he had already probably rebuilt every thing except the main body work. Glen had been urged to write a letter to British Leyland after reaching two hundred thousand miles from new. The only acknowledgement he got was congratulations and a complimentary set of spark plugs.

So off we set away up to the wilds of Weasdale at the headwaters of the mighty River Lune. Glen cajoled his old van up a long narrow lonin to an isolated bridge at the junction of what from a distance appeared to be two small valleys. On arrival however they appeared ominously large and overbearing. Once stopped, Max who had behaved almost normally apart from swearing at a farm collie now leapt for freedom in pursuit of anything that moved, this went completely over Glen's head of course. Fortunately this was such an isolated spot that no harm could be done. Glen produced a Famous army stores bait bag that didn't appear bulging with anything much apart from an antique flask and a bruised apple.

I followed suit and dipped into my flask of coffee, whereas Glen had plain hot water in his.

Five minutes was all we had and I think Glen would have foregone this if it wasn't for my presence. The fry were duly divided up before Glen grabbed my shoulder to insure full attention.

"Now then Jack will tek ten thousand a piece, with two buckets a piece and mun sure yu keeps em freshened up". I nodded compliantly with one eye on some dark heavy clouds looming overhead, the weather up these desolate dales could change abruptly, when a nice day in Kirby Lonsdale could be a hail storm up here in April.

"Tha knows aboot spreading em reet up valley dunt thee"

I nodded again and picked up the two heavily laden buckets. Glen did like wise before once again giving me the heavy stare

"Ill gan up this un, and you gan up yon un, and mek sure tha gits reet tut far end tha must spread em well out. Yull eventually come till a brig, then tha can cu back an nut a yard sooner"

He chuckled with this last instruction.

I kid you not that beautiful valley was four miles long; it took me two and a half hours and two blizzards to get to the end. The return journey was a further two hours and in wellies at that. My feet were humming, blistered, and very sore when I finally got back to Glens van. It was 18.00 by this time, no sign of Glen or Max of course, I couldn't even sit in the van to sup my tea. Glen and Max finally did appear trundling down the valley half an hour later.

" Thas made good time Jack I hope yu spread em out well enough"

I was not amused, but assured Glen that I had done what was required and his little babies as he liked to call them were happily swimming about in a freezing cold beck in the middle of nowhere. I never worked with Glen's fry, or visited Weasdale ever again but I did sleep well that night.

The policy of collecting broodstock and planting fry was eventually abandoned a few years later favouring instead a natural recruitment policy whereby the fish are left to reproduce naturally without any direct help from ourselves. The preferred option now is to improve the habitat in the rivers and streams to increase survival rates of juvenile fish. This is now done with help from other organisations and Farmers. The most popular schemes include fencing the bankside areas to create buffer zones, enhancing vegetation growth and thereby benefiting all the wildlife in that area. The population of salmon and sea trout in the River Stock system has certainly not looked back since the change in policy.

13

CHOKERS

In the hot July of 1981 the Stock estuary experienced a build up of migratory fish. Nothing new there obviously except very hot weather caused a sequence of events that caused me no end of problems for about two months beginning mid June until the weather broke in August. Fish move with the ebb and flow of the tides, backwards and forwards, day and night. The heat of the sands, plus the rapid turbidity can have a dramatic affect on a salmon or sea trout journeying in such a way, so much so that many were choking to death in the murky waters, then to be left high and dry as the tide receded. These are known by locals as "chokers or chokies". First on the scene to take advantage of this windfall are the scavenging gulls, alert and ready as ever, picking away at the corpses marooned on the sand. In fact if one is observant they give the game away and can even be observed whilst driving past or scanning the sands with binoculars. The tell tale groups of birds squabbling just like vultures over a free meal was becoming a regular sight. Unfortunately they weren't the only predators on the scene; naturally the human kind also wanted a share of the spoils. The main culprit was a retired Butcher called Tommy Dickinson who was very handily placed living next to the pub at Sandside and right on the shore. He had been taking fish this way for donkey's years without much effort and very little attention from Bailiffs. Danny was very keen to catch him however, but lacked that extra bit of guile needed for such a wily old bird like Tommy. Word was getting around that various people in Sandside were harvesting dead fish, Joe's phone was becoming red hot and of course he wasn't a happy man. Big Don was on holiday with his family at Butlins, Danny was doing early mornings so Joe set me on the day shifts for a week. I found a good point of observation from the quarry above Sandside and settled there on the Monday at four in the afternoon. It was hot and sunny and the tide was about one hours ebb, perfect conditions for the task in hand. I only had to wait half an hour until the first culprit appeared on the scene, a man in White T-shirt and shorts, followed by a yellow dog probably a Labrador, I focused my binnocs and watched him stride purposefully across the drying sands, he soon reached the periphery of the tide at the channels edge, then walked it steadily downstream. He was approaching a black backed gull about fifty yards ahead. He was at least half a mile away from my location, however with the binnocs I could clearly see him looking around. He even had a pair of his own binoculars, a sure sign of guilt. Consequently I had to be very careful even though I was well hidden behind some gorse and broom. The man reached the same point the gull had tried to occupy, whereupon he immediately picked up a fish without the slightest hesitation, an act he had obviously done before. The gull circled menacingly obviously distraught with the intrusion. The man tied the fish to a rope or piece of string, and then dragged it behind him on the sand. I watched him continue down the channel edge picking up two more fish on the way. I had to make a decision? It was definitely time for a move. I crept quickly away scurrying back to my van, I needed to be closer and in a position to anticipate his route of return. I had already decided that the car park of the Blue Anchor would do nicely and it was right on the shore by the road. I was parked up ten minutes later blending in well amongst several parked cars. Tommy Dickinson's house was next door but I detected no stir, I focused my binnocs once again. My man was already heading home, casually strolling back towards the pub. This was going well, I was reeling him in nicely. I watched patiently, he got nearer and nearer his dog was as happy as Larry loping round him in playful circles, I realised at this point the fish were actually on the dog lead trailed by his side in an inane effort to disguise them. Eventually he furtively approached the road, now was time to nail him, I made my move popping over a low stone wall and at this stage he was no more than twenty yards away. That was the moment he spotted me and immediately just let go of the lead. He kept on walking as if nothing had happened.

I made a quick interception to stop him, he was sweating and fidgety, a middle aged bald man wearing glasses, a beer gut, with a strong welsh accent. I showed my warrant and told him who I was. The man stared at me defiantly.

"I know who you are; I've seen you knocking about"

I was a bit surprised because I had never clapped eyes on him before.

"What you been on with then"

"Just walking the dog boyoh"

This I found very irritating, my face I am sure reflected this fact as I made my enquiries.

"What did you drop over there then……..Sir?"

"Don't know what you mean boyoh, over where then?"

Cocky bastard! I physically escorted him over to the spot to find a dog lead fastened through the gill covers of two sea trout and a half eaten salmon lying on the sand. His footprints almost jumped out, his face fell in resignation.

"I got them didn't I, well Everyone's doing it you know"

I did the honors as he put up little resistance from then on, it turned out he was Tommy Dickinson's next door neighbor Daffid Evans, so no guesses as to who'd given him the idea. This was an easy collar as they say, bang to rights!

All was well at this juncture so I thought. I was about to leave him there in the car park and put the fish in my van, when Suddenly out of the blue this ginormous formidable fifteen stone woman appeared fists clenched striding towards us. I was caught completely by surprise rapidly deducing that this must be none other than Mrs Evans, who immediately started firing questions at me twenty to the dozen. The woman bore down on me with a few F and B words thrown in for good measure. Every time I tried to explain my parentage was questioned in broad welsh together with suggestions as to what I should really be doing for a living. I made a sharp exit in the end followed closely by that mad woman screaming at my van window. She possessed a very embarrassed looking Welshman cowering behind.

The strangest thing was after all that he actually pleaded not guilty on the court day and guess who came with him?

The trial was quite straightforward really Victor Bailey made mincemeat of his weak defence based on why leave dead fish out there to rot when taking them home made much more sense. Obviously if this offence was not enforced any Tom Dick or Harry could turn up with bags of fish claiming to have found them or picked them up, believe me they would that's for certain. It was for this reason men like Daffid Evans were prosecuted.

The case was proven, with a £100 fine together with £50 costs…. very satisfactory! I was more than a bit concerned however about Mrs Evans who had remained ominously quiet all through the proceedings. I decided to implement a dignified low profile type of exit, but not surprisingly she was just biding her time. I reached the main foyer spying the exit doors and freedom tantalisingly close. The silence predictably was then shattered!

"… I hope yur fuckin satisfied… you piece of government Shite"

I could feel the floor trembling as she approached, I have faced some big hairy poachers in my time but this welsh hurricane was something else and regrettably she managed to get between me and the exit door.

"My Daffid was nay but out walking, what's wrong wid takin a few fish that's already deead like"

I tried explaining that we had been through all that in court, but it just made things worse. She screamed more abuse barring my exit, by now and luckily for all concerned the usher was on the case.

"Come on madam you can't harass and intimidate a witness"

She wasn't to be denied the venting of feelings by anyone at this stage,

"Fuck you as well in fact fuck you all"

She finally stormed out of the building screaming more expletives before disappearing into the car park to mine and Everyone's relief. I have never met a more formidable looking opponent before or since.

A week after nabbing Daffid Evans I got an early phone call from Sergeant White at Brockley police station.

"Mr. Carter there's been an incident at Sandside, Tommy Dickinson's with WPC Dixon can you go and assist".

I left immediately despite a mouthful of toast, it was 06.30 on a damp wet Wednesday morning. I arrived at the Blue Anchor at 06.45, where I soon spotted the Panda car alongside a coast guard land rover and a huddle of uniformed personnel. Once out of my van I spotted a disheveled little person amongst the gathering. I was amazed because there stood the elusive Tommy Dickinson, wet through covered in mud from head to foot, and shivering violently. He looked like a pathetic old man whom I suppose is exactly what he was. WPC Dixon met me as I approached, normally she was full on and cheerful, but this misty morning she took me to one side wearing a mischievous glint in her eye.

"You won't believe this Jack", she whispered, "he only got his self fast in the quick sands half a mile out yonder. Coast guard lads have pulled him out, stuck fast up to his waist he was".

I had to laugh if somewhat discreetly, but there was more. WPC Dixon took me across to her Panda car and opened the boot.

"He had these with him, wouldn't part with em, and even offered me one if I let him go"

We both giggled behind the boot lid, because in front of me was a coal sack containing three pristine salmon all around the eight pound mark and covered in sea lice. I could just picture poor old Tommy stuck fast and trying to bribe a police officer.

I carried the sack over to the beleaguered culprit and begged an explanation.

Tommy looked up coughing, trying his best to look the victim.

"Well I guess thas gettan me at last, its tekin thee long enough, you and yon posh bugger. If it wurnt furt sands tha never would av"

I took down Tommy's details and discovered he was seventy-three years old, I felt a bit sorry for him really, although he'd certainly had a good run. I took the sack of fish and left in case the dreaded Mrs Evans should make an appearance, apparently she had raised the alarm spotting Tommy in difficulty out on the sands. I wouldn't bet against one of those salmon having her name on it.

Tommy never did get to court as we put our heads together and decided a warning letter would suffice. Taking a disheveled old man to court was not good policy then and never will be, although he couldn't really complain if we had. Danny was the only one keen to see him done, naturally because he had been led a merry dance for years.

I think the experience Tommy suffered that morning frightened him more than he would ever admit because I never heard any reports of him out there ever again.

Word spread quickly about Tommy's close call yet the conditions in the bay around Sandside were still causing me some concern. The latest crew to have a go was reportedly teenagers who had latched on to making an easy buck.

I intensified coverage of this area by stepping up patrols alternating with Danny. The strangest thing happened however one lunchtime as I ate my sandwiches in the Blue Anchor car park. My thoughts were miles away, Abba playing nicely as I read the paper, I managed the occasional glance across the sands, then back to the soccer page in the daily mail.

Suddenly I nearly jumped off the seat following a loud knock on my side window; I glanced round to see the female version of the incredible hulk, the one and only Mrs Evans. Naturally I almost choked on a ham sandwich, what onslaught awaited me was my only thought. She gestured for me to wind down the window, I nervously complied but only enough to hear whatever tirade was coming.

"Tha wants to git here of an evening Lad. That's when thall get em, its no use now tha may as well fuck off till then".

I paused with uncertainty.

"Right OK"

Then she was gone. A much-needed gulp of coffee followed. Despite the unnerving source of this particular tip off, a tip off is a tip off, no matter where it comes from and tip offs are reliably worth their weight in gold.

I returned home and informed Danny that tonight after tea was the time to be out. One thing can be said for Danny he always turned out, never arguing like some that I knew. The job came first, strike whenever an opportunity arose.

The plan I devised was for me to take observation from the quarry and Danny go further downstream at Leighton. I got into my usual vantage place behind the gorse bushes at 18.30 that same evening and waited to see if the Hulks information was anywhere near the mark. It was of course never in doubt really, when soon a group of youths appeared from the general direction of the Blue Anchor. They had probably just had a few drinks. They were noisy and boisterous three lads and three lasses, walking and running across the sand towards the main channel. The tide was a neap so plenty of water still remained in the estuary, much splashing and general fooling about accompanied this little sortie. It wasn't long before they reached the channel edge following the same routine as Daffid Evans had done. A bag with several fish in was soon in their possession.

I tried to call Danny on the Radio but as usual the old Pye sets were useless, so I decided to make a move regardless.

I was in the Blue anchor car park fifteen minutes later, unfortunately my quarry had moved downstream much further than Daffid previously had. I had no choice but to follow them down along the road to a point at the shore a further half a mile downstream next to some iron railings. I parked between two vehicles hoping to blend in. In front was a cortina containing Derby and Joan, whilst behind me was an empty van. Perfect, I spanned the vastness with binnocs. Bingo the group was obligingly heading back towards me, so I waited trying to predict their route. Eventually they became close enough to see who was doing what, I honed in on one lad in particular because he was carrying what looked like quite a heavy sack. …Closer and …closer, I waited for the moment as they reached the shore, one by one pulling themselves on to the pavement, the girls fooling about around the two lads, except of course for a tall wiry lad of about twenty years old in T shirt and shorts. He held the white plastic sack, he was and looked well clued up, but he didn't spot me just yet.

Now was the moment, I leapt out of my van like a gazelle just at the time he placed the sack up on the pavement. The response was instant as we exchanged intense but brief eye contact, grabbing the sack he fled back across the sands with me in hot pursuit, I was vaguely aware of the others legging it down the road in the general direction of Leighton. My man was soon thirty yards in front as I launched myself across the sand, he went through shallow water and I was definitely gaining. I was fairly fit for my age but this lad was built like Seb Coe, every time I got near him he just seemed to accelerate, no doubt he was just playing with me. Then to my horror grinning all over his face he started to tip out the contents of the sack into the murky water, one by one sea trout disappeared out of sight. I kept gaining and falling back hampered by water, my lungs complained intensely. Finally he triumphantly threw the empty sack away and unbeknown to me we had run round in a circle. I finally caught up with him when he deliberately eased off. He stood there in ankle deep water to face me. I held up my warrant desperately gasping for air, his face was a picture, he looked me in the eye once again, but no sound left my mouth, I couldn't get the words out. This was the time I needed to announce who I was and what I was going to do with him, but I was completely and totally knackered. Eventually after what seemed like an eternity I managed to whisper

"Water Bailiff don't move"

Of course in reality it was me that couldn't move. I gradually recovered enough to get him back to shore and into my book, the detail and name he gave me was a joke, James Smith, Leighton road, Leighton. I had no means of verifying this and no evidence to seize. He was soon rescued and whisked away by his boy racer pals leaving me alone, wet, knackered, with only a false name and address for my exertions.

Danny appeared by this time, I wearily filled him in on the events prior to searching for some evidence. We searched the area for a good half hour and never found one single fish or even the sack, I was not amused.

I suggested to Danny that they had gone in the direction of the Blue Anchor, so that's where I headed.

On reaching the car park to add insult to injury two cars full of youths sped out past me shouting and yelling triumphantly. I returned home feeling very deflated, enough was definitely enough.

The following day I was again in the Blue Anchor car park taking obs, when to my horror the Hulk suddenly reappeared yet again, how was I going to talk my way round this one. She loomed at my window.

"You caught em then?"

"Er…Yes Mrs Evans"

I was just about to tell my sorry tale, but she interrupted me before I could speak,

"He's a little shit that young Spunge, It's about time he was nicked"

I looked at her and thought "blimey there is a god" go for it,

"Aye you're right, I'm not quite sure he gave me the right address though"

I was thinking on my feet here hoping to capitalise on this propitious turn of events.

"I know exactly where he lives lad, twenty seven Maple drive, in Leighton up bit Station, in fact next door to my Brother Harry"

"Thanks Mrs Evans I'm on my way".

I left immediately feeling wonderful, good old Hulk, what a result that was. I visited Maple drive in Leighton that very evening with Danny where the young Mr. Smith obligingly answered the door. His face fell down to his knees, whereas mine was grinning like a Cheshire cat.

He confessed the lot and was in fact one Robert Spunge, now there's a name you don't forget easily. He eventually pleaded guilty at Brockley Magistrates court three months later, it cost him £175 plus £50 costs and he never went near chokers again ….job done!

14

THE WEIR

In 1981 I moved into Brockley having found lodgings in a terraced house belonging to a single mother. She had two kids and even agreed to take Ben as well. This was of course a relief even if he did bite her daughter the first day I moved in. To be fair to the dog it was a playful type of bite, but did draw blood unfortunately. This proved a very convenient home and only two hundred yards from the river, even better within handy walking distance of all the Pubs. My Landlady was founder of the Brockley Gingerbread group for single parents so naturally I was soon enlisted. The social life that accompanied this organisation was geared around the kids, although we did manage some nights out for adults only as well as the monthly meetings. I found this very beneficial making a lot of friends that I still have to this day.

The other big change was Joe's retirement, which had successfully happened just before Christmas. A formal presentation took place at the area office in Brockley followed by a session at the Blue Anchor in Sandside. This was an appropriate venue for a good send off, I can vouch that there was no holding back that day. The estuary didn't get a single glance and the tide came and went quietly completely unnoticed, whilst we all drank ourselves into oblivion. It was the end of an era and time for change. Joe of course put my name forward as his successor, but in all honesty they were big boots to fill and probably just too soon in my case. My experience although good and getting better didn't really amount to enough for such a position. Joe did a great job convincing me though, so I was well fired up when the interviews came round. I was also quite confident just to get that far, the only other real candidates were Hank of course and an ex policeman who at the time was a Bailiff in west Cumbria. Nobody new anything about him apart from the rumor he had lost a Land rover to the incoming tide, hardly a good CV! West Cumbria was the equivalent to the Wild West in fisheries terms with frequent uncivilized and violent clashes between Bailiffs and poachers. We were always hearing tales about the macho men and all the cases and arrests involved.

I came to the conclusion although Brockley could be quite rough at times it was not a bad place to be in comparison. Hank badly wanted the job, but was up against quite a formidable stumbling block, Joe made it quite clear to everyone that Hank would only get the job over his dead body.

The interviews eventually came around a few weeks later on a cold wet January morning and for me went quite well. I put my case forward for leadership as best I could. I never even saw my West Cumbrian rival on the day so departed none the wiser. Hank was very bullish of course unaware that he probably had even less chance than I did.

Two weeks later the inevitable happened, I didn't get the job and for that matter neither did Hank. I was philosophical enough to realise that it was just too soon, but I knew in my heart that's where I wanted to be one day. It was worrying though, because I couldn't see where the next vacancy would come from, West Cumbria maybe? ...No thank you!

The new Fisheries Inspector was unveiled at the Brockley office in February 1981.

His name was Richard Myers, a cockney ex copper about mid forties. He was a stout fellow with a bushy beard and first impressions were of a jolly easy going man who smoked like a chimney. He was quite a contrast to Joe, but time moves on and so did we. I visited Joe once a week both as a friend and not least because Hannah cooked a roast Sunday dinner of the highest caliber. I would discuss all the latest events in the lives of the fisheries Bailiffs; Joe would torment Ben endlessly as I fought to stay awake after stuffing my face.

Dick Myers as he soon became known didn't change the day to day running of things at first so everything ticked along nicely as spring and summer approached. The thinking behind Dick's appointment was apparently down to his police background. The idea being to improve our enforcement capabilities, after all poaching incidents were still on the increase.

I considered this to be a fair proposal; we needed all the help we could get.

In July 1981 a new and ominous problem arose in Brockley, this was the development of a previously unidentified poaching method evolving at the town weir.

The weir is positioned at the north end of the town and was built in the nineteen fifties. I had never given it much attention previously and never even considered why it was there. There is no obvious reason, no millrace to be fed, so why build it? The general opinion I discovered was for the protection of a sewer pipe crossing the river at this point about twenty yards above the weir crest. That was confirmed eventually as the sole reason for the existence of this formidable structure. The weir itself is made of concrete and about one hundred yards wide from one bank to the other. In the centre is a fish pass in the form of a square box made up of low walls about half the height of the actual weir. The height is deceiving depending on the state of flow; I guess it has about a twelve-foot drop from the crest down to the riverbed.

Angling activity above and below any weir is an offence from the first of October until the following season as specified by bylaw. A person fishing downstream from the weir was the norm, but actually fishing at the weir or in the fish pass had not been encountered. Jez Bergerac changed all that however. I discovered this fact patrolling the town one evening in July. I met Jez casually walking downstream from the weir along the green, an area of open grassland running adjacent to the river. There was no panic as Ben trundled enthusiastically along beside me. Jez was carrying a spinning rod and wearing his usual childish grin.

"Hello Mr. Carter, want to see my license"

I was intrigued and not a little surprised, Jez with a license? Surely not Go on then Jez, it'll be a first"

He sniggered boyishly and produced a brown trout license; I tried not to be sarcastic

"That's fine Jez, but you know you can't take salmon or sea trout with this don't you"

"Oh yes Mr. Carter I only want a few trout"

I was deeply suspicious of this compliant stance now put forward by a teenage lad who had been bordering on the bigger portrait of criminality for a while.

Nevertheless I had no choice but to send him on his way in good faith hoping for a miracle. Two days later I got a phone call from Timmy Dunne.

"That fucker Bergerac's bin snaggin sea trout ont weir, they reckon he had five buggers last neet"

I wasn't sure what to make of this at first, so I consulted Hank and Dick Myers the next morning at the office. We had bylaws and acts spread out on the table, luckily a new brain had recently joined us in the team. Roger Mcbane became our new Principal fisheries officer or in plain terms the main boss for the south lakes. He was a decent bloke with degrees coming out of his ears, but little practical experience. He could fathom out the law though and we soon had it sussed with him on the case. After some deliberations we came up with the solution. Any person fishing in or around the fish pass or even on the weir was interfering with the free passage of fish as stated in the salmon and fresh water fisheries act. This included fishing whilst in possession of a valid license and using legitimate bait or lure at the time never mind foul hooking or snatching.

That same evening I got hold of Big Don to help me patrol the town, agreeing to meet at six o clock on Jubilee Bridge from whence we set off to walk it right through. Les Paltrow was fishing by waterflats surrounded by young kids as usual. Yuk! I gave him a wide berth. Fifteen minutes later we were positioned by the scout hut at the bottom end of the green, well camouflaged by boisterous lads practicing their marching techniques. This provided some cover and a vantage point up to the weir, roughly four hundred yards away. Don put his binocs up

"See out Don"

"Yep he's there alright, have a look for yourself"

I focused the glasses and immediately spotted Jez stood motionless on the weir crest and about half way along facing into the fish pass. He was holding a fishing rod but didn't seem to be doing anything drastic at that particular time.

I decided on a pincer movement sending Don ahead over the bridge on the right bank behind the weir whilst I would approach from the left bank.

It worked well and Jez easily spotted Don ten minutes later thus allowing me to sneak up unnoticed behind him. Jez finally turned round and faced me.

I shouted across above the sound of white cascading water holding my warrant card up in the process.

"Get yourself over here Jez"

Jez returned precariously across the weir taking care not to fall in. The drop into the fast churning water below was very dangerous on a good flow; in this case recent rain still maintained such a situation, thus forcing Jez to take his time. Once back across the familiar silly grin reappeared.

"What's up Mr. Carter you've sin mi license, I'm only after trout"

"You can't fish from the weir Jez or any where near the fish pass"

He looked at me with devilish grin

"Why's that then?"

"It's interfering with the free passage of fish"

Jez began to get annoyed, but I stuck to my guns and warned him to keep away. I also reminded him I could have booked him there and then; needless to say he wasn't impressed. I moved Jez on to go and fish elsewhere, that was that so I thought.

Next morning Timmy Dunne was back on the phone.

"What you doin he's bin back again"

"Who has Timmy?"

"Bloody Bergerac who du yu bloody think, he's sniggin ont weir after you buggers have gone".

I was not amused, Jez was now taking the piss, and not only that Timmy Dunne was bad mouthing me to anyone who would listen. This needed some careful thought and a day's deliberation.

I decided on a new plan after much consideration; I contacted Danny suggesting he go out on his tod after tea the next evening to check Jez. Big Don and I would then come in a bit later and hopefully surprise him. I was using the theory; It's the second mouse that gets the cheese. It turned out to be another fine evening with a river full of sea trout and Danny checked Jez innocently fishing a worm by the green …so far so good.

I met Don at the top end of town at 20.00 and we moved covertly downstream approaching via the Right Bank behind a large Office block known as Abbey house.

I peered round the end of the building at 20.20, there sure enough was our man stood on the weir right by the fish pass. I felt the hairs on the back of my neck rise up when Jez cast a large treble hook into the box. I watched as he reeled in his tackle with sharp violent tugs trying to make contact with any part of any fish resting innocently in the oxygen rich water beneath. He repeated the process several times until the inevitable happened; the line went taught signaling a fish was hooked. Jez gave a whoop of excitement unable to contain himself. The commotion attracted an audience on the left bank next to the weir, several dog walkers stopped to watch Jez in action. The on going turmoil quickly gained the attention of other passers by, not to mention some kids Jez had brought along to keep nicks. The crowd was growing as the scene unfolded until the poor fish made a leap for freedom out of the box and downstream. I decided it was time to make a move whilst Jez wrestled with his prey. I crawled across the bridge on all fours leaving Don to cover the right bank approach. I negotiated the bridge oblivious to any passers by and all accompanying strange looks. I finally reached refuge behind the public toilets just above the weir on the left bank still unseen by Jez and the ever-increasing crowd now totally focused on the action. I managed to peer round the toilets to get a clear view of Jez, he was standing on the wall of the fish pass still playing the fish. In situations like this when a fish is foul hooked the poor creature will fight very hard and for much longer than a fish hooked in the mouth. Legitimate fish are landed sooner and suffer far less as a consequence. I decided enough was enough at this point and dashed to the edge of the weir screaming at Jez. I ignored the twenty or so spectators, some of whom legged it immediately, while others stood open mouthed and all the lookouts yelled to him

"Jez, Jez, watch it Becky's here"

Jez swung round, he was a good forty yards away, his face was wild with shock, but not shocked enough to stop him from breaking his fishing line with a severe tug requiring both hands.

I was seething by now whilst Jez made his way very slowly back towards me, loosing ones temper with a scroat like Jez would be all too easy. I had to compose myself as the distance between us lessened, I could read his ever-nearing ugly face. The victim in all this was now away downstream with a large treble hook impaled in its side. The line would soon catch round a root or rock leaving it to become exhausted in a fruitless struggle, finally drowning or being discovered by an opportunist and unceremoniously removed.

Jez arrived back on terra firma protesting his innocence; Don joined me only to be hassled by the entourage of kids and hangers on. It is difficult to deal with someone when this is happening, so I dragged him off to one side. Jez hadn't a leg to stand on of course, so I gleefully booked him for using a snatch, even though I didn't have it in my possession I did seize his rod and find another two trebles in his trouser pocket though. I also informed him he was interfering with the free passage of fish. Whether this was fully understood by Jez was questionable, but this was the very first case of many on that notorious weir.

The events that followed were down to several factors, firstly word of easy pickings at the weir soon spread round the town despite the capture of Jez. Secondly the black market for salmon and sea trout was thriving offering good financial returns for those willing to take the risk and thirdly the number of youths and young men taking drugs was on the increase which in turn required financing.

I was now starting to realise that we had quite a problem developing, various previously unknown characters took up fishing, some had trout licenses some just didn't bother and were easy pickings for a week or two. Jez had another go on the weir the very day after we had caught him; he was a nineteen-year-old lad with not a lot going on between his ears and like many more before and since was determined to beat the systems society laid down. I of course wasn't about to let that happen ... game on!

I approached the weir again two days later at about 21.00 in the evening only this time with Hank. I don't think Hank was impressed with the job in hand, he would much prefer to ride round Windermere or sup tea with Peter Teasdale, however I was determined that Jez needed his comeuppance. Hank dropped me at Abbey house then drove his Land rover across to the left bank. Jez was back on the weir defiant as ever, only this time he had at least four lookouts all young lads in there early teens and equipped with that vital tool in such a situation... the push bike!

I had to be very watchful whilst these lookouts toured the area trying to flush out any careless Becky, but what they hadn't bargained for was Hank, simply because unlike me they hadn't seen him before. Hank reliably dressed in tweed suit, brogues and tie was just another bloke to them.

Jez was snatching away on the weir as per usual nonchalantly watched by Hank now stood on the left bank amongst half a dozen kids and spectators. I don't think this was a crafty plan of Hanks own making, more he couldn't be arsed to put himself out type of move. It was about to work in my favour however as I saw the opportunity unfold. The risk of being sniffed out by the push bike brigade meant I had to act sooner rather than later. I decided to tackle Jez head on from the right bank, approaching from behind Abbey house then down to the weir edge, of course he spotted me right away. He immediately turned round heading as fast as was possible back to the other side. The usual screaming of

"Becky, Becky" was forthcoming from the faithful push bike brigade, unfortunately Jez went straight into the arms of Hank on the left bank and this time we got rod and snatch. Jez was mortified to have been fooled by Hank,

"Who's this bugger?"

He gesticulated at Hank who now loved every minute and gladly took over the glory in all his pomp and majesty.

"Thou just listen to me young man, thas in serious trouble, tha needs to get thee sel yam and don't let us catch thee here again".

Hank sounded a dead ringer for Brian Clough with a Cumbrian dialect.

I was quite happy letting him take the glory and new it wouldn't be the last time.

Jez didn't appear on the weir again that summer but the grapevine told me he was getting experience elsewhere and learning fast.

The remainder of that summer and backend became notorious for activity in and around the weir, all interest in salmon fishing focused around this one place like any honey pot attracting both good and bad elements. There was and still are to this day good honest anglers who fish in the town stretch and in the vicinity of this weir, but the bad element gave us a real headache. The events of most days required both covert and high profile patrols, the covert patrols became more and more fruitless as the lookout system in place was usually too difficult to fool. All the routes of attack became known. The high profile method merely relied on one or two Bailiffs keeping a presence at the weir monitoring all angling activity. If a fish was foul hooked which was quite a high percentage, it could be policed in a way as to ensure it was returned with the least possible injury ensuring the survival of at least some fish. It was not uncommon to find fish dead at a later date usually somewhere downstream either with a festered wound or even with hook and line still in the carcass.

The local scroats, criminals, and druggies that never previously fished at all became attracted to the weir and its spoils. They gathered day and night stretching our resources to the limit. The night shift was the hardest to police, groups gathered and new names became a familiar sight each and every day or night. Often they would goad me as I tried every which way I could to outwit them, regrettably I was always outnumbered and not able to be there all of the time.

The Green Dragon a local pub two hundred yards up the road housed a rather nasty character called Arnold Capstick who was Landlord and ex boxer. He would often walk down or should I say stagger down at night after midnight with his dog, without exception he would home in on which ever Bailiff was unfortunate enough to be on duty at the weir. I can remember him surprising me one night as I instructed a youth to return a salmon foul hooked from the weir.

"What yu made him put it back fur yu miserable bastard, he's gitten a license I bet"

I tried to explain despite being hampered by his putrid alcoholic breath belching across my bough, but he was having none of it.

"You're just a bunch of fascist twats, if tha bothers my lad's thas goin int beck yu cunt"

He was a formidable bloke fuelled with drink and a naturally bad temper. I made a calculated retreat rather than stay to slug it out. This type of situation arose many times amongst various individuals more often than not powered by drink.

The lads that Arnold Capstick referred to were his own three sons who all took up fishing that year. They each performed on the weir most nights, becoming much more than a nuisance. I had several unsuccessful attempts at catching them; regrettably Father wasn't helping by egging them on so Don christened them "The brothers Grim". Luck went our way eventually as the law of averages dictates. I set up a patrol with Big Don one Saturday night deliberately waiting until after 01.00 in the morning, when hopefully the last revelers including Father Capstick might be past caring. We sneaked by the pub at one thirty and thankfully all was quiet. We then moved on towards the weir dodging stealthily from parked car to parked car. I peered cautiously over the back of a ford escort about a hundred yards from the front line. I could see the usual suspects including at least two of the Capstick lads.

There were obviously people on the weir, but it was impossible to decipher who was doing what. I waited a couple of minutes then whispered across to Don.

"We'll after rush em and take what we can, we can probably get a bit nearer"

Don nodded as he chewed furiously on his Wrigley's pulling down his woolly hat, he looked very intimidating…good!

I cunningly gained another twenty-five yards before nodding to Don, that was the all important signal.

I ran swiftly in a b-line totally focused, it was one of those occasions when everything seemed to go into time frame or slow motion like an action replay. I was aware of bodies peeling off on all sides, screaming youths, girl hangers on, others open mouthed and frozen to the spot. A lad on the weir stood mesmerized, his fishing line glinting under the street light, caught in two minds jump or run! I immediately recognised Graeme Capstick the youngest of the brothers grim, his rod swung slowly round complete with a big treble hook dangling with menace and guilt. Droplets of water sprayed like saliva from a shaking dog. I was gaining by this time, whereas he ran precariously along the weir heading desperately for the Right Bank and freedom. I was having none of that and accelerating over the bridge even though he'd passed half way. He was thankfully hampered by the flow and the fear of falling eventually jumping off to negate the last ten yards. The resulting splash was spectacular not least because he miraculously stayed upright, mobile and fuelled by adrenaline. His thigh waders hindered escape considerably.

Only a wall and railings remained to negotiate, but I was almost upon him until finally he fell in a disheveled heap sending the rod and line sprawling. I nailed him easily at this point. Graeme Capstick was only fifteen when apprehended that night, however the resulting decision to prosecute was not a difficult one, he had it coming as they say, the first juvenile I ever had to prosecute entirely because of his persistence and the need to win some of the battles if not the war.

He appeared in court the same day as Jez Bergerac, Victor Bailey had been primed of the need to get the magistrates convinced that the weir was a significant player in the poaching world. Capstick pleaded guilty on the day watched eagerly by his Father. The Court fined find him £30 plus £20 costs, obviously not a big fine but at least it put down a marker for things to come. Jez of course pleaded not guilty to a total of four charges, all in vain thankfully, justice was done setting him back a total of £150. I won the day and left a very happy man for the time being at least.

15

FRANKY AND SERGIO

In 1981 further incidents occurred at the town weir right into September some involving the remaining two Capstick brothers, who finally also went in my book. I was assisted considerably thanks to a character called Franky Wilson. The weir had become popular with many bona fide anglers as well as scroats, entirely due to the build up of fish in the town stretch. Franky Wilson was one such angler although strictly a worm and spinning man, he would often be found talking and fishing below or in the vicinity of the weir. He usually fished in the company of a guy called Lewis Parsons locally known as giant Haystacks due to his more than ample frame. Lewis was quite simply a very nice man and as is often the case very gentle for such a giant. I built up a cosy relationship with these two developing a trust born from their guts to spot poaching at the weir and then pass on the info to yours truly. It was down to Franky that I nailed the remaining two Capsticks, David and Ian. They had foolishly befriended him before and during snatching exploits, only for Franky to then give me the nod. Six-o-clock in the morning was apparently the favoured time when most people had drifted away. The temptation to brag about fish they had caught was obviously too much to resist, so they took Franky into their confidence as he had with me. This situation is not unusual and Franky was more than eager to help. It was for all those reasons I took Danny and Big Ron at 05.30 one wet and windy September morning when luckily both lads were bang at it in spite of the weather. They even had two salmon on the bank ready to take home. They were so busy at the task in hand we successfully sneaked up from behind the public toilets without even waking two druggies fast asleep in the ladies. The unique and revolting aroma that surrounded those toilets back then is one I will always remember. It wasn't unusual to find half a dozen spaced out individuals occupying the insalubrious premises together with so called fishermen all performing various bodily functions that don't bare thinking about.

David and Ian Capstick went satisfactorily into my book, the rods were seized together with various trebles, and the two fish, thank you very much Franky!

This situation carried right into October complete with more juicy tip offs paying dividends leading to more prosecutions.

Events took a surprising turn though on a bright October afternoon after covering the upper reaches with Danny. We had scoured the Brock and Brant all day without any success so finally headed for home. There was however a good vantage point across Gilbertfields above Brockley at a lay-by on the main road. It was conveniently sited next to a hot food van and always worth a look. I had just purchased two teas and an Eccles cake, whilst Danny aimed his binnocs across the open fields past Gilbertsfield farm towards the footpath on the River Stock. It was here in my first year that Tommy Brown nailed Fingers Jackson snorkelling in the deep pool known as Sandygorge. The pool is deep and long, a wonderful sanctuary for big salmon waiting to spawn on the broad fast stickle that drained it. I casually addressed Danny,

"Anything about Dan"

I was just munching my Eccles cake watched greedily by Ben when Danny replied,

"Yes indeed three people stood on the beck edge"

Typical, just when I thought it was safe to go home.

I grabbed my own binocs spilling my tea in the process; I surveyed the scene using the van roof as a rest. I soon made out three men; unfortunately the distance was a good half-mile, so getting an ID wouldn't be easy. Slowly but surely I worked them out, and the plot thickened?

"One of em is Sam Mcgowan Dan, and one is……. I think … yep its Les Gaunt, can't make out the other but he's got a rod that's for sure".

Danny took a hurried gulp of his tea whilst I meanwhile weighed up form. The only way of approach to get there quickly was what we lovingly described as route one, which literally meant walk straight in, the shortest route. This was always a gamble because we would be negotiating two open fields divided by dry stone walls, followed finally by a further big open field that unfortunately contained a large flock of sheep, a factor I overlooked for some reason in the excitement. The theory assumed that the three men would be watching the path rather than the open ground to the rear, Of course if they did happen to turn round the game was up in a flash, the only option then would be to rush in and grab whatever we could.

We were soon on the move traveling the short distance on the back road to Burndale, Danny of course was having a quick St Bruno fix, whilst Ben polished off my Eccles cake all over the back seat. I parked by the wall, and then carefully scanned for our men again. Danny sorted out his various sticks, glasses, notebooks and general paraphernalia that always seemed to be required. I could see the glint of a rod and line in the sun but still didn't know the identity of the third person.

"Are you right Dan?"

The reply was whispered in typical public school twang,

"Yes alright what's the plan?"

Dan was a trusted back up, as reliable as anyone in such a situation providing he didn't have to think or plan tactics; he would do exactly what you told him to the letter no matter what.

"Route one Dan, that's our easiest, quickest, and only option"

"Oh righty ho"

Dan grinned in his own inimitable way and off we set, Ben barked his annoyance at being left behind in the van, fortunately we were too far away for this to be a problem on the day. I walked in the half crouch position to keep below the stone walls and hopefully out of sight, I gained the first wall in about three minutes, Danny was of course right there next to me. The gate was opened and shut without fuss, and then it was off across field number two, again half crouched until reaching the next wall. This took a further five minutes. We stopped to breathe and regain composure; I was sweating like a pig already.

"I'm just going to try and put the binnocs on em Dan"

I quickly found a suitable point for a quick scan across the last open field and that's when I finally became aware of the damned sheep. Sheep are a nightmare obviously, easily panicked into rushing becoming very visible and a dead give away. I managed to get a look across to the beck without any obvious alarm in fact one or two of the nearest sheep did see me but didn't seem concerned.

Sam McGowan was about a hundred yards away as the crow flies; as per usual having very little grey matter he was left to keep nicks. The waft of cigarette smoke was just about reaching my heightened senses and I watched Sam look up and down the footpath, his attention was drawn irresistibly towards Les Gaunt leaning over an elderberry bough to peer through his Polaroid's into the beck. Nothing new here I thought, that was until the third man came into view. I nudged Dan violently, it was none other than Franky Wilson blatantly carrying a spinning rod, and he even looked my way so I had to duck back behind the wall pronto.

I turned to Dan in confusion

"You'll never guess whose carrying the bloody rod, its Franky flaming Wilson"

I positioned myself again to observe from the wall as I tried to make sense of this development because Franky was now snatching with the best of em.

"The two faced bastard"

I was murmuring away and more than a bit angry; here was what I thought was a good mate bang at it with the two well known miscreants.

After a couple of minutes assessing the situation I psyched myself into a state of readiness before turning again to Danny.

"Right Dan we need to nab this twat, all we can do is try and plop over this wall and walk straight in, can't see another way round it"

Dan nodded his agreement as we prepared to go.

I watched as all three men began another examination of the river bank, then carefully picked the moment and sort of slithered over the wall landing with a soft thud in the short lush grass, I was quickly followed by Dan. Standing upright I slowly commencing the hundred yard walk with Dan in my wake, the sheep broke away inevitably right down the middle about twenty going left and another thirty flying off right, a small flock of starlings rose in unison and disgust at the intrusion. I kept on going eyes fixed on my prey, yard by yard it felt like a western. John Wayne walks across an open space expecting to be shot at any moment. I was convinced one of them would surely turn round. Eventually the hawthorn bushes on the beck edge looked ever welcoming, the sheep were still flying off in both directions, twenty yards to go, surely not possible? I somehow made it to those bushes completely undetected with good old Dan at my heel. All three men apparently so engrossed they never even looked round once.

I don't think route one has ever been more outrageously exploited as it was that October afternoon. The three poachers now performed at our mercy, all I could do was wait for a result.

We both got nicely hidden only about twenty yards downstream from the three men, Les Gaunt was stripped to the waist by now, he was actually wading in the water and heading my way, I could even hear what he said.

"Here, here there's a fuckin big bastard just here, pass us the rod"

Franky obliged and Sam lit another fag, some use he was. Les Gaunt successfully launched his apparatus violently into a seven-pound salmon before handing the rod back to Franky amid much splashing and confusion; I was poised like a spring, my heart pounding in anticipation. The fish was played laboriously for several minutes until exhausted, before it was unceremoniously yanked violently on to the bank by Franky. Sam rushed over to rapidly dispatch it with a crushing thud to the head courtesy of a handily placed rock. When I suddenly sprang from the bushes with Danny we were only ten yards from the crime scene, it was one of those best feelings as a Bailiff moment, the shock horror expressions of poachers in situations such as this are inimitable. Les Gaunt glared in disbelief.

"Oh fuckin hell not you again"

Sam shrugged his shoulders and would have walked off if I hadn't put a hand on him.

"Better not Sam eh lad".

Wilson eyed me warily I could see the cogs of his mind turning; desperately trying to see a way out of a very embarrassing mess.

His final reaction was to clam up altogether despite my remark emphasising that I knew who he was any way, so his non-actions only made matters worse.

He eventually gave me his details rather than risk being done for obstruction, but he wasn't happy about giving up the rod and line which turned out to be his. I thought for a moment he was going to turn nasty, however his mixed emotions were obviously clouding any reasonable judgment. I think this fact slowed him down just enough to complete the business and allow our departure triumphantly, complete with both rod and fish. This incident was run of the mill for Les Gaunt and Sam, just another fine mess to add to the ever-growing list. Franky was scuppered though and whatsmore his cover of squeaky-clean angler was blown right out the water. He did fish the town again for a while, greeting me venomously on each occasion, he was eventually fined a £100 for that little escapade. On the court day he became very hostile towards me, so much so that several weeks later I walked past him in the main street of Brockley and was subject to a verbal assassination outside Woollies.

"Thas cost me a hundred quid yu bastard, a hundred fuckin quid"

That type of reaction did occur from time to time, however Franky bore a grudge against me for about ten years, never failing to greet me with a snarl and abuse on the few future occasions I was unfortunate enough to bump into him.

I didn't see him for a long period at all until the late nineties, I was sent one day to pick up some oxygen cylinders in Sedbergh and low and behold there he was. I recognised him straight away immediately wondering, would he still bear a grudge after all this time?

I needn't have worried he had obviously mellowed.

"Now then Mr. Carter long time sin yu pulled us int it"

"Aye Franky how's it going"

"Can't complain tha knows, by the way I was bang out of order that day yu know"

I didn't really want to go down that road, so I nodded cautiously, he grinned at me.

"I were a reet Pratt wunt I"

He laughed out loud heartily this time.

"Never mind eh"

He laughed again as he loaded me up with two new cylinders.

I left fairly quickly extremely pleased he had finally come to his senses if somewhat late in the day.

1981 was a significant year for another reason, poaching seemed to increase annually, but strangely so did the health of the river, gone were the days of the plaguesome UDN. The numbers of salmon and sea trout increased throughout the eighties despite many removed either by angling, commercial, or illegal capture. There was by this time another player up-and-coming, the one and only Sergio Ferraria. This guy was not a formula one driver or open golf champion as the name suggests but a scoundrel from the council estate in Burndale. The family was of Spanish origin and his parents emigrated to this country after the war plying their trade in the ice cream industry. Sergio was one of four brothers and two sisters, all of whom were basically honest and hard working causing no problems to anyone. Sergio turned out to be the classic black sheep of the family, first coming to my attention via new boss Dick Myers. Dick would sometimes patrol my patch on days when I was off duty, or after I had been on nights with Don or Danny.

I didn't catch on for a while, but it seems that Dick would stop in Burndale near the chip shop and check the River Brock at a point opposite the allotments. It soon became clear Dick had a style of anti poaching all of his own. Don sussed him out first during a patrol of the area above Brockley. One afternoon when I was on leave they planned to split up mid way through a shift, allowing Don to look down the bottom end and estuary leaving Dick to cover my patch.

Don couldn't wait to tell me?

"Guess what, Myers left me at Croftgill bang on 13.00 to patrol your patch whilst I went down the estuary, and do you know I hadn't even got away from Bampton hall when didn't I see the bugger on his way home. How long had he been away do yu think?"

I had no idea

"One hour! One bloody hour that's friggin all".

I was taken aback to think that he was patrolling the whole of my patch in an hour then going home. This was possibly the first sign that our boss was not all he had been cracked up to be.

This ex policeman, legal expert, macho man, going to clean the place up single-handed type of bloke, apparently not!

I was thankfully aware of all this of course when Dick described his encounters with Sergio, who was obviously working that particular bit of river in Burndale. Sergio had easily spotted Dick Myers as he drove through or pulled up at the bus stop to peer over the wall into the beck. Dick had fortuitously observed Sergio running or walking away carrying a rod on one occasion and actually carrying a fish. I made a mental note of the fact that he hadn't bothered to actually do anything about it at any point, I found this to be a bit disconcerting to say the least.

I decided to spend some time in that area myself, so to this end I parked up on a sunny August afternoon about half way between Brockley and Burndale. I chose a shady street and settled Ben as best I could before walking the half-mile into Burndale. I passed the loathsome Les Paltrow who seemed to be all over the place during this period, he was fishing just below the confluence of the Brock and Stock. He was alone thank goodness, probably all the kids would be at school and he was wearing the same scabby, filthy raincoat I had seen him in on our first encounter. He had peeling filthy skin on his baldhead, which I personally found quite revolting. He never failed to head my way in some vain attempt to show me a license that I definitely wasn't keen on seeing. I brushed him aside to proceed earnestly upstream hoping not to be further distracted from my task. I reached the bus stop rather faster than first intended which proved to be my undoing. I circled the wooden shelter to get a good view upstream, only to be met by the unnerving sight of a sea trout flying through the air about fifty yards upstream. My eyes briefly met those of the man I now know to be Sergio Ferraria, he was yanking back on a spinning rod violently. He reacted very quickly at this point disappearing across a short field and into the maze of Ashfields the council estate before I had time to respond, the sea trout shot past me downstream thankfully still very much alive.

Of course I didn't know who this guy was at that point, but two days later our paths crossed once again.

On this occasion I staked out the same area at about 14.00 only instead I used the opposite or Right Bank courtesy of a blackthorn thicket. Poachers who have regular honest employment rarely perform in the morning. My man duly turned up walking down the left bank accompanied by a black and white mongrel and obviously he was in no hurry systematically examining every bit of river and obviously after fish. I got a good view using my binnocs; He looked about mid thirties, well built with evil dark eyes. He moved slowly downstream allowing me ample opportunity to cautiously pursue him. I stalked him down for a good half hour eventually positioning myself directly opposite, I watched as he crouched down peering under roots frequently looking up and down the bank in case the likes of a Bailiff was around to spoil his efforts, a mute swan with three well grown cygnets cruised innocently past dissecting the pair of us. In time he produced a wire snare, which was attached to a stick broken from a sycamore branch close by. He had several attempts to locate a fish before moving off once again. I followed for another twenty yards, but his pace was increasing so I decided it was time to jump him. To do this effectively I had to wade the river and consequently he easily spotted my advancement. Surprisingly he didn't panic or run off, only his dog barked on seeing me splash through the swift flowing warm water. I had my warrant out in my hand ready during the approach.

"Water Bailiff can I have a word"

The reaction took me by surprise,

"Don't you come across here harassing me I'm only walking my dog, if you come near me again I'll throw you in do you understand".

He was blazing by this time and quite a formidable foe, nevertheless I still asked him about the snare,

"What snare? What fuckin snare?"

He dramatically opened his black tweed jacket turning out the pockets in a violent sort of come and look for yourself action.

I ended up with nothing except a bruised ego, whereas he just stormed off.

I had several subsequent sightings of Sergio over the following couple of weeks until one afternoon I dropped on him at Elmbank almost by accident, in fact I am not sure who surprised who the most. I had patrolled all day and was just checking the old weir with Ben. He appeared from nowhere clutching a spinning rod equipped with everything except any form of bait or lure. I tackled him head on,

"Got a license for that then"

He spun round defiantly, his beady black eyes penetrating my return stare and obviously annoyed with himself for the surprise attack.

"Cause I have, but I ain't fishing am I?"

He was reasserting his bullish style, confidence now replaced the surprise.

"You're about too, so that's good enough for me, where is it?"

"At home mate"

I explained the requirement that a valid license should be carried at all times whilst fishing and issued him with a ticket. "The ticket" or "failing to produce notice" to give it the correct name allows an angler seven days to produce his license to the area office.

I took down his details, which he gave as Clive Webb living at a house on Ashfields.

I had no way of confirming whether this was in fact the right name and address or not. The police and criminal evidence act would come out in later years and change all that, but for now I had no choice but to believe him despite grave doubts as to its validity.

The following two weeks not surprisingly didn't see the production of any license. I was consequently handed the task of tracking him down by Dick Myers. This proved quite easy as the nice Lady at the Burndale post office recognised my description with ease.

"That'll be Sergio, he's a dammed nuisance, if you catch up with him remind him he owes six weeks paper money."

I went straight on to Ashfields and knocked at the door of number forty four. I decided to try the back door because the street Mafia seemed keen to take an interest on my arrival, I knocked and waited, it was 09.30 in the morning. A dark attractive woman around forty answered the door she was clad in a dressing gown and not much else. I composed myself as best I could, clearing my throat rather nervously, while the woman smiled obviously enjoying my discomfort.

"Does a Mr. Ferraria live here please?"

"He's not in will I do?"

"Are you Mrs Ferraria?"

"Something like that, he'll be back later though, do you want to come in and wait?"

I declined the offer as the dressing gown began to slide open rather invitingly.

"I'll pop back later"

I reached my car rather flustered and felt the whole world's eyes on me during my escape. I did return that evening just when Sergio attempted to take his dog for an impromptu walk.

I quickly collared him to successfully report him for not having a licence on the previous occasion and also providing false details…He was not amused.

In late September I had a second confrontation with Sergio on the R Brock at Brock Mill. Finding a meaningful position for covert observation in the vicinity of the mill was not an easy task, not least due to an unpleasant guy working there that I occasionally came across fishing the town section in Brockley. The old mill had been one of the many used during the industrial revolution, but alas was now just a paper recycling plant and rather an eyesore at that. The on going litter problem in an otherwise pristine environment often brought confrontation with the parish council. The only manual worker there was one Paul Cranston notorious for his reputation as the main Friday night brawler in Brockley; he was a bald headed guy with a distinctive small but badly broken nose. He would have been better advised to take up boxing professionally had he the common sense to do so. His physique was impressive and his deportment was a tad unfriendly to say the least, so caution was the order of the day when one was around Paul.

He certainly didn't like me that's for sure, or any other Becky that patrolled the riverbank between Brock Bridge and Elmbank. He never failed to spot the enemy, sounding the hooter housed in the mill, thus alerting everyone for miles that the Becky's were about. It took me a while to grasp what was going on here not realising I was wasting my time as soon as the dreaded hooter went off. Once the penny had dropped however I began approaching the area from different angles with more stealth taking up to an hour sometimes, I secured a good hide directly opposite the mill on the left bank and overlooking a long deep glide full of sea trout. I used to enjoy testing myself to see if I could gain the satisfaction of not hearing that bloody hooter.

It was during such a sortie one afternoon that Sergio actually showed up, I had been tucked away for over an hour lulled by the gentle gurgle of water as it trundled out of the pool and gently away towards Burndale.

The only activity of note revealed Cranston briefly taking his fag break along the footpath; it was during long stints like this when the rhythmic sound of flowing water was uninterrupted for several hours that a strange thing happened. I am convinced it was some form of self hypnosis, because I went into a state of not actually being asleep but somewhere very close to it. The funny thing was, if someone or something appeared on the scene the even rhythm was interrupted by whatever noise they contributed. That immediately broke the spell allowing me to fully check it out. That soporific state proved fool proof over the years greatly assisting long weary stake outs. A similar expedition in a hedge on the River Brant produced one magical moment I will always remember. I had sat for three hours without moving when I became strangely aware of another presence, how I knew is a mystery, but something caused me to turn round. Incredibly I was two feet away from a silent, pristine fox, two perfect black shining eyes met mine freezing the moment. A fox is a very curious animal and he was no exception, then seconds later I was alone again.

Another thirty minutes passed at Elmbank before Sergio's ugly face appeared on the opposite bank out of nowhere. The adrenaline kicked in while I strained to get a good view and his mongrel cocked a leg on a well-used tree with casual indifference.

The next action was a first however; Sergio spent several minutes examining the pool before retreating downstream about fifty yards until out of sight. What should I do stick or move? The temptation to move early presents a dilemma in situations like this one, on this occasion Sergio made my mind up for me. The sound and sight of rocks being hurled into the bushes and trees was both alarming and puzzling. The sound got ever louder and nearer. I soon realised what was happening, Sergio was actually trying to flush me out, and he was stoning the bushes in case a Beckwatcher like me happened to be lying in wait. I made the dubious decision to stay put, even though the air raid continued moving closer and closer, several minutes later he was dead opposite. I sat tight making a quick calculated guess that the odds of being hit were probably about fifty fifty, moving out of the way would certainly have handed round one to Sergio. I kept absolutely still whilst rocks and stones rained down, I'm not sure how close to me the nearest rock came, but it was a bit hairy that's for sure. He worked his way upstream about a hundred yards before returning to the pool, where I doggedly remained in one piece fortunately.

I could clearly see the steely grin on his face when he stared in the pool; he was also now suddenly joined out of the blue by Cranston the ugly man number two. The game was definitely in progress; Sergio waded into the river to a large lump of bedrock jutting proudly out of the stream. He straddled the rock rather akin to mounting a horse before taking a final look round. I carefully focused my binnocs on the scene ready to watch the show, Sergio was wearing a tatty dark jacket like some sort of blazer, I had seen him in this jacket several times before and assumed it to be his regular poaching attire together with his tracksuit trousers. He didn't disappoint me soon producing a snare from his inside pocket, while Cranston tossed him a stick crudely snapped off a nearby hazel bush. Oddly Cranston departed at this point probably due to the inconvenience of his day job. Sergio assembled the device on to his stick and commenced a very close examination of the beck in and around the rock. Several minutes passed by but no fish was forthcoming prompting Sergio to egress from his perch and depart downstream rather faster than usual only to be rejoined once again by Cranston. I made a quick decision to get help, I didn't fancy taking on these two on my tod. I made a hasty dash to the phone box conveniently placed near Elmbank cottages. I got straight through to Brockley Police station and asked for help, PC Jonty Jones the Bobby assigned to Burndale village fortunately happened to be in the station. He was as ever very obliging agreeing to turn out and start walking upstream from Brock Bridge leaving me to follow them downstream. I immediately left the phone box and headed back the short distance to the river, then carefully stalking my way downstream. I spotted the two men about quarter of a mile further down, although now on the Right Bank. I approached warily not expecting Jonty for at least another ten minutes; the two men were well engrossed in their task so time wasn't a problem. I followed another couple of hundred yards approaching a long deep section of river much favoured by poachers; the beck edge was well trodden due to overuse. Where was Jonty? I maintained my distance until once again events took over. Sergio was once again collecting rocks ably assisted by Cranston, however at this point out of the corner of my eye I saw Jontys uniform materialise through the trees. In the same instant Sergio and Paul Cranston began to bombard those same trees and bushes with a hail of rocks. I looked on in amazement as a very startled Bobby dived for cover; this although alarming at the time was going to work very much in my favour. The onslaught eventually stopped, allowing the two villains to move in to the river, I too made a move not knowing if Jonty was even still in one piece. It soon became obvious that he was very much so and not a happy bunny, he came striding forward from behind an oaktree stopping at the waters edge with a face like thunder. I think he almost waded straight in but thought better of it at the last second. Sergio was midstream by now, Cranston just evaporated into thin air. I joined Jonty growling menacingly at Sergio.

"What the hell are you playing at Ferraria, just what the fuck are you bloody doing, you nearly bloody killed me, it.....it.... Felt like world war three! Just git your sen out here you bastard".

I really wanted to laugh at this point but Jonty was so mad anything could happen.

Sergio was a whiter shade of pale by now,

"I'm sorry constable we were trying to flush out crows that's all"

Jonty moved closer and for one moment I thought he was going to deck him on the spot, but fortunately he was just starting to cool off a bit,

"Yur in for it now lad, assaulting a police officer and no doubt Mr. Carter here has something he wants to say"

Sergio was cringing and almost in tears. I turned to him; I was starting to enjoy myself.

"Where's the snare then Sergio"

No heroics this time no "what fuckin snare" more a last request, he duly produced the offending article from the same pocket I had seen him use by the mill. I booked him for the use of a snare and throwing stones in a pool to facilitate the taking of fish. Jonty simply arrested him for obstructing a police officer. Later that afternoon Jonty went with me to apprehend Paul Cranston who was warned about the company he kept, however I still booked him for stoning a pool, together with aiding and abetting Sergio.

16

CONTINUED GRIEF AT THE WEIR

The following spring Sergio appeared at Brockley Magistrates court for the first time on all three charges of fishing without a licence, possession of a snare, and stoning a pool by way of his rock throwing escapades. He arrived on the day back to his usual bullish self. Cranston arrived straight from work in his scruff, typical of many such offenders. I was always amazed by this; after all here was the one chance to make some sort of a good impression in front of the people who mattered most. Cranston not only turned up in filthy jeans and a T shirt, which may once have actually been white, but the accompanying smell of stale wastepaper pulp hung round him assuring his isolation in the waiting room.

Sergio was the complete opposite giving a hint of things to come, this day in court laid no doubts in my mind that Sergio was quite a character.

He was all smiles, giving it Mr. Carter this and Mr. Carter that, almost as if I was his best mate, he wore clean corduroy trousers with white shirt and tie plus an almost smart tweed jacket. It was soon obvious that he was enjoying himself immensely even puffing his chest out to announce he was representing himself, undoubtedly because all the Solicitors in Brockley hated him, I wonder why?

Cranston was first to appear at one o clock exactly, he pleaded guilty as charged and in addition I could see he was chewing gum. I immediately recalled what happened that day when poor old Rusty Butler appeared doing likewise.

Mrs Briggs didn't disappoint jumping on him right away. Cranston obeyed instantly getting the message in no uncertain terms, the usher rushed obediently forward to take the offending substance away in a piece of tissue, dramatically holding it aloft as he did so.

Cranston was leaning forward with both hands on the witness box in a manner close to slouching, Mrs Briggs barked at him in Thatcherite venom, Cranston stood to attention as the reality of this formidable opponent kicked in.

"Stand up straight at once young man, I will not have such slovenly behaviour in my court do you understand?"

The case commenced by way of Victor Bailey outlining the facts regarding Paul Cranston, who by now was a humbled wreck awaiting sentence with little or no resistance.

Victor smoothly outlined the circumstances as he paced confidently around the room in his own Perry Mason style. Cranston was destroyed in ten devastating minutes compounded by a list of previous convictions, entirely showing a colourful history of violence and theft.

I was given the evil eye as the bench retired to fix sentence, not long after that a fine of £200 with costs of a further £50 ended Cranston"s agony. He retreated meekly to lick his wounds. I made a mental note to give him a wide birth as much as possible in the foreseeable future, hoping the sentence would deter him and maybe even silence that exasperating hooter at the mill.

Sergio of course pleaded not guilty, so I was summoned to the witness box immediately, thus allowing Victor to lead me through the facts. I really laid it on thick, detailing the rain of stones and rocks aimed my way. PC Jonty Jones gave his account in similar fashion, laying down the facts with all the enthusiasm of an episode of Z cars; however Sergio seemed unfazed while he patiently waited his turn. His chance came to cross examine me when Victor stated he had no further questions. Sergio stepped forward with a Perry Mason manner all of his own, is this guy for real I wondered? Doesn't. he realise he's in big trouble, and this is no game? He approached engaging my stare,

"Mr. Carter on the day in question did you see me catch any fish"

I looked anxiously at Victor, but he ignored my glance choosing to thumb through his papers as if plotting his next strategy. In truth I think he was as unsure of Sergio's next move as everyone else was, I answered as simply as possible, no point in complicating what lay ahead,

"No"

"Of course you didn't, and did you see my camera?"

"I beg your pardon"

"A simple question Mr. Carter Did you see my camera? The one I produced from my jacket pocket"

I turned and faced the bench, Mrs Briggs smiled, surely a good sign

"No your worships all I saw produced was a snare"

I said this with assertion so as to try and emphasise how ridiculous he was being.

The bench went into a mini huddle nodding and murmuring discreetly, another good sign I told myself. Victor continued scrutinising all his paperwork.

"What you saw on the day Mr. Carter was me trying to photograph the salmon that were indeed under that rock I was on at the time. The reason being Mr. Carter is because I am doing a research program into the life in our rivers for the Open University".

I just stared at him in total amazement, what is this guy on? The silence that followed was prolonged while every person in the courtroom took in the bizarre story Sergio had cooked up. I was thrown quite a bit myself I must admit, so I just reiterated the fact that a wire snare did indeed get extracted from his inside pocket, which was a fact, it was my word against his.

I finally sat down when the argument didn't really go anywhere; Sergio continuously gave vague and unlikely reasons for his actions that day. He puffed out his chest still full of himself as I found my seat.

Sergio took the stand himself next totally at the mercy of Victor who took his time quietly stalking slowly round the courtroom, Sergio's eyes followed every step warily, but still with a faint hint of cockiness. Victor paced across the court before deliberately returning slowly back to his table, whereon after a lengthy pause he turned smartly like a Sergeant major slapping his papers on the table with a bang. Everyone jumped, not least myself, all the bench, and even old Fred the normally sloth like usher,

"Do you honestly think Mr. Ferraria, that this or any self respecting court in this country would honestly believe that you were actually straddled across a rock in the middle of the river to take photographs of fish for some fictitious university course"

Victor stopped, and then looked across at the bench for a reaction. They in turn were fighting back grins and smiles that would appear both unfair and unprofessional. Victor continued to pick at and ridicule Sergio; yet another defendant was getting the treatment from this sagacious operator.

"What proofs have you of this course? Have you brought any of the work for the court to examine"?

Sergio shuffled rather sheepishly at this point,

"Well no I didn't think......."

"What about the snare Mr. Ferraria? Where did that come from, or has Mr. Carter imagined it? It was found to be in you're pocket after all, your lying aren't you? It's all baloney. What about your accomplice? And for that matter why were you hurling rocks into the bushes?

To his credit Sergio fought back as best he could, but of course he hadn't any sensible explanation for any of it, I became increasingly confident as Victor landed punch after punch.

"There was no snare actually used, it was just in my pocket like, Carter is lying, Paul only came to look, the rocks were just to flush out crows and stuff, no intention to hurt anyone like yu know"

Sergio was sweating by now and I loved every minute of it, justice at work!

Victor just emphasised the lies that came pouring out of Sergio's mouth one after another before finally calling a halt. The bench were starting to loose interest, glancing at watches and even up at the ceiling. This I learned was a good indicator; they had obviously made their minds up some time ago that Sergio was a serial liar and deserved all that was coming to him. The usher stood up obviously relieved,

"All stand please"

The Magistrates retired at last, it was four thirty in the afternoon, Sergio strolled out still seemingly unworried about his fate, and he obviously had a very thick skin.

I didn't have to wait long for their return, the Bench settled back in their seats, workmanlike once again and Mrs Briggs fixed a cold stare on Sergio's greasy features. She addressed him with stolid efficiency,

"Mr. Ferraria we have heard the evidence given here today and find you guilty as charged on all counts."

I gave an inner cheer to myself and smiled willingly at the bench, all that remained was to read out his previous convictions and his financial status. The details were relayed to the magistrates via the court clerk. Sergio was a shift worker at the paper mill in Burndale and actually on quite good money. He had many convictions for motoring offences, theft, plus one very strange incident when caught breaking and entering the house of one of his own brothers.

The bench retired yet again to decide his fate, this time taking about half an hour to reach a decision during which time Sergio was joined by his wife for comfort. He was visibly wilting under the ordeal. Finally Mrs Briggs fixed her stare on Sergio one last time before coolly imposing a £200 penalty plus £75 costs. Sergio took a sharp intake of breath looking suitably humbled for once. He was ordered to pay the full amount within twenty eight days and I must admit that irked me somewhat. The fact that this scroaty bloke could wipe off such a fine in one go. I just hoped that it wasn't poaching gains he was using. His wife led him away without even a glance in my direction, which suited me just fine.

I was in the process of buying my own house in Brockley at this period in time, which I finally acquired at the princely sum of £13,500. The house was a small two bedroomed terrace only two hundred yards from the Green Dragon, then another two hundred to the weir. I was back to paying a mortgage, but didn't care at least I was on the housing ladder even if it was a little too close to the beck. I was also dating a lovely lady called Margaret or Maggie as everyone called her; of course we met at the Gingerbread club hitting it off straight away. I also inherited a spaniel bitch called Jewel in to the bargain. I was consequently often now seen around with two dogs instead of one.

That year the problems at the weir in Brockley got even worse when more individuals became aware of the gains available if they were prepared to take risks.

Harry Lawton a new young lad appeared on the scene from the notorious Cinderbarrow council estate. He was fifteen years old; he had a long pointy nose and greasy long black hair. He fished too much and at all hours, I took the liberty of trying to direct him down the right path. I even took him to one side on several occasions because he had developed an unhealthy habit of foul hooking fish. I made him return those I was fortunate enough to witness. I tried pointing out that he was mixing with bad company and his fishing methods left much to be desired. Harry Lawton became a fixture at the weir, but the weirdest feature about this lad was his appearance at every landing of a rod caught fish followed by his unhealthy desire to whack it on the head. In fact he would run hell for leather just to be there demanding to be the one who dispatched the unfortunate beast in some sort of personal blood lust.

This was strange behaviour to say the least. I managed to stamp some authority on the situation as he proudly showed me a license to fish one evening.

"Mr. Carter, Mr. Carter look what av gitten, mi old man subbed us, says It's to keep me out a bother".

I had taken the trouble to visit Harry's dad one evening because I could see that Harry wasn't getting the message regarding the necessity for a rod license, the last thing I wanted was to see another young lad in court without giving him a chance. Most young lads only need telling once, but Harry was one of those few that chose to bury his head in the sand when authority wagged a finger. I had warned him at least three times before finally putting his name and address in my note book hoping this would scare him sufficiently. Unfortunately the next day he was back as large as life and still without a license. The company policy was of course book everybody, then maybe let them off with a warning later if all parties thought this to be the best course of action. Personally I have always found a trip to see a parent often did the trick, indeed in Harry's case his Father had no idea that Harry was becoming a serial angler with weird psychopathic undertones. Harry's dad had naively assumed he was innocently keeping out of trouble. Jim Lawton was a single parent typical of many council house occupants on Cinderbarrow, his wife had disappeared years ago leaving poor old Jim to cope with three kids. Harry was the eldest with two younger sisters. How a man copes in such a situation is baffling, but the down side in this case was the fact that Harry got complete freedom with little or no opposition from his Dad. The evening I knocked on Jim Lawton's door a very meek and harassed looking guy answered, he wore a white t-shirt with sweat marks round the neck and under the arms, drips from his last meal decorated his torso. I introduced myself before outlining what Harry was up to, poor old Jim wilted visibly when another social problem presented itself adding to his domestic plight, he sighed heavily.

"Thad better come in then lad"

I entered another world; the smell hit me like a storm cloud, I tried hard not to show it despite breathing erratically. It was sort of stale sweat and fried food meets tired socks and underwear, I almost panicked when he offered me a brew just recovering enough to politely refuse, instead saying I was due home in ten minutes, which was a total white lie of course. The lack of a woman's touch had never been more obvious than there at Jim Lawton's council house. We finally parted on good terms and Jim promised to reel in Harry and get him sorted.

The result was very satisfying when Harry waved his new license about showing it to anyone who came within earshot.

Nothings ever straightforward of course!

"This license only allows you to catch trout Harry, you know that now don't you?"

"Aye Mr. Carter that's all as after, or at least when you're about"

Laughter greeted this remark not only from Harry, but several onlookers as well, although not me naturally.

Harry laughed the loudest and I knew that my good work may be in vain, but at least I'd tried.

The weir took up a lot of my time that summer as fish moved up the river becoming abundant by August, all the usual suspects were on the scene, Gaunt, McGowan, Jez of course, and little Harry "the assassin" as we now called him, more eager to kill fish than ever.

I patrolled days, nights, afternoons, early mornings, any time to try and outwit them, but the numbers of anglers, scroats, and hangers on increased daily and even more by night. Drug dealer's, users, and anglers all seemed to merge into one long nightmare; goodness knows what was happening elsewhere on the river.

Prosecutable offences became harder and harder to detect because the criminal element was getting wise to what they could get away with. They all purchased trout licenses which made them legitimate anglers up until the point they took a salmon or sea trout, this they obviously did when no Becky's were about. They used a sophisticated grapevine and lookout service, some even slept in the public toilets until we had gone. Those toilets disgusting as they were became even more frequented than the previous year, forming a depot for these guys to smoke pot, have sex, and even gut any fish caught. The remnants of innards could be regularly found in and around the hand basin. Some realised It could even become worthwhile upgrading a license to take sea trout and in some cases fish were actually caught fair and square with a licensed instrument. When the river rose after rain the activity increased even more putting further strains on our resources. I think we actually coped really well, but not without some notable hiccups. One night I had my youngest son Robert staying over with me during a weekend off, he was eight years old. It was Saturday night at 22.15, my lad was fast asleep and I was just about to watch match of the day. The phone rang and I was greeted by the unmistakable voice of PC Jonty Jones.

"I've had a woman on Jack, she's on about fish being snatched at thweir can you deal with it, I'll come down and help if you wants"

I explained about my babysitting duties, but good old Jonty had the answer!

"We can put him in the riot van till we're done if you like".

I could hear faint laughter in the background, but I hadn't a better idea and time was always of the essence in these situations

So it was, I woke a sleeping son and outlined the situation, Bob was well chuffed of course, the thought of a ride in a police riot van in the middle of the night to an eight year old was too good to miss. The van arrived ten minutes later and off we went with Bob planted on the back seat. We arrived at speed to implement a surprise attack,

Jez Bergerac, McGowan, and Gaunt were all fishing in front of the weir, but predictably they saw us coming. The Police presence was enough to send them scurrying frantically away, unfortunately no illegal activity was discovered, and undoubtedly it would have been going on prior to our intervention, so Jonty invited us back to the nick for a brew. Bob got an impromptu tour round that provided a night he has never forgotten.

We increased the effective strategy of using one man and vehicle parked on the wide section of pavement by the weir just to observe and police any caught fish, making sure that any foul hooked victims were returned as soon as possible hopefully not too badly injured. This policy had worked quite well during the previous year. The action some nights was actually very quiet with little activity; this could cause boredom to set in for both ourselves and the attendant riff raff. One such night I was sat in my van about 03.00 yawning and guilty of clock watching, when suddenly there was a commotion, Sam McGowan began playing what appeared to be a sizable fish, I must have been miles away because it wasn't until they began shouting that I twigged anything was happening. I came to my senses and peered through the van window to see Sam about fifty yards downstream holding his rod and line considerably bent with the strain. Several of the usual suspects were in attendance, so I quickly made my way down. Ben was barking by now in amongst the general mayhem contributing to the excitement. I was soon in a good position when Sam turned to me grinning in the street light.

"Must be a whopper Mr. Carter what do yu reckon"

"Aye looks a good fish lad"

Harry Lawton and Cliff Woof plus a few more were all crowding round and jostling for position.

The next thing to happen was the last thing I ever could have anticipated, unexpectedly Sam yanked hard on the rod and an object flew out of the water right over my head missing me by only a few inches. I ducked instinctively, spun round to see them all facing me jeering and laughing. There on the bank and fixed firmly to his hook was an old leather boot playfully dragged around by a now hysterical Sam Mcgowan. I was suitably embarrassed to be caught out this way and must have looked pretty helpless while they danced around me. In the end all I could do was laugh with them until they eventually drifted off home, if I learnt one thing that night it was a timely reminder to stay alert at all times.

One night about two weeks later Danny was given a turn at the onerous task of night watchman, he set himself up adjacent to the weir in his Morris thirteen hundred equipped with his pipe, stick, flask, and butties. I always had my doubts as to whether this was a sensible move, but Dick Myers argued that the staff you had were the staff you used, which is a fair comment I suppose. What actually happened that night I learned through the ever active criminal grape vine, whilst out for a drink in the Blue Anchor I was informed that apparently Danny had survived unscathed until about 02.00. He had been watching the likes of Jez and company until sleep of course finally overpowered him; I am convinced this won't have been the first night he succumbed. The scroats had watched with amusement as Danny slumbered, It wasn't difficult to picture Danny slumped head back in the seat with his pipe in some state of abandonment. They would probably fish for a while, or just watch from the toilets until he drifted off. Danny's car wheels were then chocked with large stones out of the beck; all four wheels were given the same treatment, meanwhile Danny slept in blissful ignorance. When he finally awoke it was daylight and not an angler in sight. Six in the morning and the coast clear, Danny decided enough was enough and time to go home. Beady eyes lurking in the public loo glared with expectancy when Danny fired up his motor. He stalled three times in as many attempts to reverse; Dan was baffled as to why the car would not move? Eventually even Danny figured he'd better get out and see what the hell was going on. He could only stare in bewilderment, until abruptly jumping out of his skin when half a dozen youths burst out of the toilets laughing, screaming, and pointing before finally running off down the green. Danny spent half an hour checking his car before gingerly retreating with his tail firmly between his legs. Dan never ever mentioned the episode, but it was the worst kept secret in Brockley.

A week later I was with Danny again on the Friday night just after midnight, the river had dropped back from a fresh leaving it ideal to snatch fish. We were in Danny's car parked nicely up by the school and I was keen to try a new night sight for the first time. These devices are very clever using an image intensifier normally associated with military rifle sights; I guess the troubles in Northern Ireland would have sped up the development. I have used various devices over the years, which in the eighties were not that brilliant to be honest, whereas now we use some super gear that gives excellent night images creating a great advantage in many situations. The one we trialed that night was a Mclennan and worked so well we still have them around today. The background street lighting that night was a bonus adding to the quality, I focused on a regular customer present at the weir, definitely an up and coming poacher, namely one Clifford Woof. Cliff was a very thin gaunt looking guy who looked as if a few fish suppers were just what the doctor ordered. I had caught him twice the previous year, once fishing without a license, then again tickling sea trout out of the weed in the town. He was the type of lad that never showed any tendency towards violence preferring to take his capture on the chin without fuss. It was for this reason I was not alarmed on seeing him.

We left the vehicle and crept stealthily between parked cars, carefully and slowly lessening the distance between us and him. This took about fifteen minutes until all that was left was open ground. I raised the night sight and peered into the gloom before turning to Danny.

"He's bang at it Dan, snatching like buggery, there's another guy sat on the bench, haven't a clue who he is, maybe just watching".

I watched for a couple more minutes whilst Cliff snatched away without success.

"Let's go for route one Dan"

Dan nodded his agreement while we readied ourselves for the mad dash at our man. I fixed all my gear, made a mental note of where my bits and pieces were stashed and in which pockets, then gave the nod. I made the ground in no time completely surprising our man, Danny lunged into the water and grabbed Cliff's rod and attached large treble hook before he could blink.

"Stop Bailiffs!"

I quickly outlined to Cliff what we had seen ushering him up on to the footpath.

The man on the bench hadn't moved and what's more I hadn't paid him the attention I should have. In these situations I have always found it best just to home directly on the miscreant concerned rather than complicate things with person or persons not actually committing an offence.

I was watching Danny take on the task of cautioning and booking Cliff Woof. Cliff of course was fine until Danny seized the rod and line, then all hell broke loose! The man on the bench suddenly came to life, it was

non other than Cliff's brother Alvin, I recognised him immediately. I
new this meant trouble, Alvin was a thug of the highest order and owner
of a string of convictions for violent crime. Tommy Brown had dealings
with him prior to my employment handling the situation pretty well
by all accounts, but here and now it was stick up for kid brother time.
I swore to myself in frustration at being caught out like this, but it was
too late now he was right on us.

"What's the problem with our kid like?"

I turned and faced my antagonist.

"He is being reported for snatching fish"

I new as I spoke the words this was red rag to a bull time... still in for
a penny!

"Like fuck he is, give him his rod back"

Danny took the rod and turned as if to leave, but Alvin intercepted him,
grabbing him by the throat as he did so, things were going pear shaped
very fast.

"Woh woh you cant do that Alvin"

Danny was no match for Alvin and neither was I if it came to a brawl.
The next thing Danny broke free and the rod clattered to the floor, Cliff
immediately picked it up. I spoke first as it all hung in the balance.

"We are seizing the rod and I'll call the police if you obstruct us in our
duty"

Who was I kidding I told myself. Danny moved toward the rod again
and Alvin jumped on him, they both went down. Danny was up for the
fight despite his age, I had to admire his guts. I thought about what Joe
always used to say about such a situation-

"The worst that can happen Jack, is tha gits a black eye"

I dived in separating them in the process, it was at this point Cliff
grabbed his rod and set off for home at a great rate of knots.

"Danny go and call the police"

I faced Alvin fully expecting to get a right hook at the very least and more than likely Joes predicted black eye, but the sight of Danny entering a phone box probably saved my bacon. Alvin prodded my chest so hard I nearly went down,

"Wur not done you fuckin bastard, I'll have you, yu cunt"

He then legged it after his brother leaving me both shaken and well stirred. I briefly composed myself before heading off towards Danny, who was now emerging from the phone box.

"They're on their way"

This had all the makings of a cock up, so we spent a few careful minutes getting the facts and events down on paper. Jonty Jones arrived in less than five minutes.

"What fine mess have you got us into now Jack Carter, most people are asleep bi now you know, not waging mayhem in the middle of the night."

Jonty was grinning and loving every minute. I outlined the facts as quickly as I could under the circumstances. In the background his radio began to blare out the name Alvin Woof, Jonty Smiled.

"Well well then guess whose just been picked up?"

It was music to my ears; both Woofs had been arrested and were on the way to the nick. The rest was a formality and I finally got the rod. Alvin graphically reminded me of our unfinished business when they eventually left the nick at about 05.00 in the morning, I would have to watch my back with that one that's for sure, adding him to an ever growing list.

17

BLACK SUNDAY

In September 1982 the weir in Brockley became an even bigger drain on our resources mainly due to unsettled weather producing fresh after fresh. I was down for duty on a beautiful Sunday morning when autumn had just started to take hold; the sun was shining after a rainy night typical of recent weeks. I drove through Brockley making a quick check at the weir in the process. The river was pristine slightly on the up with a hint of colour and the suns rays bounced off white water pierced occasionally by the salmon fighting for a safe route upstream. It was nine in the morning and the vultures were gathering to feast on this seasonal abundance, Timmy Dunne was there full of wind and piss as usual, he did have a rod himself, but it rarely got wet. Big Lewis Parsons was also there but too embarrassed to talk due to his association with Frankie Wilson, Ben "fingers" Jackson came to chat

"Thas goin to have thee work cut out today Becky int yu"

"Aye I guess you're right"

I noted fingers had a fly rod, so no problem there then, unless it was some cunning plan to make me think he was being a good boy today. Ben Jackson was a typical crafty country poacher of the old school. The sole purpose of his forays was entirely to feed his ever growing flock of siblings. It was strange therefore that he had a reputation as an expert fly fisherman and could have probably fed his flock by this method alone keeping out of trouble into the bargain. He finally went off downstream to practice his art. The status quo that exisisted at this point was not causing me any major concerns, so I afforded my self the luxury of heading off towards Burndale for some respite. I parked up and took Ben for a good walk foolishly thinking this was to be a fine late summer day out on the river. I headed up from Brock Bridge to Elmbank without seeing a soul. Not even Sergio blackened my path; I was in danger of becoming relaxed. I returned to my van an hour later, I even contemplated eating my bait there at the bridge, but my conscience was telling me: go forth to the weir young man. I just couldn't settle so return I did just after noon. The river had lifted a bit further and fish were leaping for the whole world to see. The same people were fishing as before with the exception of Timmy Dunne who had left to give his mouth a rest. A dozen or more Joe publics had gathered on the edge to watch fish jump these included kids, dogs, grannies, as well as a few scroats. I parked by the pavement adjacent to the weir, opened my bait box and sat back munching a banana sandwich. It was a satisfactory state of affairs, plenty of people but no real action, I just wanted to see out the day watch a few fish caught then drift off home, after all it was Sunday.

By one o clock the river was running at its peak and clearing, anywhere else on the river the pure art of fly would be the choice, but not here, just an abundance of anglers keen to exploit the conditions amongst the fast white turbulence. People just kept on arriving, whether they be families out for a walk or anglers previously unseen. They appeared out of the woodwork one after another; soon I was backwards and forwards checking hitherto unseen licenses, or even making sure any foul hooked fish were returned at once. By two o clock twenty five rods were fishing from the weir and downstream for a hundred yards on my side alone. Ten more even set up on the opposite bank. The spectators numbered at least another twenty, so the action was intense. I monitored Harry Lawton having a field day as chief executioner, Fingers Jackson foul hooked two fish within five minutes and I struggled to fight my way through so that I could get to see them landed. Every time a fish was hooked the mob closed in to get a good view. At one point three fish were hooked at the same time within yards, it was becoming impossible to police. I was now starting to get extremely stressed, one young lad hooked a fish up the arse and as he returned it to the river under my close scrutiny an evil little weasely man laid into me big style.

"you fuckin Bastard, what you made him put it back for, yur wus than Hitler, bloody Hitler that's what you are".

I ignored him as best I could under the circumstances retreating to my van for a much needed brew. The numbers grew even more until a total of forty one anglers fished shoulder to shoulder including ten on the right bank huddled under the weir. People and lines even became entangled as the sheer numbers encroached causing minor scuffles and altercations, still at least that took the heat off me I suppose. I had never experienced anything quite like it, or since for that matter. That day is etched in my mind for ever. I made a promise to myself, this situation could not go on and I would press for a byelaw to be introduced at the earliest opportunity. I telephoned Dick Myers at three o clock to make that very point, I told him I needed help desperately.

Big Don arrived just after half four by which time I was a mental and physical wreck. Fortunately for him and me some folk were drifting away by this time and I made sure I was one of them,

The Brockley weir was now worse than ever and a continuing major drain on resources. I lobbied my peers and line manager endlessly to seriously consider my proposal to introduce a total ban on fishing within close proximity to the weir. The general opinion by this time was turning my way due to the gravity of the situation. Consequently I was summoned to the office in Brockley by Roger Mcbane mid week after Black Sunday specifically to discuss the problem. I didn't pull any punches, I had quiet a bit to get off my chest. I needn't have worried because Roger was well on side by now, probably due mainly by the amount of phone calls received at the office. Members of the public had been complaining repeatedly about the general unsocial behaviour as well as the fishing. All this was helping my campaign of course and I was a much happier man I can tell you when I left the office that day. Unfortunately there would be many hoops to go through before a byelaw could be implemented. The wheels of progress in such matters turn very slowly so the problem would be around for some time yet, but at least it was a start.

The following week I had another snatching case at the weir which has always stuck in my throat due to the unsuccessful outcome.

Two brothers had joined the ever growing list of scroats fancying their chances at poaching the weir; in fact they were twins Warren and Pete Thomson. Warren was considerably taller than his brother and if truth be known had more brains as well, he was also quite civilised if in fact he spoke at all, and Big Don soon had them christened "the Thomson twins". I had obtained Warrens identity a week or so earlier when he produced a trout license, but Brother Pete at this point was unknown to me or any of our team. This all changed the Thursday night following Black Sunday. Pete was fishing on top of the weir at three in the morning. I was working with Big Don taking advantage of a large pile of earth on the green. This had been obligingly heaped up by contractors laying a new sewer pipe. We managed to crawl on to the top and observe activity only about fifty yards downstream from the weir itself. Warren Thomson was sat on the first seat on the green with a girl and definitely not the slightest bit interested in fishing or whatever his brother was up to.

I may not have known Pete Thomson's identity at this point; however I did recognise another guy fishing next to him. David Grimshaw had been on the periphery of trouble for some time having sneakily fished with a trout license all season, I had reluctantly put up with his over active mouth on many a night while he drank and smoked pot in and around the public toilets. Grimshaw was not a pretty sight, his long greasy hair and pock marked face was probably the remnants from an acne affected child hood. He was always however in the company of an attractive girl, but even more remarkably she was obviously expecting his child in the not too distant future. It amazed me how such an ugly specimen could have a partner who was obviously both pleasant and good looking, why would she hang around with such a waster? Still who was I to judge because Grimshaw and his partner are still together to this day? I think the relationship was spawned at school when David was the big hard man.

Pete and David were bang at it snatching like hell on the weir, but Don and I quickly nailed them with total surprise. Grimshaw was bang to rights but the other guy was having none of it. I was fascinated by his voice of all things; it was sort of deep, loud, and croaky, definitely unique for a small guy. He argued black was white despite having a large and lethal treble hook dangling at the end of his line. I got a name and address out of him after much shouting and threatening on both sides, he said he was William Smith, which lets face it is not convincing. I was so concerned that seizing the rod became a priority, big Don made this happen despite some argy bargy, which involved our culprit removing the reel from the rod, then stuffing it down the front of his trousers. I told Don to report him for obstruction as there was no way either of us was going after it down there.

During this entire activity brother Warren remained preoccupied and never showed any inclination of coming to his brothers aid, this was pre planned I suspect.

The following day I visited the address on Waterflats that so called William Smith had given me, surprise surprise it was totally wrong. The door was answered by another long haired scroat who new nothing of my wanted man. He was somebody that Thomson obviously set up for such an occasion.

My next stop was Brockley Police station and a chat with Jonty Jones. I described in detail the youth I had booked the previous night, Jonty shook his head vacantly after each detail was relayed until I mentioned his voice. Bingo!

"Sounds to me like Pete Thomson from Cinderbarrow, only person I know with a fog horn like that".

I returned home and phoned Dick Myers he gave me the nod to take Big Don after tea and try to nab our man whilst the scent was still warm. I have always found the longer you left an ID unresolved the harder it was to follow up.

Jonty had armed me with Thomson's address which was not that far away from the false one he himself had submitted. Thomson's actual date of birth also matched the one supplied on the night; this often proved the case in such circumstances. It was obviously easy to supply a false name and address but a false date of birth nearly always proved too big a challenge when put on the spot.

We approached 55 Wells Avenue with some caution at six o clock and parked a few doors away. It was a rough end of town even for a nice place like Brockley. Bedraggled rough cast council semis with unkempt gardens decked out in rusty bangers, or assorted bike parts. Snotty nosed kids eyed us up as possible aliens.

I worked out which house belonged to our man and we moved in. The gate fell off as I entered the garden causing a rather gruesome German shepherd next door to vent his feelings, consequently any form of surprise was now gone. I knocked firmly on the door and heard movement within. The door was finally opened by our man; however I was immediately thrown by his appearance. His hair was cut short, he was clean shaven, and smartly dressed. He grinned at me as I produced my warrant; I was hesitant glancing worryingly at Don who also looked perplexed. Was this really him I asked myself?

I questioned the guy rather gingerly.

"Hello my names Jack Carter I'm investigating an incident last night at the weir in town".

The next door neighbour a rather colourful punk rocker watched the proceedings as he reigned in his slavering dog.

Thomson put on a convincing stare of innocence,

"What's it to do wid me like"

I watched his face carefully looking for any signs that it was indeed our man, these strange situations came up from time to time over the years, usually when I was not sure of a positive ID, and after all it was night when we collared him. My subconscious however kicked in, I had little voices telling me, "yes that's him" his eyes, his nose, and finally there was the voice of course, resounding and never to be forgotten.

I went for the jugular!

I looked him straight in the face eyeball to eyeball,

"You are the man I apprehended last night at Brockley weir; I am reporting you for using a snatch and unlicensed fishing"

He gave the same back albeit in the form of a lengthy stare, followed by his reply short and to the point,

"Bollocks to that you twat"

I took down his details under a hail of abusive denial.

"It weren't me I was here all night ask her"

I was presented with what was presumably his girlfriend; she was a plain girl about nineteen with short brown hair, she meekly nodded in agreement to every word he said.

"Can I take your name Miss…?"

She immediately looked horrified and vanished without speaking a word.

I left with a feeling that although we had caught up with our man it hadn't really gone all that well. The street was full of aggressive onlookers when we departed, the situation called out for refuge with a couple of pints in the Blue Anchor, a welcome respite before I dropped Don back at home.

The case against Thomson and Grimshaw went through our legal department in the usual way on the basis that we had identified our man beyond reasonable doubt. I had carefully considered the incidents both at the weir and at Thomson's house the following day. It is very easy to raise doubts in your own mind if dwelt upon too much, however his distinctive voice was unmistakable and reassuring.

The trial was down for January 15th 1983, a Monday, Grimshaw pleaded guilty and was fined £50 with £15 costs. Thomson stuck to his guns and pleaded not guilty in confident style. His case was adjourned for two weeks. The day of his subsequent trial I and all the rest of our team remained confident as proceedings began. The chairman of the bench that day was a Farmer from Hincaster. Les Parkinson was a robust country Gentleman and a character in his own right. Thomson had half a dozen of his scroaty mates in the public gallery, his girlfriend and Grimshaw were absent for obvious reasons. Victor Bailey plugged away at Thomson for nearly an hour trying to trip him up, but all he got was that same old tale of being somewhere else. I just stuck to my facts also swearing on oath that he was the man apprehended that fateful night, which indeed he was. The odd doubt still irritatingly played on my mind though and threatened to undermine my self belief. I had not seen Thomson since the time of the offence, so when he entered the witness box I was relieved that I recognised him immediately.

The rod and line I had seized was exhibited to the court still with a large treble hook attached, but minus any reel. Thomson was asked if the rod was his but of course he denied any recognition or claim of ownership.

The bench finally retired and everyone relaxed, Thomson gave me the evil eye as was the norm in such circumstances, and then confidently turned to his band of followers for moral support. The Bench was still out forty five minutes later and I was beginning to worry. It was after an hour that they eventually re-emerged, faces blank and void of any emotion. There was no sign or hint that may have betrayed any on going heated debate.

The verdict was clinically read out… not guilty!

The gallery gave whoops of delight crowding round their hero and escorting him out past the bench.

These things do happen I suppose, but we were all very surprised and Victor Bailey was livid implying that the bench had proved weak; he was not a good looser.

The only consolation we got was the forfeiture of the rod and snatch.

Some months later I attended an evening at the Court house where our legal team addressed the magistrates to try and educate them on fisheries law, this was an excellent and successful evening. I enjoyed being able to speak to these people hitherto so untouchable up in their lofty seats. During all this I spotted Les Parkinson and the Thomson case got an airing during our conversation. Les was obviously troubled

"We just weren't sure that it was him, I was pretty sure, but the other two believed there was some doubt, you know, so I was a bit snookered".

I shrugged my shoulders and smiled

"Don't worry about it Les he'll come again, shit always floats to the top you know"

Les looked at me long and hard, apology written all over his anguished face,

"I have to say though Jack we definitely got it all wrong"

"Why do you think that then Les?"

"Well you see… when the bugger was leaving he had to walk right past me and that's when I knew see, as he went past he said…

"What happens too mi rod now can I have it back?"

Well, there's a surprise all we could do was both laugh.

18

SERGIO GOES TOO FAR

1983 was thankfully the last year fishing at the weir was legal; the wheels were in motion within The Ministry to get the new byelaw passed. The number of prosecutions kept on mounting and probably our successes contributed to reduced activity during that year. Several regulars still persisted however, including the Thomson twin's and yet another band of brothers from yet another of the pubs in Brockley namely the notorious Cowperthwaites, Mike, Gerry, and Brian. By August not a single case of snatching had occurred at the weir, but the Cowperthwaites all believed they could fish without a license, so consequently went in my book one by one. The hot weather that was prevailing coincided with a good run of sea trout and the water levels in the Stock were dropping fast. My luck changed on a routine patrol one Saturday night in early August whilst out with Danny. I was sneaking quietly up the Green via the Scout hut, and then a few minutes observing to the weir drew a blank. I signaled Danny to edge forward carefully picking our steps as we progressed. The first section consisted of a grassed area up to the footbridge which formed a steep banking down to the river. We crouched double almost crawling along this ridge and had nearly reached the bridge, I paused to put the binocs up and scan the remaining Green up to the weir. I was so intent on this task I didn't immediately see what was right there in front of me. I was soon woken from this state by Danny who prodded me, he then dramatically pointed to four men sitting doggo amongst the long grass on the riverbank. Just who surprised who at this point was debatable? They didn't move or make any attempts to hide, or indeed do anything. It was some time before I regained any sort of composure before turning and walking quietly forward covering the few feet between us and them. I recognised every one of them, firstly sat just off the pack was Grimshaw cross legged clutching a can of McEwen's, he seemed almost comatose, satiated with beer and whacky backy. The other three were huddled together in a similar state, namely Mike Cowperthwaite and both the dreaded Thomson twins. I tried to weigh up what was going on here, at first I thought maybe they'd decided just to get spaced out on a hot summer's night and who could blame them. The next thing I saw however put things into perspective, Danny triumphantly produced two fresh hewn willow sticks with wire snares attached. He discovered them only a few feet away. I moved in assertively now flashing my Warrant card at the four men. Warren Thomson seemed to be fairly compus mentus so I concentrated on him, the others just looked on vacantly.

"What are these then Warren?"

"Fucked if I know Mr. Carter"

Grimshaw managed to stand up with some difficulty before almost falling as he lit a dog end; I noticed he was wet through from head to toe.

"You're a bit wet David lad"

"Aye bin swimming like"

The reply was drawled without animation.

Mike Cowperthwaite was also wet, Pete Thomson wouldn't look at me not surprisingly, but I was of course desperate to make up for our previous encounter. I decided to move the process forward and booked them all for being in possession of an illegal instrument namely the snares. They all livened up somewhat during this process, but still seemed too doped up to kick off. They denied ever seeing them before of course, but as far as I was concerned this was decisive, condemning, circumstantial evidence. I could even see the broken willow branches from where they had obtained the two sticks. The four men finally trundled off delivering muted insults and claims to innocence as they departed. Danny and I then started searching the surrounding area. We hit the jackpot in under five minutes. Lo and behold there in the grass well hidden about ten yards from the scene were five crisp, clean, and very fresh sea trout.

Danny gasped,

"The bastards Jack look yu here, their rowed up like sardines"

He was right the fish were laid side by side meticulously in a crude shallow hole scraped out hurriedly, then neatly covered with dry grass. I quickly retrieved the fish placing them in a plastic bag noting the snare marks on the tail of each specimen; we made some quick notes then went in pursuit of the four men. Finding them was easy, as expected they were up at the toilets by the weir. They showed no signs of concern when I displayed the fish. Pete Thomson grinned in his own annoying way.

"Tha won't pin that lot on us yu twat"

Pete was as charming as ever complete with that unique voice, he really did get under my skin more than most, and the hairs on the back of my neck were up as soon as he spoke.

"I'm having you this time mate" I murmured to myself.

I was convinced that we had a stone wall case that night and left to bank the seized fish and snares at the Office. The gang of four went to ground for the rest of that year and only the Cowperthwaites ever really troubled me again. Mike Cowperthwaite went down hill fast with drugs and further more not helped either by a good hiding behind his Fathers pub the following Christmas. The Thomson twins just vanished off the scene like many more before them, not to be missed I might add. Grimshaw had his family responsibilities and blended back into Council house land, like many more of similar ilk and adequately supported by the tax payer of course.

Many Months went by after that incident and despite my many inquiries made to our legal department nothing ever seemed to happen. In hindsight I probably didn't pester them enough. The case just never materialised, it was as though we had never even been out that night at all. Eventually after about nine months I worked it out, Cowperthwaite senior a renowned member of the licensed vitulars association and respected Landlord of the Golden Lion in Brockley was also a freemason and Grand Master no less. I have it from a reliable source that wheels within wheels turned the hand of fate against us. I suppose that's life as they say, but Pete and Warren Thomson walked away for a second time and as far as I'm concerned that was twice too often.

In 1983 Sergio was still bang at it utilising the River Brock as a supply line for his fish sales, unfortunately however his adopted family had joined in as well. Sergio had three step sons all living in the same three bedroom semi on Ashfields estate. The eldest son John Simpson was nineteen and owned a car making him very valuable to the other two. I don't think he himself ever actually went poaching once, but I am sure he made many a trip to pick up fish after a days work engineered by his two brothers. The two younger ones were Alan the main poacher and Sammy who was just easily led. I had received a few tip offs about this crew plus heavy rumours and sightings by the ever watchful Farmers of Brockdale. The law of averages and lady luck usually play a part in this type of activity and for the Simpson brothers this was about to happen. The back end of 1983 produced a typical frosty spell during November causing river levels to fall thus leaving all spawning fish extremely vulnerable. It was no surprise then when I got a phone call at just after six on a Monday night. I had literally just sat down to a plate full of liver and onions swimming in gravy, savoured with creamy mashed potato. I answered the phone only to hear the dulcet tones of Eddie Downham from Well head farm.

"Yon buggers are upt valley tha needs to git up here reet now they're in a Cortina"

He put the phone down emphatically; I glanced longingly at my tea knowing my fate was sealed.

This was all the info I needed, now was a time for action, no messing just drop everything and go.

I phoned the police and within ten minutes I was togged up and on the move, Ben was left totally pissed off with only the smell of my tea to comfort him. I picked up my old friend PC Tanner at Brockley nick. Ten more minutes and we were headed up the valley armed with no plan in particular except to look for the Cortina. The big plus in Brockdale was the fact that it is one long cul-de-sac, so if they were up there, then they were well hemmed in. Twenty five minutes on from the initial phone call a red Cortina faced us with headlights blaring mid way up the valley. The driver was none other than John Simpson. I was out of my car and at him immediately, he hurled expletives at me while both his brothers sat tight. PC Tanner joined me and John Simpson's face dropped like a stone. The power of a policeman's uniform never ceases to amaze me.

"What you on with John?"

His face was nearly in the foot well and the reply was beseeching to say the least.

"Just out for a ride Mr. Carter"

PC Tanner ordered the two remaining brothers out of the car, I gazed inside greedily, but nothing much seemed amiss.

"I am going to search your vehicle John"

"What for we aint done nowt"

Buoyed by my police support I went ahead, I checked amongst clothing scattered randomly around the vehicle and noted the familiar smell of fish, I even checked the glove compartment, and then I lifted the front seat. I couldn't have wished for more, it was all there in front of my eyes. Five very coloured sea trout lay in a heap, milt and eggs oozing out on the mucky floor. Black bruise marks and bloody wounds were easily visible. Three stricken faces looked on,

"What's this lot then lads?"

Prolonged uncomfortable silence greeted my question until John Simpson coughed in disgust

"We should have bin quicker I guess"

I booked them all and even found another fish hidden in a manky anorak in the boot along with a blood stained gaff. The charges just kept mounting up, unlicensed fishing, possession of an illegal instrument, taking fish during the close season, and last but not least taking unclean fish.* which these clearly were. These unfortunate animals had been deprived of the final act of life, I always took this sort of offence badly despite the obvious delight in lifting these low life's for committing such an act. There is no more a depressing sight than part spent fish lying on a slab.

Two days later at a similar time in the evening I got another tip off, this time from a friend of mine who owned a game dealing business near Sedbergh. Weeks could go by without a sniff of a case then just like buses two come along at once, I was on a roll. Alan Jones sounded very animated on the phone.

"Jack you won't believe this but I've just had a woman at the door with a boot full of fish, …she wanted me to buy them there and then".

I took all this in while he explained how she turned up as bold as brass in a red Cortina, of course he had sent her packing in the nicest way possible way, not wanting to alarm her unduly. Obviously I now had a fair idea who we were dealing with, two red Cortinas within two days was too much of a coincidence and amazingly stupid.

"Thanks Alan I think I know who we're dealing with, I'll try and get the police to intercept her"

Fortunately I had eaten my tea on this occasion and watched half of top of the pops including legs and co; nevertheless I had to act immediately once again. I got hold of Jonty at the nick who immediately alerted Traffic to find the Cortina. I managed to get hold of Hank who was willing and sober and arranged to meet him also at Brockley nick. I arrived at the police station within ten minutes to be greeted by Jonty Jones grinning all over his face.

"It seems you were spot on Jack, traffic have just lifted yon woman in the main street by the town hall, they're bringing her in now"

No sooner had he finished talking than the traffic car appeared followed by the same red Cortina we pulled up in Brockdale a couple of days previously. Mrs Simpson emerged in a tearful state and I couldn't help but feel sorry for her. The cool slinky lady I had first encountered was now a bedraggled wreck. I was joined by Hank at this point looking as immaculate as ever.

She began spouting profusely blaming Sergio for everything; I was in heaven, what a turn up for the book.

"He made me do it cause I complained about no room in the freezer, it's bloody well full of manky bloody fish. He filled the bugger switched it on, but never put a fuse in the damn plug so it began to stink dint it, we thought we'd better shift em"

She was blubbing big style, I had to move, strike while the iron was hot.

"Are you saying that there is still some fish at home Mrs Simpson?"

"Aye lad cause there is, loads flippin loads; please please do him proper this time."

I took a deep breath, looked at Hank and he winked while Mrs Simpson was taken down for interview.

I knew we had to move fast, after all here was a chance to nab Sergio as well, let's go for a full house; it was too good to miss.

Jonty gave us a young Bobby called Tony Fleming so we headed straight out to surprise Sergio. We were camped outside his door in less than ten minutes; Hank was in full flow completely taking over as usual when the odds were in our favour. It was Hank who hammered on the door and Sergio that promptly answered; needless to say he went spontaneously white on realising that his beloved wife had come seriously unstuck. His words were those of a condemned man,

"What the ell's appened?"

Hank waded in to him in true senior Bailiff mode outlining the events of the last forty five minutes. Sergio knew the game was up so we walked victoriously into the wash house to examine his infamous large chest freezer. Hank instructed me to lift the lid. I obliged approaching with trepidation, the contents were a mixture of frozen chips, peas and of course fish, quite a few at that and the smell was just as his wife had described. I lifted them out, both salmon and sea trout, I laid them out across the wash house floor. Ten fish were removed six salmon and four sea trout, some unclean, some with snare marks and all between three to ten pounds. The freezer was switched on, so it would be fair to say Sergio had been active somewhere on the River Brock during that very same day. Hank sighed and tutted dramatically milking every moment.

Sergio went gratefully into my book just at the point Mrs Simpson returned, she looked very relieved it was all over and even made us a cup of tea while we packed up all the fish. Sergio just couldn't help himself and began to boast about his poaching skills despite his present downfall. I nodded at Hank thinking we should quit while the going was good.

Sergio and his family became very quiet and inactive from that point which was the most satisfying part of the whole scenario. The number of fish saved and left to procreate is unknown, but it would add up to a fair few without Sergio pestering them. Their day in court the following spring was quite unique because both cases were heard on the same day. The whole family lined up and pleaded guilty like naughty children. Mrs Simpson was cool and composed once again and got away with a ten pound fine for trying to sell the fish, proceedings were influenced by a tinge of sympathy from the bench I suspect. Still never mind justice was done with total fines of around £200 plus costs of £100. The environmental impact of losing so many fish was unquantifiable in those days, however today a salmon has an environmental value estimated at above £700 per fish relating to the financial factors such as license fee, my wages, anglers equipment costs, and tourism value etc.

* Unclean fish are fish that are spawning, about to spawn or not recovered from spawning. (Salmon and freshwater fisheries act 1975 sec 2)

19

THE BROCKLEY PSYCHO MAFIA

The following year 1984 was a milestone, the long anticipated new byelaw to ban fishing fifty metres below and twenty above Brockley town weir came into effect. This had previously only been the case during October in any year at all weirs. The ban was total and in the case of Brockley weir the effect was massive, just like turning off a tap. I painted white markers on the concrete path edging, after carefully measuring it out with Big Don. Timmy Dunne was there and even he seemed impressed.

"That should show the buggers and if I sees any yan tryin it I'll scop em in Jack"

I nodded at Timmy politely, who was I to spoil his street cred, even if he was the biggest coward with the largest mouth in Brockley.

My job has been infinitely more enjoyable since that day, not least because I could spend more time covering the rest of my patch.

The runs of migratory fish improved year on year in the eighties, which naturally led to higher rod catches. The angling grapevine between Brockley Angling association members was always rife with who took what and how many, but more worryingly who took them by fair means and who took them foul hooked?

Anglers can be sorted into two categories, firstly sport anglers who fish purely for pleasure. These are generally good people who don't even worry if they never actually land a fish, but just love being on the river in a position to appreciate the environment. They usually fish fly, the purist form of angling requiring the greatest skill and patience. Spinners and wormers can be included in some cases. I have thankfully made many firm friends over the years that fit into this category. More than adequate numbers of fish are caught by these people based on a total skill and no greed basis. Unfortunately I have to mention a third type of angler who bases his fishing on financial gain and total greed. These anglers were numerous on the R Stock in the eighties; I referred to them as the Brockley psycho Mafia. They often fished in little groups or cliques, especially so at the two main troughs on the Stock. Haig Trough directly below Haig Bridge was the most favoured, closely followed by Stanwick weir and Stanwick trough further downstream, close to our own Croftgill building. I loathed these men especially when they greeted me like a best friend, then fish like saints until I moved on. Left alone or in groups they would be foul hooking with the best of them. Like minded individuals would join in, each one queuing up for a turn at drowning a worm through the fast water in the neck of a trough. The chances of foul hooking were always fairly high without having to try very hard, but if fish were scarce blatant snatching occurred. Treble hooks were not always necessary, legitimate single hook rigs were very effective especially if the bedraggled garden worm was threaded well up the shank of the hook to leave the main working part lethally bare. This meant to all intents and purpose what you had was a legitimate Gentleman angler innocently dangling a worm, when in reality he was a cool sly cheat yanking out as many fish as possible. Such like individuals were despicable in my book and far worse than a conventional poacher; at least he was up front and new the score. The number of anglers selling their catch was on the up, so I tried to increase my time policing that particular problem. This proved by far the most difficult dilemma to address for several reasons. Firstly just getting near the action was a major headache. I had several avenues of approach, sometimes I would just go in make small talk weigh up who was there, then leave signifying I was going elsewhere leaving them to assume the coast was clear. I would then return say half an hour later and stand on the bridge just observing, quite often I would stand over them in a similar fashion to the long days and nights implemented at Brockley weir. If a fish was foul hooked at least I had the satisfaction of seeing it returned. I even released some fish upstream to prevent recapture. This would really piss them off, in fact several would pack up and leave if I just turned up. To actually catch an angler take a foul hooked fish required hours of work and I was rarely successful, however I always felt compelled to keep trying. I had certain special sites of concealment allowing observation close to the action, although getting to them was extremely difficult and nigh on impossible much of the time. Haig Bridge was such a location; I used a hide about five yards downstream from the buttress of the bridge on the left bank behind a sycamore tree. The base was thick with leafy side shoots, which gave me some cover. To get there required leaving my vehicle concealed at least a mile away before making the journey on foot across country to the wood below the bridge. The remaining distance was then negotiated Indian style wearing a camo jacket complete with binocs, flask, and notebooks, one yard at a time, carefully making sure no ever watchful angler spotted me. The whole process could take in excess of an hour especially if the area was busy. It was difficult to always be successful, so there were occasions when I was spotted, this was obviously highly embarrassing, but unless I got close to the action there was no point in even being there. My success ratio for remaining unseen however was pretty good. I cherished getting a meaningful position against the odds, a skill at which I became very competent. The key was making the extra effort, putting myself out often paid dividends. It was hard graft and time consuming, but I loved every minute rain or shine.

Once in position the show would begin, I would get into a shallow hide cramped up in some contorted state providing as good a view as was possible without compromising my presence. I would try and weigh up the number of anglers present then most importantly who they were. The Mafia members are too numerous to name, which shows how big a problem this was. If a fish was hooked a well worked routine took place. The guy with a fish on would yell out, and then his closest ally would go to the downstream side of the bridge buttress, take hold of the straining rod complete with fish attached, the angler then came round to retake hold of his rod. The fish was then played for several minutes depending on its size and where it was hooked. A foul hooked fish fights long, hard, and would nearly always travel downstream in the process, and conveniently away from any disapproving eyes up at the bridge. Eventually it would either get off or retreat further downstream, or more than likely be hauled in by two or three furtive henchmen. The fish was then quickly dispatched probably marked in the mouth to fake a fair capture, and then finally scurried away into the boot of a car. I watched many of these escapades, but usually the fish quickly disappeared downstream only to be landed before I could creep into a position to see where it was hooked. This proved very frustrating, seeing a hook actually somewhere in the body of a submerged fish was almost impossible, especially sufficient enough to repeat under oath. Often I would get just a glimpse and nothing else. I did have success on a few occasions however. In August 1984 I was after one individual whose name just kept cropping up, phone calls from genuine anglers who had observed him snag fish right in front of their eyes, complaints about him whilst routinely checking anglers, there's no smoke without fire I concluded.

The angler in question was a Mafia leader in the name of Dennis Blake nicknamed by Big Don of course as "Dennis the menace".

Dennis fixed Domestic appliances in his day job using an escort van with his name all over it. Annoyingly as he was self employed, the gains from fishing at the time were obviously better than mending washing machines, which consequently meant most days he was down at Haig Bridge his favoured pitch. He was a big bloke, tall with a red face and curly short hair. I had tried and tried to nail him or one of his cronies, but I just needed a break. I waited for hours on some occasions with aching limbs to prove it; I was going through a lot of radox at the time. One sunny Friday I set out again on yet another mission to hopefully nab him. I had been told that a consortium was pooling fish and my man was transport manager taking boot loads to Lancaster market. I was powerless to intervene as this was perfectly legal, not even club rules prevented such an enterprise in those days, and this is not the case now thank goodness.

I left my car in Croftgill, Frankie goes to Hollywood had just been on radio 2 playing "Relax" fat chance of that I thought.

I wormed my way to the hide below Haig Bridge, and then sorted my bits of gear. I could hear voices and laughter so I got into a kneeling position and waited. The job was amazing sometimes, I had barely got settled when a shout broke the rhythm of gurgling water. I focused the binocs and peered forth. It was unmistakably Dennis, the sunlight seemed to accentuate his ruddy features and contorted face, his rod was bent double he yelled with glee,

"Wahoy lads" fish on, fish on"

Game on more like as far as I was concerned!

The rod was passed to an accomplice; one Reg Daly another Psycho Mafia Godfather. Daly was a worker at the Insurance Company in Brockley, who also seemed to have a lot of dubious spare time. I suspect his employers never new where he was half the time; he was obviously always one jump ahead of that particular game.

The rod was passed back to Blake in the usual manner and the inevitable journey downstream began. Progress was slow however, I could see the line glint in the sunlight, my heart was racing, I was struggling to keep my binocs steady. Suddenly the fish leapt for freedom straight up and out of the water, Dennis groaned with the strain and concentration, Daly was in close attendance carrying a landing net and offering advice. It was at this point I got my break I could clearly see the hook and worm impaled in the body of a fine salmon flashing like a bar of silver. The hook was embedded mid torso and just below the dorsal fin; this was gold dust, a clear uninterrupted positive view. The poor beast returned to the water with a resounding splash while the bent rod was maneuvered along. I crept on all fours through ferns, nettles, and dog shit, but never lost sight of my quarry. Ten minutes elapsed before the end was in sight; I was a stinging, stinking, and sweating mess when the fish finally tired enough to be removed. The two men were concentrating too much to bother whether or not Becky was around, this was the norm in these situations, and complacency was fatal which ever side you batted for.

Finally the fish surrendered, exhausted by the lengthy struggle, Daly was able to slip his landing net beneath her pristine shape before lifting the gasping listless body on to the bank, most critically at this point not only did I get a second glimpse of the offending hook. I watched Dennis Blake struggle to remove it from the cartilaginous flesh below the dorsal fin. The fish was hastily dispatched with a well worn priest then carted away smartly up the footpath. I was on the move as well by now, I didn't want these two pillocks driving off before I got to them, care was still paramount, no need to alert the remaining troops. I eventually popped out on the bridge just in time to see the two men stood behind Blake's van. I must have looked pretty gruesome homing in all fired up like that. Blake certainly had the fish in the van before I got there, but I was ready for anything, months of hard work lay in the balance here. I approached making a b-line for the two men. I could see their brains working overtime weighing up the odds, had I already seen them or just arrived? This I soon put them right on, warily the two men followed my every move.

"Now then lads how's it going?"

They seemed to relax a bit at this point, probably thinking they may be safe,

"Its quiet Mr. Carter ave na but just arrived"

The lying bastard thought he was home and dry,

"What about you then Reg?"

"Aye me an all Jack"

He was smiling like an innocent child, I try not to lose my temper with anybody during an incident, but here were two blatant liars trying to conceal the act of treachery I had been so fortunate to witness. I was boiling up inside trying my damndist to keep a lid on it.

"So you haven't caught owt then Dennis?"

I looked him in the eye, he shuffled nervously scratching his head removing a flat cap in the process, his forehead was as white as his face was red. He hesitated nervously.

"That's reeet, had yan yesterday though about ten pund"

I couldn't contain myself any longer,

"Not so Dennis I've just watched you take one and whatsmore it was foul hooked, and you Reg? You netted the bugger"

Silence reigned briefly while both men took in what I said, both faces sank to the ground, but it was Reg who spoke first.

"I only netted it Jack, just doin a favour for a mate, never sin where it were hooked"

Dennis looked in disbelief when his partner in crime showed his true colours; his hands were shaking as the realisation sunk in, he new he was being hung out to dry.

"Better open the van up Dennis"

He briefly showed defiance,

"No way Mr. Carter thas not getting in there"

I was having none of that, so I made the decision to call his bluff, walked over and opened the rear door. The fish was laid out on a black plastic bin liner. Dennis never moved. I examined it soon finding a tear mark exactly where I had seen the hook impaled.

I let him have it with both barrels:

"You're a disgrace the pair of you, call yourselves anglers, this fish was foul hooked I wonder how many you've had before, you should be thrown off"

I was angry alright and they knew it, consequently no further resistance followed. I booked the pair of them although I new Reg Daly would never get to court; still I could at least let him sweat for a few weeks. The news of Dennis Blake's comeuppance spread like wildfire through the fishing grapevine, as a result Haig Bridge went quiet for the remainder of the year, but I wouldn't go as far as to say all fish would be taken fairly. It was encouraging to note that plenty of legitimate anglers returned catching a decent number of fish into the bargain.

20

THE GRAVE YARD SHIFT

The backend of 84 approached with several regulars already in the book including Jez Bergerac, Lesley Gaunt, and Cliff Woof. The likes of Rusty Bentley and Len Dixon appeared noticeable by their absence at this time. In fact I often saw Rusty knocking around town, usually with his wife and kids; I was greeted like a long lost friend. He always wanted to reminisce and assure me that his bad days were behind him, I just hoped this would be the case.

Propagation work was taking up most of our time in late October much the same as any other year, so night work had been somewhat neglected, that was until I got a phone call one Monday morning, it was non other than the dulcet tones of Eddie Downham at Well Head farm.

"Hello Jack I thought you should know we've had visitors up the valley last couple of nights, theys comin about half eleven. They're in Church dubs lights flashin all oeert spot"

I thanked Eddie promising to give it my full attention. I sat at home and worked out some sort of strategy in my head prior to informing Dick Myers, who at once agreed to assist me that same night. I wasn't over the moon at this arrangement due to Dick's style of play, but necessity was the order of the day and he was the Boss after all.

I traveled up Brockdale that afternoon on my own to check Church dubs for any signs of last nights activity. The Church stands midway up the valley heading a stretch of deep water just upstream notorious for poaching activity. The pools are close to the road and have good tree root cover ideal for day time snaring or lamping during darkness. I found footmarks, broken sticks and general paddle over a length of about a hundred yards, backing up Eddie's information. I wanted to plan the operation in advance to make sure we would be well prepared, I decided that my best vantage point was in the church graveyard because it was up on a hillock giving a clear elevated view of the pools upstream. I had often used this place as a hide and oddly rather than finding it spooky I considered it comforting sitting against a headstone by the wall. I knew all the names and details of quite a few graves, these consisted mostly of farmers who had lived and worked all their lives in this beautiful valley. I would sometimes say hello to individual graves on arrival and ask them how the occupants were, not before making sure the Church was empty of course. I never did see anybody else alive on any of my visits, a resident black cat being the exception and he was more than a bit spiritual in my eyes. Next to the road adjacent to the river was a track up to a barn, this I decided would be an ideal position for Dick Myers to sit with his vehicle hidden.

I returned home and relayed my plans to Myers, he as usual just agreed with what ever was suggested, this was no exception, he arranged to pick me up at 22.00 that same evening.

Dick Myers arrived half an hour early another predictable feature of his behaviour; of course I had worked this into my plans. In fact I always arranged to meet him half an hour after the desired time; I found it very irritating to have him sat in his vehicle outside the house for thirty minutes until I ventured out.

We arrived at the church bang on 22.00 without meeting a single vehicle, in fact very few vehicles ever stirred up the valley after dark. Only the odd farm lad whizzed by, sneaking home from the pub. Myers sped off to get in position by the barn, I could hear the gears crunching as he fought with reverse in his horrendously crappy Polonez estate, Myers was the hardest person on a vehicle I have ever known. The Polonez was abused on a daily basis; it had my utmost admiration because somehow it seemed to just keep going. One day at a filling station in Coniston, Dick rammed it in Reverse with his big dinner plate hand only to be left holding the gear lever when it snapped like a carrot. For most people that would seriously spoil their day, not Dick, he just laughed and threw it on the back seat.

I settled amongst the graves sat upright against the wall, then did a radio test with Dick, it was 22.10. The moon was nearly full briefly until cloud cover gave total blackness; a tawny owl screeched close by like some forgotten ghost, the scene was set. Nothing stirred until 22.55 when the calm was rudely shattered by not one but two cars hurtling past the church, I was startled by the sudden intrusion, like waking from a dream. I quickly shuffled into position ignoring stiff complaining muscles. The two cars stopped directly opposite the barn where Dick Myers was hopefully concealed. I could hear voices, car doors slamming and then a bright light was scanning the field by the beck, it seemed like total chaos with disregard for any form of caution, my peaceful location had been transformed by what sounded like an army, it was quite extraordinary.

I called Myers on the radio, but alarmingly all I got was absolutely nothing. A gang of poachers were working the river and Myers was AWOL!

I soon twigged that he probably hadn't charged his radio battery, so I was perilously isolated, in a dilemma the words of the song came to mind "should I stay or should I go"

I watched as the men progressed menacingly downstream, I made a quick decision to move in and hoped Dick Myers was on the ball. I crawled on all fours two hundred painful yards out of the graveyard and down the road. I arrived at the two cars, a mini and an escort each hemmed in the dyke next to the field gate. The gang was moving back upstream by this time, I could see a person actually holding a large fish silhouetted briefly in the light beam swinging haphazardly on water and field. The next thing that happened caused me to swing round in disbelief, there was Dick Myers still sat half in and half out of his Polonez door open and lit up like a Christmas tree, he was happily calling the police on his radio. The bugger hadn't even bothered to hide his car behind the barn, preferring instead to sit in comfort as I huddled amongst the graves. Needless to say we were soon rumbled when four men returned to the vehicles. I immediately recognised Ian Capstick and Jez Bergerac, but the other two were newcomers. Dick Myers waded in snatching the car keys off one of the unknowns which kicked off an immediate reaction prompting shoving and pushing all round until I bellowed for all to stop. Once some kind of order was established Myers foolishly gave back the car keys, which invited all four to jump in and drive off, which is exactly what happened. This by now had all the makings of a complete cock up. I bit my lip after all Myers was still the boss, I walked off into the field determined to have his job one day given half a chance. I arrived at the beck edge whilst Myers treated himself to a fag. I scanned the well trodden waters edge and was soon rewarded; the spoils were laid in the grass right where the gang of four must have dumped them on spotting Dick Myers impersonation of Blackpool illuminations. The large fish I had eyeballed briefly was bleeding, very dead and laid out in the grass. A powerful torch with crude battery was a few feet further on, and then would you believe it I found a garden fork with spear and Jackson clearly labeled on the front. I was joined by Myers

"What the hell's that Jack?"

"It's a bleedin fork, they've used the flaming thing to spear the damned fish Dick"

Myers whistled in disbelief

This was a first for me and never to be repeated, the tines were bloodstained into the bargain, that fork had speared that salmon. The fish was around the eight pound mark and had several puncture marks in its body; considerable force would be needed for such an act.

"One thing Dick they'll be as sick as parrots to lose this lot"

We gathered the evidence and left, I wasn't too worried that they had done a runner as I knew two of them anyway. I rounded up Jez and Capstick without much bother the following day, needless to say they both denied the evidence, but couldn't deny actually being there. One man never did surface, but the other couldn't keep his mouth shut relaying the tale to all his workmates in the paper mill in Burndale, he was a one off and owned the mini.

Our day in court was entertaining when exhibit A one garden fork was displayed in front of the bench. All three members of what became known as the gang of four were fined £50 each plus £100 costs split equally between them at thirty three pounds thirty three pence each, another first!

I wonder if the fourth man ever contributed. I'll never know.

21

MAGGOTS

In the November of eighty four we moved house again to a super property just off the Green in Brockley, complete with view looking right up to the weir quarter of a mile away. I was so confident in the byelaw becoming effective I believed living in such a location would not be a problem. This proved to be the case most of the time, in fact I really enjoyed the close relationship with the river, I could walk out anytime with my dogs and check levels, pollution reports, watch fish running, and generally be right up to speed with the state of play. In the following year however I came a bit unstuck one warm summer Saturday night, Maggie's Nephew Tony from Workington was staying with us with a view to getting a job and a fresh start. We all went out for a meal and a few drinks, naturally getting rather merry in the process and of course the route home at around midnight took us right past the weir. On our approach we encountered a gang of lads that regrettably included Grimshaw, several other scroats, and two more brothers I had concerns over for fishing activity at Jubilee Bridge. These were namely

Simon and Chris Wightman, both as it happened were in possession of a rod and stood by the weir. The river was fresh and abundant with fish. I approached with the bravado typical of a man fuelled by drink; of course Maggie was furious and left me to it with a stern warning not to get involved in my time off. Tony remained in the background as I laid into the youths. I gave Chris Wightman the full blast of my feelings, as far as I was concerned nobody tries to fish at my weir. I was finger pointing and generally asking to get chucked in.

"You know there's no fishing here lad, look there's even a sign on the railings telling you just that, are you blind or what?"

He turned round impassively to face me, he was literally two feet from the North West Water Authority sign clearly stating byelaw 19.

"I know there's a fuckin sign but I can't read or write can I?"

The others surrounded me and laughed, but I was livid,

"Pull the other one lad do you think I was born yesterday, I'm going to get the police …come on Tony"

We made a semi dignified retreat because it finally dawned on me that the odds were not really in my favour, I phoned the nick at Brockley as soon as I was through the door, quickly relaying the situation to Jonty Jones. I laughed sarcastically as I related the comments of Chris Wightman.

"He says he can't read or write just because he was next to the flamin sign"

The reply was delayed and not what I wanted to hear, it totally floored me,

…"He can't"

"What do you mean he cant, he can't what?"

He can't read or write, he was telling you the truth Jack, Chris Wightman can't read or write a single word, never has and never will I reckon"

His words hung like a death sentence, I had been way too keen and fired up even to consider that he might actually be telling the truth. Not only was I totally demoralised on hearing this, but by the time I returned to the weir with the Police they were long gone and that was that, a lucky escape for both sides I think.

The main Lakes of Windermere and Coniston always provided a welcome change of scenery, plus the still water fishing environment was also challenging at times. Coniston was a particular concern early in the year from March onwards due to the spawning habits of the Arctic Char (*Salvelinus alpinus*). This fish is a member of the salmon family that formerly migrated back to the sea, only to get land locked following the ice age. Charr live in very deep water only coming close to the shores and shallow water to spawn. In fact remarkably two separate sub species exist spawning either in the back end or in the spring. The big concern to us was the spring spawners because they were very vulnerable to exploitation by unscrupulous angling techniques. The bona fida anglers used traditional wooden boats with specific long wooden Charr poles and metal lures fished at depths of ninety feet or more. This traditional method goes back several hundred years.

Our problem was off comers, mainly Wiganers plus others from other Lancashire towns like Liverpool, St Helens, Nelson, Colne, and Manchester. The problem was at its peak in eighty five …the reason? Because Char are a delicacy and in those days worth at least £2 per pound. Gangs of these anglers turned up regularly in ever growing numbers to fish early doors or even all night. The method was easy, deadly, and devastating to Char stocks. Maggoting on a vast scale was both illegal as hook bait, or as ground bait, the reason being primarily to protect stocks of young fish. Juvenile salmon, trout, and char feed voraciously in the spring and maggots are just plain irresistible. The physical damage done to a juvenile fish even when caught and released is immense. The good news was byelaw 18, this effectively banned Maggoting during the course fish close season both as hook bait, and not on or attached to a hook, in other words used as ground bait. The bad news was most of the traveling throng were prepared to use maggots and risk being caught. Both lakes became well populated by anglers in the eighties especially at first light before the hoards of speed boats and water skiers ruined the peace and tranquility, I could never understand how they got away with it on Windermere, the noise and smell was overpowering at times.

Further bad news was the fact that Char had the same close season as trout, which finished at midnight on March 14th. This gave the unfortunate scenario of fish that could be technically unclean but in season. In the early eighties most anglers on Windermere and Coniston fished from the shoreline, boat anglers were few and far between. I patrolled both lakes usually at weekends with steady success picking off maggoters as and when detected; sometimes this depended on how much effort I was prepared to put in. The biggest obstacle was actually locating the store of maggots in use by an individual or group. If I was very lucky, or the angler was naïve the maggots would often be kept out in the open, usually in a standard plastic bait box, more than likely however they would be concealed in a fishing basket or tackle box, then furtively removed and placed in plastic swim feeders or straight on to the hook. A swim feeder is a simple but clever device that consists of a small plastic pot with holes in. This is attached to the anglers rig and filled with maggots, these then wriggle about gently floating out of the holes into the water to be gobbled up by ever growing numbers of hungry fish. A catapult is another sure sign of skullduggery; these are used simply to fire maggots out into the water, and then cast a baited hook amongst them. Cunning ploys to pull the wool over a Bailiffs eye were numerous, for example having a worm on the hook but also ground bait on the sly using maggots. The necessity to creep up on these people was paramount; this gave me chance to locate any secret stash. I have seen maggots produced out of pockets, flasks, sandwich boxes, fag packets, hats, almost anything would do. The most satisfying part of the whole process was a down trodden face when I uncovered the hiding place.

Disabled anglers were another anomaly in those days, half of Wigan appeared to be disabled, and this was often used as a ploy to gain the sympathy vote if trouble was brewing. I remember sneaking up to a guy on the east shore of Windermere on a beautiful Sunday morning in May. He was blissfully unawares sitting back on his camping chair listening to radio 2 at six a.m. I watched him reel in his line complete with swim feeder full of maggots. Ever so carefully I moved in just after he'd rebaited, not surprisingly he spotted me when I was still about twenty yards away. The man leapt off his chair like Lynford Christie in a frantic effort to sabotage the line. On my arrival I easily recovered the offending mess complete with all the trimmings. He immediately began breathing heavily, gasping and feigning an Asthma attack. He was even trying to feign a bad back in the process. He was a typical pathetic individual caught with his trousers down, and waving his disabled badge in front of my nose. I gave him the same treatment as everyone else of course. If he had been seriously ill and not trying to con me I could have had a few awkward questions to answer I reckon, instead he got humiliated and a fine in court just like he deserved.

Quite often I would team up with Hank because Windermere was his patch after all. This meant many a Saturday or Sunday patrol commencing with a very early start. This suited Hank down to the ground he was a stalwart morning person who liked to get home for lunch and have the rest of the day to himself. This would always be spent in his working men's club. Never call Hank after lunch was the unwritten rule; a fact acknowledged by everyone in the team especially after Joe Marwoods day.

Patrols with Hank meant he drove his land rover while I did most of the work. This didn't bother me at all; in fact I preferred it that way. I developed a reputation in the team as a deadly force, as indeed Hank had been in days gone by and to be fair he would chip in if there was more than I could handle at any one incident. I never went with Dick Myers if I could help it because we would be back home by ten, usually after another whistle stop tour and that would undoubtedly include both lakes. I wanted to boost my CV after all, and be ready to wear his shoes if and when the chance arrived. So it was Hank and I that pulled dozens of culprits on the shores of those lakes in the eighties, including some who had caught Char. The lucrative gains from char fishing also brought unscrupulous boat anglers to Coniston with the sole intention of exploiting this fine fish. The main area of concern was an area just off Peel Island; a beauty spot used in Ransom's book Swallows and amazons. The drama was still very much around although, if in a some what different form. Groups of mostly working class Lancastrians migrated at weekends to the lakes with the sole intention of catching char on rod and line from a boat. They turned up one after another launching flimsy little fiberglass dinghies at both sides of the lake; each boat was gently rowed across to Peel Island. A small Armada built up, the numerous boats formed a circle rather like covered wagons and anglers were even draped on the rocky outcrops facing west from the Island. A situation developed whereby Maggots would be scattered all around in a mass ground baiting excersize, which catastrophically attracted large shoals of char. Each angler hauled them in tag lag, the aim being to get a sack full as quickly as possible, then take it to a hotel or supermarket, and sell the lot for cash. Once the gains had been pocketed they would disappear back where they came from and probably drink themselves into oblivion. The only problems they encountered was either hopefully Bailiffs or bad weather or both, the latter often severely tested inadequate equipment, I once witnessed four burly men set sail in a pram dinghy so low in the water it had barely inches of clearance, they actually used two spades for oars. Huddled so close together I was convinced an impending disaster was just round the corner, how they spent the day like that was astonishing, it looked like four men in a dustbin with fishing rods poking out at peculiar angles. The lure of rich pickings drove them and many more like them on to take such risks. Catching anglers Maggoting along the shoreline was a doddle compared to boat crews, we were very much a shore based force at this time, seeing worthwhile evidence was almost impossible. A typical patrol would have me arrive with Hank in his land rover at Sunny bank lay-by directly opposite Peel Island. Here we would sit and observe the carnage through binocs unable to identify what type of bait was being used, or by whom due to the half mile or more distance between us and them. I would swear at them as each fish came out then make notes. Hank loved it he would happily sit there all day caressing his pocket watch as the hours rolled by. A lunch allowance was always a priority for Hank, this was payable when a shift went to six hours or more which was most days in these circumstances. In those days a breakfast could be claimed on early shifts and that paid an even higher rate, a fact that Hank made the most of. It was right up his street, plenty of action but no need to get involved. This scenario was no good for me of course; I wasn't going to rest until this butchery was sorted.

We did get odd cases when anglers fished close to the shore, generally because we were either very jammy or they were a bit naïve. Just being in possession of maggots was not an offence and still isn't to this day, so stopping them coming ashore was mostly a waste of time. I have seen bags full of char with live maggots actually crawling out from their mouths, the usual explanation was:

"They must have eaten someone else's ground bait before I caught them"

Or words to that effect, there was nothing I could do about it.

The first major success involving boat anglers however happened on a Sunday in March 1985, I had decided a fresh approach was needed. I worked out that getting onto that bloody island was imperative to obtain any sort of view of what was going on. I badgered Dick Myers into borrowing a small inflatable boat from our hydrologists. Peel island although half a mile from the west shore is only about two hundred yards from the east shore. I had a plan that required two people, I and one other could carry the dinghy through the woods, launch, and quietly row across. The island is unfishable from that side due to rocks and shallow water; consequently it was totally ignored by any anglers. My idea was to land and then carefully crawl up through the vegetation made up of mainly bracken, juniper and other small trees.

The Sunday in question was ideal; a cold high pressure dominated the weather so visibility would be good and the chance of offenders high. I was in good spirits not least because United had beaten Liverpool one nil on the Saturday. I left the dogs with Maggie and picked Danny as my accomplice for the day, at least I knew he was keen. We arrived during darkness around three in the morning. Parking and carrying the boat was a mammoth task in itself. We had to negotiate two of the roughest fields in Cumbria and also scale a couple of dry stone walls. Eventually totally knackered we reached the waters edge opposite the island. A few graylags stirred and croaked in annoyance, but no alarming panic occurred, instead they just grumbled and swam gently south. We took a timely breather drinking in the cold air; I was sweating heavily having gone from frozen to boiling in just a few minutes I looked across the lake as my eyes adjusted to the darkness. The island was just visible looming like a large battle ship moored in the mist. I helped Danny load our gear into the boat at which point he whispered that she was a bit soft round the sponsons. This was not a cause for concern, Danny calmly produced the little foot pump and carefully pumped her up, I was worried by the noise but the need outweighed the danger. It was 04.00. When we quietly set sail, I rowed gently and slowly watching the first signs of daylight flicker across the tranquil lake. We safely landed within minutes carefully stashing the boat between two rocks protected by a stunted overhanging oak, the last thing we needed was some marauding scroat to find it. We gathered our essentials before crawling slowly and steadily up on to the apex of the Island away from the numerous little footpaths created over many years. I found a soft spot in the undergrowth behind a convenient low rock allowing good vision across the Lake. Straight away I could hear faint voices together with the significant whiff of cigarette smoke. I adjusted all my bits of kit and even managed a crafty sup of tea from my flask. Danny was a couple of yards away in a similar spot.

The daylight gradually began to increase revealing two small boats already in position. It was 05.45 and all was well until a third boat appeared, its little outboard spluttering gently through the calm waters like a bumble bee. The boat moored up about thirty yards from my hide, it was a small dirty white fiberglass tub containing two men and a small boy. I put my binnocs on it and immediately eyeballed a large blue bucket centre stage amidships, no prizes for guessing what was in there. I also realised that I knew one of the men, I couldn't put a name to him but our paths had definitely crossed at some point. He was around late forties wearing a blue bobble hat and camo jacket, his mate had a green floatation suit on and black wool hat. The young lad had a typical green parka and already looked fed up. The same young lad soon caught a char which he knocked on the head in ruthless fashion, before then gutting the fish. The two men both catapulted maggots into the lake from the big blue tub, no surprise there I thought. I could even hear them talking, complaining that some fish were getting off despite landing several more as I watched. This was beginning to look very promising; the extra effort was finally paying off. I swapped positions with Danny and took down some notes, then suddenly I heard the clunk of a boat against rock, Danny gave me a kick,

"There's someone coming on the island"

I looked up in panic

"Shit"

We both ducked down in the scrub only seconds before a bloke walked past to relieve himself, he was still only about twenty feet away. This turned out to be a very tricky moment, fortunately after what seemed ages he returned whence he came. Of course he was only joined by a mate, and next thing we knew they had a fire lit. Soon the heady smell of fried bacon wafted all around, it was too much. I made the quick decision that we had gathered all the evidence needed, which was just as well because the white boat was on its way back to the shore. It was time to move, and quickly.

"Come on Danny lets go for it"

Danny was not always the sharpest of athletes in such situations, but I needn't have worried. We sneaked back to our boat carefully avoiding master chef and his mate. I hurriedly dragged her out and dived in, it was at this point I noticed that the sponsons were down again, only now time was not on our side.

Danny was aboard grasping the oars, the steely look on his face told me he was more than ready,

"Go Danny, go like hell"

I have never witnessed a man row like Dan did that morning; his arms were just a blur fighting desperately to make the shore before we sank. It felt like an age until slowly but surely terra firma beckoned, I was certainly never more glad to be on dry land,

"Too close for comfort that Dan"

He barely nodded; he was too knackered to speak.

"Leave all the gear Dan we need to get going"

Grabbing my notebook I ran hell for leather north to the Gondola pier.

Two men and the boy were busy unloading stuff on to the pier without a care in the world; I reached them some distance ahead of Dan,

"Stop Bailiffs"

They each looked up and it was then that I recognised the guy in the bobble hat; I had only nabbed him using maggots the previous year on the R Stock down at Bampton Hall water.

I approached the boat to find all the maggots in the world crawling around on the floor, The man in the green floatation suit tried to conceal a large plastic sack which obviously contained many char. Warrants were produced before I looked in the sack, it was a sorry sight, containing around fifty or sixty char plus maggots dead and alive in abundance, also some of the fish were unclean, loose ova and milt was also present. They were bang to rights of that I was certain, these fish could probably be cashed in at the very least for a hundred pounds, not bad for a mornings work. The man I knew was Terry Wiggins with son Alan, the other guy was Philip Robinson all from Blackpool. I asked what they had been using for bait and as usual I got a complete denial. Terry Wiggins did his level best to act hurt and victimised at my accusations.

"I can't think wur them maggots ave come from Mr. Carter, they must of gotten em fromt tuther boats". I seized the blue tub that was still containing a small amount of its deadly supply. Both men had licences so ID wasn't an issue. I let the young lad off even though he was twelve at least.

The following autumn they duly turned up at Hawkshead court to plead not guilty, it was a strange case because after much deliberation the bench seemed to get rather bogged down. The result included a conviction for ground baiting, due to the best evidence but an acquittal for the use of maggots as hook bait. The Magistrates couldn't seem to grasp the fact I had been able to see maggots actually on the hooks. I was mortified at this verdict, reminded once again just how fickle and unpredictable some courts could be. Never ever count your chickens in a court of law. This roller coaster day seemingly going pear shaped then took another twist when both defendants were surprisingly fined a whopping £200 each for the ground baiting offence with £25 costs on top. I almost yelled out, but managed a discreet fist clench of triumph behind the seat instead. The two defendants went pale with anger and any passed pleasantries for the day went out the window. The only thing in their favour was the fact that the fines were to be paid at a measly five quid a week. The char were donated to Brockley general hospital because they had been in deep freeze since the day of the offence, there looked enough to feed the five thousand. The char situation had become another serious fisheries problem, not only to the survival of the species, but on our resources as well, just as the weir in Brockley had been previously. This prompted the team to push hard for a change in the close season with yet another new byelaw. The following year thanks to more sterling work by Roger Mcbane this came into force resulting in the close season thankfully extended to April 30th .This now allowed char in the most part to spawn and return to deep water away from the pernicious maggot brigade.

Wiggins and Robinson were not done yet though because they appealed against the sentence, a scenario I had never previously been troubled with. Three months later in January 1986 it all happened again at Crown court in Barrow. The Judge for the day happened to be non other than Judge Franks, a regular angler in Broxton Park no less, and whatsmore I had once brought him luck. I had routinely checked his licence during friendly conversation and was just leaving when he successfully hooked and landed a fine salmon, I could only hope he would remember. The proceedings began with Terry Wiggins Barrister outlining the personal circumstances of his client. Our Terry was, apparently disabled of course, nothing new there then. He had no job due to his bad back and crippling arthritis, funny how that didn't stop him freezing his bollocks off on a cold March morning for hours in a small boat. He also supposedly had six kids ranging from six to sixteen, no problem with his reproductive functions seemingly, then to cap it all he was illiterate unable to read or write. He survived on £50 a week benefits etc etc .This blurb took quite sometime while his Barrister spun out the hapless lifestyle of his beleaguered client. Finally Judge Franks intervened, he had heard enough before announcing that Mr. Wiggins had better enter the witness box and take the oath. Terry Wiggins limped pathetically across the court, then up into the witness stand to face his tormentors. The clerk asked Terry to state his name and address; the court usher held up his piece of card enabling Terry to read out the oath. Terry Wiggins took hold of the card, and duly repeated the contents standing almost to attention. What followed was a hung silence that seemed to last an age, until finally broken by the Judge himself. Judge Franks peered across the court over his half rimmed glasses and directly at Terry's Barrister.

"I thought you told this court your client couldn't read or write"?

The penny dropped, out of the blue amongst muffled laughter Wiggins had been shot down, both he and his Barrister had been made to look ridiculous. I don't think what followed was anything more than going through the motions, in fact Judge Franks not only upheld the original fines for both men, but added insult to injury by putting a further £50 on to the original fines together with upping the payments to £10 a week.

I loved British justice at times like this, it gave me such a boost in my fight against crime, it made all the hard work and effort so worthwhile, spurring me on for more of the same.

22

ALL IN A DAYS WORK

A Constables notebook contains cotemporaneous notes for his entire working life, in my case as a Water Bailiff, details of every movement, plus each and every offence reported. My own book was constantly supplied with an assortment of names and offences, either rod and line or poaching related. The mid eighties turned out to be the most productive of my career and fish stocks continued to increase. Our Bailiff team struggled to keep on top of the ever increasing poaching problem in south lakes. It was an ever growing challenge on which I thrived. I was ambitious too, despite the few opportunities that arose in the career building stakes. During 1984 an Inspectors job became vacant in South west Cumbria due to the sacking of what was hitherto considered to be a top man, the main man in fact. The Inspector in question Reg Smith was himself yet another ex cop, he had for a few years conducted all the Bailiffs training sessions, he new the law inside out and had that golden gift of the gab. He was arguably a bit too cocky for my liking. It eventually and regrettably came to light that many of the nights anti poaching patrols in South west Cumbria were actually done in the pub. The consequences were not hard to figure out! Legless Bailiffs and no cases. It wasn't until a van got rolled over on Corney fell that the truth came out. Smith obviously had to go, together with his senior Bailiff, it was high time for a clean up. I applied for the vacated post despite the fact that south west Cumbria was not really where I wanted to be, but I felt I had to make an effort and show I was ambitious. My main rival was a Bailiff on the River Lune.

Frank Bell was about my age built like a tank and an ex soldier. He inevitably got the job; apparently I was sussed out by Roger Mcbane who later informed me that during the interview it became apparent I wasn't in love with that particular part of the world. I was disheartened, but not too much so because the job I had my heart on was of course that currently held by my own boss Dick Myers.

I put it behind me becoming even more determined to build a good reputation, hopefully helped by the plethora of offenders out there, especially on Windermere. It was areas like those that Maggoting and various byelaw offences seemed to grow on trees. Hank of course was happy to let me roam his patch like a free agent, so I made the most of every possible opportunity especially when Hank was off duty. Throughout the late eighties I couldn't go wrong, I just had an instinct and a nose for where they would be. I could pick them off when others would drift by with an empty book. It was always down to effort, never go home when there could be a case round the corner. The other Bailiffs just didn't do it; they got the odd ones or helped me, or got them because they were out with me. The exception of course was Danny, he was as keen as anybody, but unfortunately he was just too slow at times.

Other events happened too; four of the main weirs on the River Stock were refurbished with new fish passes built during the summer of eighty four. This proved a major upheaval; however this has since allowed improved access for migratory fish to spawning areas. The work instigated a major increase in fish stocks in the upper reaches. During the January of eighty six The Bailiff team itself completely repaired another fish pass situated on the last upstream weir in Crossley. This type of work was a welcome change and made for good banter or team building as it is now referred to.

Winter work in the hatchery across on the Lune was another variation during really cold weather. The main job we were called upon to help with was picking whites; this entailed picking the dead or white eggs from each tray of salmon or sea trout ova. Standing in an ice cold hatchery could be an ordeal at times though; one winter in particular produced a big freeze that threatened to cut off the entire water supply. I spent days hacking away at the massive lumps of ice to maintain the vital supply of water, I could have been in the North Pole.

In the spring of eighty five Maggie began a B&B business in our house by the Green in Brockley. In time this proved to be an excellent little earner despite getting off to a somewhat tricky start. The very first couple we took in started having sex almost as soon as they got settled, locking themselves in the spare room. I hardly slept all night, kept awake by the varying noises generated by bonking in the bathroom, then the bed room and most of the night. I was up at four in the morning to do a patrol on Windermere. All I could remember was the sound of the radiator banging in rhythm against the bedroom wall as I left. The last thing I said to Maggie before leaving was,

"Whatever that guys on I want some".

Fortunately most of our guests after that were absolutely fine; it was just an unfortunate start.

I had seen a lot of mink that year and came to the conclusion that some effort at trapping might not go amiss. I visited my old mate Glen Bracken to obtain a couple of traps and a rough guide how to use them, mink were a particular problem on the three rivers around Brockley in the eighties, reaching record numbers. The unfortunate situation arose following the release of many mink from fur farms by well meaning but ignorant people. I managed considerable success, although disposing of them humanely was a problem. I used a standard cage trap, which could then be dropped in the water subsequently drowning the offending beast. I only performed this method once because it was too distressing; the whole process just took too long. The method I settled on was one of canine utilisation, in other words I let Ben have them. This was easier said than done, you try holding a rampant terrier whilst at the same time trying to release a screeching mink from the trap. It proved a bit tricky to say the least. Ben could kill a mink in an instant and I defy anyone to argue against this method. I have heard of gassing mink on a car exhaust, but again this was not particularly humane. I only ran into difficulties once, when a released mink managed to shimmy up a tree before Ben was quick enough to nab it. The little beast screeched its head off leaving Ben yapping helplessly on the ground; eventually the mink quite remarkably dived thirty feet down into the river and swam for freedom. I suffered thefts of traps on several occasions, so after a few months I gave it up as a bad job, not least because my employees didn't condone mink trapping in any shape or form.

October eighty five was proving a challenging month even though fishing in the proximity of weirs was routinely prohibited, problems still arose, I couldn't afford to take my eye off the ball for a single day. The psycho Mafia still hammered the troughs as well as the weir at Stanwick. This weir is a flow measuring device rather than impoundment therefore didn't come under the byelaw restriction in October. The Mafia anglers however had covertly implemented the placing of stones discreetly below the weir at its right bank side, and these could be hard to see in higher flows. Fish would rest in eddies formed around these stones which of course was the whole purpose of the exercise. This facilitated exploitation by my good friends from the Brockley AA. This was yet more hassle, but also hailed the arrival of a new player. Thomas Williams was unfortunately another of those people that got under my skin, I hated him. He was Lancastrian but lived in Crossley. He had a twiny, annoying, loud deep voice, that never shut up, Big Don soon had him weighed up and christened him "pig eyes" for obvious physical reasons. Williams was a wormer never fishing anything else, he always had a licence, always turned up where the most fish were and specialised in befriending land owners of salmon rivers. He was very adept at achieving this of course both the worming for fish and the worming his way on to somebody else's land. He would promise to supply a percentage of his catch to the persuaded party before hammering it so much, that eventually they saw through him and chucked him off. He would then repeat the process somewhere else in the area. He was also well in with the Stanwick weir mob which really irritated me. He was in his own eyes a budding country gent, but I knew better he was Mafia through and through. I was of course keen that he should get his comeuppance and my lucky break eventually came on a wet October afternoon whilst checking various fish passes monitoring fish movement. I was not in enforcement mode at all when I walked happily across a couple of fields by the R Brant. I was well up the beck at a secluded stretch housing an ancient weir from centuries back. The ancient structure had stood the rigors of time well with its sloping stone face a good vantage point for watching fish run. The fish pass itself such as it was looked like some kind of guilty afterthought. Weathered concrete moss covered and broken in places the pass formed a crude channel down one side. I was approaching accompanied by both dogs ahead eagerly tracking rabbits, or mink in the hope of some sport. My attention was alerted though as the weir came into view, I glimpsed a rod tip poking up at intervals from a point about ten yards downstream and in the beck bottom. I quickly got my two companions on a lead and parked myself by a wall fifty yards from the beck edge. Once organised I quickly put the binnocs on the weir. I couldn't believe my luck, there was good old "pig eyes" happily worming under the weir. He must have worked his charm on yet another Farmer; I watched him for about five minutes before walking quietly in.

"Now then Tommy any luck"?

"Aye aye Jack, as had a couple uv sea trout"

I could hardly contain myself; there is a God after all!

Tommy turned quite nasty on the day when he went in my book, but never mind he had it coming, he swore blind he hadn't read the byelaws, tough shit I thought to myself. He still managed to befriend several more Farmers over the next few years until like many others he drifted off the scene; he married into money needless to say and now prospers in real estate.

In November eighty five with help from big Don I managed two good poaching cases in a single afternoon. We had cruised around all morning seeing nothing untoward, so ended up parked in full view in a gateway half way up Brockdale. We ate our sandwiches listening to Fleetwood Mac on the tape player in my newly acquired green Morris mini metro. I was watching a flock of long tailed tits flitting through the blackthorns whilst pouring out some coffee, I recollected to Don an instance when a flock of twenty seven long tailed tits crossed my path in the wood close to Dick Longhorns place, it was then that we were suddenly disturbed by a tatty brown Ford Granada that shot past. It contained three very rough looking blokes, Don was not impressed.

"What the hell are they doing up here Jack?"

I wasn't overly concerned but Don was spooked,

"Better have a gander Don in a bit when we've supped up"

Ten minutes elapsed before we followed slowly up the valley, five minutes after that, there was the Granada parked up in a passing place, Don gasped

"Look ye there Jack yans running upt field"

"Aye Don the buggers got a fish an all"

The guy was legging it back to the road carrying a small sea trout by the tail, whatsmore he jumped in the car with it and set off with spectacular wheel spin. Don spoke first.

"Now what Captain Mannering?"

"Don't panic they cant get past us Don"

I proceeded slowly up the valley and it wasn't long before the car approached. I stopped in the middle of the narrow country road, Ben was growling menacingly in the back.

The Granada stopped inches in front us, and out we got to confront three very rough looking characters, I went to the driver's side and Don to the passenger side, not one of them moved or even opened the window. Without warning, the driver a man well in his fifties slammed it in reverse, but as luck would have it just at the right moment a land rover was traveling down the valley, which left them well and truly hemmed in. This development seemed to break the ice, there was quite simply no where else to go. Slowly the driver's window came down and the older guy tamely capitulated.

"Looks like we've bin nabbed ave we"

I produced my warrant and asked them to get out, at which point one of the younger men produced a small sea trout from his rucksack.

"I guess you'll be wanting this marra"

More traffic built up both in front and behind, which all seemed to work in our favour whilst inquisitive residents frowned on the assembled raiding party. The three men were all Mitchell's from Ambleside, Father and two sons. They were builders working at Crossley, who ill advisedly thought a bit of poaching over lunch was a good idea. Once the formalities were dealt with Don determined we had better leave the area before anything else happened, I was in total agreement. I drove three miles across to The R Brant and parked up at Fossil Bridge mid way up the valley. Brantdale differs from Brockdale in as much that the Brant has more tributaries than the Brock, thus offering greater spawning potential for both salmon and sea trout. Fossil bridge is so named because of its limestone construction complete with numerous fossilised remains easily found by anyone keen to look hard enough.

Don was into his flask and we were about to write up our notes. I needed a pee, so went down behind the bridge. I was midstream and going over the afternoons events in my head when my attention was diverted. Half hidden in the bushes I could see the backend of a BSA Bantam. I spoke out loud.

"Jesus that's all we need"

I knew the bike; it belonged to non other than Jez Bergerac. I hastened back to my car and relayed the good news. No time for anything other than to get straight on the case. Don went off downstream and I headed up banks. The Radios we now had were new, compact, far superior to the last lot, and actually worked quite reliably. It wasn't long before Don relayed the good news.

"Romeo 6, I have Bergerac and Wheatley walking upstream toward the bridge,

Romeo 6, Wheatley has a heavy looking rucksack on his back"

I set off in a hurry towards the bridge, my car might give the game away, but there wouldn't be time to shift it. Instead I managed to get just downstream enough to intercept them. It was one of those priceless moments; everything had gone our way for the second time in a day. I popped out from behind a bush just as the two men walked passed. They both nearly burst into tears when confronted. Big Don was closing down the back door, resistance was pointless. Wheatley sweating profusely and out of breath let his precious cargo slide to the floor. Two capitulations within hours, and another bag of fish. Wheatleys rucksack contained seven sea trout all taken recklessly off redds, the fish were spewing out eggs and milt in the bag. I was livid, I could never understand why such stale unappetising fish were worth getting caught for. They were cutting their own throats by preventing spawning potential. I believe that such fish are sometimes used to feed dogs such as lurchers or hounds; the value for human consumption is negligible.

Needless to say after the two men had been successfully processed Don and I went straight home to make up our notes, we couldn't guarantee not having another encounter that day. In truth it would be weeks of effort before we struck again.

23

THE FALL OF JOHN BARKER

In November eighty five a particular line of enquiry bore fruit after some weeks of speculation and evidence gathering. Sergeant Jonty Jones had contacted me in October full of a story passed on from a colleague up in Workington. Allegedly a gang of salmon poachers on the River Derwent were selling fish to a game dealer in Windermere. I informed Jonty that the only supplier in that area I knew about was "Cumbria Farm and fish" on Royston drive, Bowness. The proprietor was one John Barker an infamous alcoholic in his mid fifties. Barkers name had cropped up a few times that year in connection with shady deals involving venison, fish and just about anything edible that once moved or roamed our sacred county. I was very keen to obtain some concrete evidence to bring him down. Jonty was keen as mustard as usual, so it was no surprise when I got a phone call one Wednesday afternoon about a delivery in the last few days from up west. Jonty sounded really wound up.

"My mans just let me know Jack, cant say exactly when they came down but it was possibly only last night, a van full apparently".

I agreed to meet at Brockley nick to plan our attack. Dick was away so I called in Hank, unfortunately Hank's wife Jane told me he was asleep and out for the duration.

I went to the nick anyway to plan our strategy. It was agreed we would bust them the next day at noon. This suited me just fine; I could get Hank before he dissolved into the bowels of his club for another afternoon session.

We all assembled at Brockley Police station the following morning at eleven o clock, Jonty led Hank and I into the canteen for a brew. PC Tony Fleming greeted us waving a search warrant triumphantly. My only worry was the possibility of this being just another false alarm, the number of tip offs that didn't bear fruit made me feel a bit sceptical at times. Jonty appeared with the look of a man who meant business.

"Have you got that warrant Tony Lad?"

Tony waved it round in a circular motion for the whole canteen to see... we were ready!

We pulled up outside 22 Royston drive at bang on midday. Jonty hammered on the wooden double door, eventually the scruffy lanky frame of John Barker opened up, he was a dead ringer for Richard Harris. His long wavy hair was white, wispy, and balding, a fag hung precariously between thin stubbly lips.

"Yes what's to do"

The words were coughed rather than spoken, his wretched frame racked with the inconvenience of effort.

Jonty boldly held up the search warrant before introducing us all in turn, Hanks chest was puffed out like a rooster.

"This is a warrant to search your premises for illegal salmon"

Barkers frame racked under the strain of another cough and a nervous half smile.

"Thas nowt illegal here Officer, this is a legitimate business"

Jonty brushed him aside so we followed him in. I carefully weighed up the scene as Jonty questioned Barker. The large room seemed full of freezers; I counted four chest freezers and a walk in job. Hank gave me a hesitant look when I lifted the lid on the first one.

…Wow, it was full to brimming with salmon, all eyes zoomed in. The fish were laid neatly but loose. I beckoned Jonty. He whistled in surprise and turned on Barker.

"Where did these come from then Mr. Barker?"

This was certainly no blind alley that's for sure, we had hit the jackpot. Barker lit a cigarette, coughed then reluctantly gave his explanation.

"I get them from a guy up west like"

Jonty was into him like a ton of bricks,

"Who is that then?"

"I don't know his name he just drops by now and again"

Jonty looked him in the eye with utter contempt

"My arse he does Mr. Barker there's bloody dozens here"

The fish were neatly laid together but not in bags, they were poor back end fish, dark in colour and obviously hadn't been there very long. I pointed out to Barker that I was of the opinion these fish were recently purchased. He coughed nodding in agreement at my analysis.

"Aye lad bought em last week, then had another lot yisterdy"

He was playing the innocent shop keeper, moving gingerly to the walk in freezer, he opened it to reveal a heap of salmon at least twenty deep.

"These is yisterdys, I avent had a minute spare to bag em yet"

I couldn't believe the scale of events unfolding even Hank was lost for words; Jonty started eagerly examining the invoices, whilst Hank assisted me looking in all the freezers. The heap of salmon stacked in the walk in freezer even had grass amongst them, not to mention the tell tale black net lines on every fish. I could picture the scene when a lethal net would have been hauled on to some grassy bank by the River Derwent during the dead of night, the culprits bagging the catch in glee. I confronted Barker,

"Mr. Barker these fish are obviously recently caught, where have they come from and how were they caught?"

He stared vacantly at me whilst the questions registered, finally pacing around in discomfort.

"I only buy the bloody things, how should I know, they didn't swim in tut freezer did they lad?"

Barker almost laughed at his own little joke,

Hank moved in for the kill as only he could.

"Mr. Barker unless you can prove these fish have been caught legally, and before the thirty first of August you have committed an offence"

Barker was really getting twitchy at this stage,

"What do yu mean what yu on about?"

The actual offence is buying, selling or having in possession for sale salmon or trout after the last day in August in any year. This was our only charge prior to the salmon act that came out later in 1986. This offence also had the unusual feature of being guilty until proved innocent. PC Tony Fleming put the lid on it as he waved the firms invoice records in front of Barkers now runny nose.

"The last record of salmon purchase was last April mate, where's any paperwork for this lot?"

Barker winced and coughed yet again as his situation worsened, shaking his head in despair, he had no proof of purchase and getting receipts from the nice men of Workington would not be very good for his health. He was all alone and bang to rights. We seized fifty six salmon and fifteen sea trout, Hanks new Land rover was brimming with frozen fish, Jonty took the books under vain protest from Barker. Hank moved quickly as the fish were becoming more slimy and smelly as the day wore on. We arrived at the office at three o clock that afternoon to leave three fish for forensic tests. Roger Mcbane frantically rang round frozen food wholesalers to arrange interim storage for the fish. We ended up taking the whole lot to Garstang for safe keeping. Hanks new vehicle was well christened and stunk for weeks. The fish weighed in at just under four hundred pounds weight and probably worth £3 to £4 per pound

The court case the following February was fairly straightforward, Barker pleaded guilty as was expected. He was charged separately for both the salmon and the sea trout resulting in a fine of £125 for each plus £49 storage costs and court costs of £150. I was well pleased as was Jonty Jones, £449 just about finished off John Barker, he went out of business a few weeks later with debts and ill health.

I only hope our joint efforts with the police deterred any further trips from our friends in west Cumbria.

24

CALL OUT BAILIFFS AND P.A.C.E.

1986 proved a milestone year for fisheries enforcement because it saw the introduction of the much publicised Police and Criminal Evidence act, better known as P.A.C.E. My powers as a Constable brought me nicely under the umbrella of this ACT, primarily introduced to bring the Police into line when stop and search operations were carried out. The tendency had been for stereotyping certain minorities such as coloured or ethnic youths, then subjecting them to search and interrogation techniques that left much to be desired, or so we were led to believe. The big plus for Water Bailiffs was section 25 that allowed arrest under certain circumstances, significantly giving a wrong name and address, showing a threat of violence and becoming a danger to themselves or other people. Over the years the Bailiff teams throughout the north were trained in all legal matters under the guidance of the infamous Reg Smith, so it was no surprise that this new ACT would require similar guidance. The training sessions were penciled in for April at the Black moss Hotel near Ambleside. It was a good chance to meet all the Bailiffs from the Eden, Derwent, Lune, and Ribble, exchange opinions and generally have a good crack. The Ribble lads were the most entertaining by far, with their jolly Lancashire accents and happy disposition. My introduction to Ribble temperaments back in 1978 was during my first union meeting at the old hatchery; Joe Marwood had taken us all there to discuss terms and conditions. I was given a lesson in moderate militancy hitherto never heard off in the world of fisheries. Max Hibbert the Fisheries Inspector led the show in a manner Arthur Scargill would have been proud to claim. The end result however gave us a five day thirty seven hour week plus alternate weekends off, which still applies today.

Max Hibbert and his men livened up many a Bailiff training day especially during tedious theory sessions. Len Ibbotson was a Bailiff who never failed to entertain, he was the biggest comedian as well as the smallest bloke in the whole team best remembered for telling jokes virtually none stop all day, he always reminded me of a very small version of Bernard Manning. Included in the training sessions that year was a practical exercise whereby a mock poaching incident was to be enacted by Bailiffs and their trainers on the Banks of the River Rothay below Grasmere. This was the brain child of Roger Mcbane, we were assembled at seven o clock at night on a fine cool April evening. Roger Mcbane would with other members of the management team play the part of a poaching gang and actually set a net across the river. The plan was then for each team in turn to creep up on, and deal with each event. West Cumbria lads went first with Frank Bell gaining the distinction of first to fall in and get wet, drowning his new radio in the process; this was a bad start and didn't go down at all well.

We went next and to be honest I thought it went pretty well, except for Danny getting lost in the woods of course, also my night sight died half way through for no apparent reason. Consequently management was getting a bit hot under the collar by then. The Ribble lads went last, seemingly with hardly any decent gear, full of scepticism and apathy and determined not to comply as was their normal attitude at such events.

Two sprained ankles, three wet Bailiffs, one bad back and much leg pulling later saw everyone sat in a room at Ten thirty at night supping lukewarm coffee and very ready for home. Roger Mcbane was not giving up yet though. He demanded we all open our pocket books, then write down a brief summary of events highlighting the benefits and lessons learnt from the exercise. This was then to be followed by an example from some poor sods notebook picked at random. Fifteen tedious minutes later had Roger stalking round the room hands clasped heartily looking for a victim. We all tried to look inconspicuous as he paced around, eventually he stopped in his tracks and turned, he was looking straight at little Len Ibbotson,

"Len, enlighten us from your notes"

Len shuffled awkwardly for a few seconds in his chair hardly looking up, until slowly opening his pocket book and coughing slightly as he breathed in. It was all an act of course. He held the book aloft reading out his prognosis of the night's event in sombre Lancastrian monotone.

"No torch, no radio, no phone, no night sight, and no hope!"

Briefly you could have heard a pin drop, disbelief written across the face of every person in that room. Inevitably this was soon superseded by unbidden and prolonged laughter lasting five minutes at least. Roger Mcbane grimaced in facial pain completely helpless and deflated; we had no alternative other than to drift off home.

In 1986 not only were we now armed with the wonders of P.A.C.E. we also gained another string to our bow in the form of "call out Bailiffs". These were essentially part timers taken on to help specifically with enforcement work. The only temporary staff used prior to this had been "Honorary Bailiffs", the difference being they were unpaid and used only for rod and line work and assigned to a specific angling clubs waters. They had been eventually scrapped due to various forms of mild corruption, such as turning up on waters they weren't supposed to be on or becoming power crazy and violent to innocent members. We got various complaints about heavy handed tactics on venues like Windermere enforced by Honorary Bailiffs who should have been down in Manchester or somewhere on the Ribble.

The decision to have paid call out Bailiffs was considered a bit radical in Water Authority terms, but most welcome none the less. They were actually officially classed as reserve Bailiffs and had a remit of working only with a full time Bailiff. This ensured they were permanently supervised and under control. The first reserve Bailiff to be taken on in Brockely came highly recommended by none other than Bob Harmer. Malcolm Spedding was a self employed builder who lived on Cinderbarrow council estate; he allegedly loved fishing but never had time to do it. He had successfully navigated himself through two days of training with the other new recruits under the directions of Roger Mcbane.

I arranged to pick him up at his home address on a July evening at ten o clock. His house was just round the corner from the notorious Pete Tomlinson so I approached with some trepidation. I was surprised to see his bran new Tranny van parked with an American monster Chevrolet outside what can only described as a hovel. It was obvious where his priorities lay. Malcolm was a jolly giant of a bloke even though he wasn't tall he was massive, built like the proverbial brick shit house. He greeted me with a gripping hand shake that left me wincing despite my cover up smile. He grinned through minced teeth that he apparently damaged falling forty feet off a ladder from a roof job onto the pavement. Evidently he just picked himself up and carried on working. Malcolm was a seriously hard bloke of that there was no doubt. I decided that if we did come across any poachers he would be Dirty Harry personified, which was really quite comforting. His only obvious fault was a horrendous cough that lasted a year; this of course was not an asset when sneaking around in the dark. I spent many an hour with Malcolm and found him spot on, even though he was a bit of an enigma.

Billy Ferguson was the second call out Bailiff I worked with, he was by far and out the best. He was keen beyond belief, so much so that he put most full timers to shame. Billy was also a self employed builder, I could never understand why a lad who worked twelve hours a day would then willingly come out at Ten o clock at night, work with me, then go home at four a.m. Billy would sleep till seven if he was lucky then get up and do another twelve hours at the day job. I did keep an eye on this situation though as Billy would often fall asleep on the job, which lets face it was hardly surprising. I had some good cases with Billy mainly because he was prepared to come on the lakes at weekends. It was on one such patrol that we came across Steven Hammond. I had arranged a patrol on Windermere to check for maggoters, Hank had observed some anglers fishing regularly on Rampholme in the last few weeks. The Lake wardens had passed information to Hank that maggots were being used on a regular basis. Rampholme is a small wooded island mid way between the east and west shore close to Bowness. Hank had taken great pains to point out how he had been powerless to get near them in their splendid isolation. It wasn't long after the highly entertaining finale to Bailiffs training that Billy and I did this particular patrol. It was a five a.m. start covering the west shore; activity was brisk with a couple of routine maggot offenders nabbed at Graythwaite in a typical pincer movement of stealth and teamwork. We were both well fired up on a beautiful spring morning, a small herd of Graythwaite red deer hurdled a fence before crossing the road in front of my car. I was driving down the hill from Sawrey toward the ferry when it became obvious there was activity on Rampholme. I stopped the car to check it out. Never rush or panic when observing on going events, so we had a brew and brought our notebooks efficiently up to speed. I had to teach Billy the finer points of this particular art; he was a quick learner fortunately. I got out of the car to enjoy the warm early sun in my face. Billy was already scanning the island.

"What do you see Bill?"

"Two men and a young lad I think all on this side"

I looked across and confirmed his analysis

"There are more than a few rods an all, and they're sitting in the sun just like the flaming untouchables"

I sat to chew things over for a few minutes, there were two choices. We could make elaborate notes, sit, observe, swear under our breath, and then bugger off, or go for the second pro active option. It was no contest these lads were obviously taking the piss.

"Bill I've seen enough, that Dinghy's still at the boating centre in Coniston I think we should go for it, these buggers look set for the day".

Billy was well up for it. We returned to the scene an hour later at around eight fifteen, everything was as we had left it, just as though we hadn't been away and all three suspects were still in place. I drove down to the shore and we quickly launched the boat. The sponsons thankfully had been repaired since the near miss on Coniston with Danny, and the little four horse outboard fit like a glove. We were soon speeding effortlessly across the lake resembling any other boat owner on the water. We could easily have been on our way to one of the many yachts moored offshore; instead we were our own version of the SAS on a covert mission. I took a roundabout route enabling a silent beaching on the east side totally undetected. The shoreline was ideal having an inviting shingle approach. We moved on to our quarry very quickly implementing total surprise and taking a man each, the small boy was left isolated to watch the show. Pots of maggots, worms, and bran littered the immediate surroundings; it was obvious that this was blatant disregard for the law. I kept half an eye on Billy while he booked the first guy, who as it turned out had a rod licence, so no problem there with ID. He played the ignorant victim as was par for the course. My man was much laid back sat in his deck chair; he was about forty and looked fairly well off. He had that sort of polished look with accompanying suntan, expensive clothes, and top of the range gear. He too pleaded ignorance despite having three rods out, I inspected each rod finding maggots on them all, plus a catapult that lay on top of his bait box. His demeanor became cold and calculated; he spoke in a sophisticated boardroom language, which I found a little unnerving at the time. The worrying factor was that he amazingly couldn't produce any ID; I was starting to get wary. The next few minutes were spent on interrogation, but with little success, he was a cool customer. I was given a very plausible name John Robinson at an address in Poulton-le-Fylde. D.O.B. 18-12-43. I seized four maggot pots, his catapult, and six pristine brown trout, the smallest being about a pound and a half. Windermere trout are some of the worlds finest fish and don't deserve to die at the hands of maggoters from Blackpool. The only clues so far to the mans ID was confirmation by his mate. I did have another vital lead however, moored nearby was their transport a small wooden boat with the name *"blue minnow"* clearly visible on the hull. I had no reason to doubt Robinsons details at this juncture especially when he gave his occupation as a company director. We left the scene with what appeared to be a pretty good case.

The paperwork for the case was processed as usual resulting in Billy's victim routinely attending court in August that same year; he pleaded guilty and was successfully fined. The summons to Robinson however came back as "not known at this address". I was mortified was this cool dude going to get away with it? Not if I could help it. I liaised with Dot Squires in legal, but no joy even with the voters register, or any other enquiries for that matter. I carefully revisited my pocket book where of course I eventually found the name of the small boat. I had forgotten about this clue, so the following day I visited the Lake Wardens Office for a brew and presented *"blue minnow"* to Albert Palmer. A quick check with the register produced nothing except a strained look on Albert's face

"I wonder, I just wonder"

"Come on Albert what's on your mind"

"Well I think yon lial bugger just might belong to anuther yan"

I was intrigued as Albert tapped his fingers on the table to try and stimulate his memory cells, then he looked up.

"Aye Aye, that's it, that's it Jack, yon lial boat belongs wid *"out of the blue"* a posh yacht int marina"

Right, so now we were making progress, my man was the owner of the yacht *"out of the blue* and the yachts tender was *"blue minnow"* bingo! His name came back as Steven Hammond from an address in Blackpool and as was often the case when on the wrong end of a porkies ID, the date of birth matched up, it had to be him. I thanked Albert for solving the case and left in good spirits.

I waited till my next working Saturday before traveling down to Blackpool to surprise our man, I took Billy of course and during the journey we had an argument about what the guy looked like. Doubt about recognising offenders is a common cause of worry to any Bailiff, but usually as soon as they are clocked again it all comes flooding back. The exception was of course in my case Pete Thomson back at the weir in Brockley. I was worrying about this guy a lot during the journey down to Blackpool. The house proved easy to find in the salubrious surroundings of the stockbroker belt. I knocked on the front door of a mock Georgian house of some splendour. The woman that answered was about thirty five and drop dead gorgeous. She was also extremely pleasant and helpful and obviously totally unaware of her husbands fishing misdemeanors. Despite the almost overwhelming distraction I learned that her husband was actually away, but would however be visiting their beloved boat at Bowness the following Sunday. I left after promising to visit him there to clear everything up. Progress was at last being made, even if it did mean waiting a week and changing a day off.

It was mid September as Billy and I eyeballed a man on a large sumptuous yacht, when we approached he didn't bat an eyelid, was it him? Nearer and nearer, until only a few feet separated us.

"Good morning, Mr. Hammond"?

He nodded but didn't make eye contact or even look up, I had a flash of recognition or so I thought. I introduced myself and Billy before outlining the reason for our visit. I was trying to decide if it was definitely him. In my subconscious I knew it was, but doubt can grow like a cancer, I exchanged brief discreet glances with Billy who was obviously going through the same emotions. Next I decided to go for it!

"You are the man I reported on Rampholme using maggots, not producing a licence, and failing to state a correct name and address"

He looked up then alright, I definitely had his full attention at that stage. His face was familiar, he was the one, and I was sure feeling convinced at last.

"Not me lad never go fishing these days, sorry can't help you".

Well that was pretty clear, message understood, but never mind stick to your guns I told myself. I checked his details which he couldn't deny, cautioned him and told him I was reporting him anyway. He wasn't happy that's for sure, his gorgeous wife looked mortified and shocked when his name went in the book; I surmised a substantial row would be on the cards after we had made our retreat. On leaving I turned to Billy as soon as we were out of earshot

"Well Billy what do you reckon"

"I'm not sure Jack"

I could have throttled him, still in for a penny. I was sure, but for some reason doubts lingered, I asked myself, could I still be wrong?

The day of the trial eventually came and no plea or even acknowledgement had been submitted from Hammond. I didn't sleep the night before, what if I had fucked up big style?

I was actually present at court ready for a brief with Victor Bailey, I was pacing round the foyer, I was very worried, and could it really be that it wasn't him? It was 09.45 for a 10.00 start when Victor strode casually in. He looked at me dead pan.

"Has our man turned up yet Jack?"

"No Mr. Bailey, not a sign

"Well well that's a pity"

I was sweating buckets at this point; Victor gave a wry smile, then gestured and put his hand on my shoulder.

"Jack lad don't fret yourself our mans capitulated, he phoned in at half nine and entered a guilty plea"

I let out a relieved whoop and everyone looked my way in disgust, I turned on Victor,

"Never in doubt Mr. Bailey, never in doubt".

25

THE YEAR OF TROUGHS

1987 proved to be another pivotal year for varied reasons primarily because of a phenomenal run of fish into the Stock system, the river was still improving satisfactorily year on year, a fact that the whole team took great satisfaction in. The first few months were none descript apart from a new store erected at Croftgill. Big Don and I demolished the old one, which was a welcome diversion during the quiet spell after Christmas. The task required hours of physical labour, smashing all the old asbestos sheets, putting them to one side and supervising their removal. I don't think we would get near such a task today; this work would be assigned to a specialist firm at great expense no doubt.

A new like for like concrete sectioned building was soon erected and stands to this day. The work was completed in February the day when Ian Botham stuck it on the Aussies giving us all a big lift.

The salmon season began quietly with very few "Springers" in evidence, these fine fish are the first to enter the river on the quest to spawn in the back end; they are understandably much coveted by anglers due to the immaculate condition in which they arrive, well fed and fresh from the ocean. Their value is immense not just for the quality of flesh, but significantly for the financial rewards they also bring. In my early years of employment spring run fish were more common with most taken in February and a handful in March. They were nearly always caught in the long dub, the exceptions being those taken downstream in Broxton Park. The sight of a springer laid on the bank is the finest sight any angler could hope for, bringing a much needed lift to the entire angling and Bailiff Fraternity. The poaching population as with most things changed each year and 1987 was no exception, a couple of new juveniles appeared on the scene in the spring. Firstly a lad of about fourteen materialised amongst the members of Brockley AA. He just appeared from nowhere, he innocently watched the Mafia worming at Haig Bridge, or fly fishing in Bluebell meadow. Nobody bothered to ask him why he was there, who he was, or what he wanted. It wasn't until April that events moved on, the lad actually began fishing for himself, but still he wasn't challenged. Eventually Bob Harmer phoned me one morning about various club matters and this lad's participation cropped up. I had already concluded that he was just a kid and not worth the bother, but Bob wanted him checked out any way. I came across the lad at Haig Bridge later that very morning, he was not huge on communication, however I did establish his name was Thomas Thackeray and that he was fourteen years old and of diminutive stature. I struggled with pleasantries leaving him to be aware that I at least expected him to buy a fishing license as well as making peace with the association to obtain a permit. Complaints continued regarding this lad however who apparently was still fishing without any form of the required paperwork. It came to pass that Brockley AA members led vociferously by Thomas "pig eyes" Williams among others eventually chucked him off. This only drove him on to the town stretch where our paths would soon cross again of course. I asked him nicely again and again to get a license, but I somehow always felt he wasn't taking it in. Subsequently I visited his mother soon after, she was suitably horrified assuring me in no uncertain terms that all would be sorted out. In June he officially became a nuisance due to his over enthusiasm with fishing all day and everyday, even when he was supposed to be at school. I didn't need that particular hassle of an errant schoolboy. The next phase saw him worming at the railings on Railway dub despite a byelaw stating fly only. I warned him yet again until finally two days later I had no choice but to book him for the same offence. Big Don was with me and christened him "Tom Thumb". He inevitably graduated on to snatching after forming several casual associations with the likes of Jez Bergerac and Les Gaunt of all people. Also of course the loathsome shape of Les Paltrow was still on the scene, this resulted in a terrible discovery one July afternoon. On my return home I was informed by Maggie that during my absence that day Paltrow himself had actually had the nerve to walk up my garden path and then knock on the door. Maggie had answered with her two lads standing behind. I listened in horror while she recalled how this scabby little man had informed her that this was in fact the house he was brought up in. I couldn't believe it. The cocky bastard then went on to openly admire her two lads with perverse enthusiasm. Fortunately Maggie was no fool and soon realised who he was from our conversations previously. He even tried to wheedle his way in to see his former abode; I needn't have worried because Maggie sent him packing. I know if I had come home to find Paltrow still on the premises I might have had serious difficulty with any form of self control.

Things did come to a head with Tom Thumb in August, when I again caught him snatching on Railway dub. He was just such a weird lad, conversations were always minimal on his part, and he had the personality and demeanor of a drug laden slug.

I approached him more than somewhat annoyed by his disregard for my presence; he blatantly trotted a worm at the end of his rod with total disregard for any laws.

"Now then Thomas, what the hell are you on with, don't you ever listen"

"Fuck off and let me alone, go and harass someone else"

I was quite surprised; this was the longest sentence he had ever said to me.

This pathetic little lad with an iron face was still so defiant against society. I was taking out my book yet again when things rapidly got a whole lot worse, out of the blue and on to the scene came none other than Paul Cranston, ex stone throwing, hooter blowing, poacher hard case.

"Carter leave yon lad alone or Ill deck you, you Bastard"

It was obvious Cranston was well wound up at this point, tattoos throbbing, and long hair blowing menacingly in the hot summer breeze. Tom Thumb was laughing, a phenomenon I had never witnessed before.

I was obviously in trouble, nevertheless I ignored Cranston and started to book the lad anyway, regrettably Cranston then made a lunge at me grabbing my shirt collar in the process. He was twice my size so I was in deep brown stuff at this point. My saviour turned out to be two men who just happened to be walking down the path, their presence prompted my assailant to literally put me down on the spot. I decided at this point a tactful retreat was required. Brockley police station was only yards away and it was here that I urgently sought the help of my good friend Sergeant Jonty Jones. Ten minutes later I returned to the scene with Jonty to find both Tom Thumb and Cranston amazingly still there. I then managed to do the necessary including booking Cranston for obstruction, during the process he threatened to kill me at some future date. I needed several beers at the end of that day I can tell you.

Poaching during the late summer that year was as bad as ever with cases against Bergerac, Sam McGowan, and Cliff Woof already in the bag for use of snares.

Les Gaunt, Sam McGowan, and Jez Bergerac formed a working alliance with the aid of a three wheeled Reliant van circa "Only fools and horses".

I chased the shadow of that motorised shed around the south lakes for quite some time; I even searched it twice without success. The whole episode had the air of a TV sit com, the damn vehicle was turning up all over the place, and once they even waved at me passing in the opposite direction. I eventually did manage to bring them down; the buggers were poaching lake trout that had moved up into Troutbeck to spawn. It was the first week in October; I had arranged to pick up Billy Ferguson at his home address at eleven thirty one Saturday night. I arrived at Billy's road end togged out in full camo gear and wool hat, only to realise I wasn't completely sure which was his house. I narrowed it down to two finally going for the one with a light in the front window. The guy who answered was to my dismay not Billy at all, he stood there absolutely terrified weighing up what to all intents and purpose looked like an urban guerrilla.

Eventually I persuaded him of my good intentions; apprehensively he then informed me that next door was where I needed to be. Billy was mortified when I confessed my mistake.

The decision to go up Troutbeck was based partly on seasonal timing and partly instinct. The gut feeling was subconsciously telling me to venture that way and follow my nose. Troutbeck like Brockdale is a cul-de-sac so if anybody ventured up they were trapped. I drove circumspectly up the valley without lights, it was twelve thirty a.m. It wasn't long before I spotted a tell tale light flash close to the river bank. I parked up and we walked slowly in, the trotter type vehicle was only two hundred yards upstream in a gateway. I gestured to Billy that we simply wait at the van. Inevitably it wasn't long before the three men returned. It was a lovely feeling intercepting them on their return; needless to say they were bang to rights. I relieved them of five mature trout, each around two to three pounds weight together with, one gaff, one landing net, and a lamp with battery. No threat of violence was offered, which fortunately was the norm with those lads. The Trotter van never surfaced ever again after that night thankfully. I suspect that it was probably near the end of its natural life anyway.

In the late summer and early backend of that year the two main troughs at Haig Bridge and Stanwick experienced phenomenal runs of fish, which in turn was attracting most of the Mafia from the BAA. I had no choice but to up the anti and spend more time in those areas. The main ring leader was my old friend Reg Daly. Reg was just plain greedy, it was unfortunate because he had fished the R Stock all his life from boyhood. Reg new every stretch, every pool, and every living creature in that particular environment. The real tragedy of this situation was the very fact that Reg could catch fish fair and square, as well as, if not better than anyone on the river. I have seen anglers fish all day drowning worm after worm at Stanwick trough and in perfect fishing conditions, but never land a single fish, and then at ten past four Reg would drop in after work. He would imperturbably tackle up, amble down to the water, roll a fag whilst listening to a catalogue of excuses from the assembled group as to why not a single fish had been bagged. Reg of course was weighing up form before strolling across to throw his first cast …and Bang! He was into a salmon straight away, more than likely but not necessarily hooked fair and square. This of course could be too much for those watching on, they just couldn't handle it, tempers flared, jealousy and arguments developed. How could this man come out of the blue and catch fish so regularly. If only they had just stopped to think, Reg had a lifetime's knowledge, he was the King.

The worst scenario at the troughs sprung from little "cliques" that developed, the right or wrong people together, depending on which side of the fence you stood. Certain liaisons flourished and encouraged foul hooking more than others. If a decent bona fida angler was fishing he would usually report that many fish had been returned, which was the legal requirement, and simply due to his presence. I had seen for myself the manner in which this was often performed. It was not unusual for salmon to be unhooked then just kicked casually back over the edge into the river, or thrown unceremoniously into rapid water. The survival rate of returned fish depends a great deal on the method and care used by any angler.

My considerable efforts in this area were helped a great deal by Bob Harmer the Gentleman farmer and teacher of animal husbandry in my former life. Bob and I became very good friends strengthened by a resolve to stamp out the callous actions of some members of the Brockley psycho Mafia. When October arrived continuous periods of wet weather brought more fish through the troughs, especially Stanwick due to its downstream first come first serve advantage. Reg Daly was making a fortune taking up to four and five fish each evening. He was not alone, with early morning shifts also landing a fair supply. The art of foul hooking was refined almost entirely by Reg, he perfected a method hitherto never seen before. Stanwick trough was essentially a narrow neck of water at the top that plunged into a lower, wider and slightly calmer section. The banks are made entirely of steep limestone and treacherous to the unfamiliar. Anglers could either fish in the lower section where very few were landed, or queue to fish the much coveted "top draw" as it was affectionately known. I was so concerned by this time about activities there; I consulted Dick Myers and Roger Mcbane about bringing in legislation. Bob Harmer was backing me to the hilt, which put his standing within the BAA at some risk I might add. Poor old Bob was fighting against the tide because most committee members were bang at it themselves anyway. Roger eventually decided that a byelaw may be the answer, to ban worming and spinning, now that would be nice.

The whole business came to a head during mid October when I discovered that Reg Daly had refined the process even further. He used his depth of knowledge to develop a unique process in the Stanwick trough top draw. It materialised that in the very fast water of the neck close to the top lay a substantial lump of rock. Reg had observed salmon actually using this rock as a resting place whilst negotiating a route through on migration. This situation allowed him to cast a line upstream, and then use the current to float it past the mouth of a resting or traveling fish. The line then actually ran through the mouth of the fish hooking the unfortunate beast from the outside in. Remarkable as this may seem, this is what actually happened resulting in most salmon ending up foul hooked in the mouth, or in other words even though the hook was technically in its mouth it was still foul hooked. I ultimately got wise to this con trick of course through my powers of observation. I had some difficulty in convincing anyone at first, until first Dick and then Roger Mcbane both witnessed it for themselves. I got together with Bob Harmer who called an extraordinary BAA committee meeting to discuss the problem. This was quite animated whilst good argued against evil; fortunately Roger was there to add his persuasive arm of Authority. We won the night, but only just, by a narrow vote to return all fish not hooked within the mouth. This was a start but not nearly enough in my book, unless a bailiff was actually present to witness the act, most fish would still be knocked on the head. The water Authority was still going to push for a byelaw and introduce a fly only rule on both troughs, so it was still game on.

The situation worsened right to the end, I will always remember the final wet miserable day of the season in October 1987. A huge coloured spate brought all the Mafia men to Stanwick trough, I spent ten hours policing them and saw over thirty foul hooked fish returned not to mention all those kept. The river became so high that only the calm back eddies could be fished. The die hard including Reg Daly stayed to the bitter end, I was disgusted with the lot of them. The byelaw had been up for recommendation in mid October, but Roger Mcbane was on leave at the critical point. This was a cruel turn of fate. His stand in, a District fishery Officer drafted down from Carlisle was definitely got at by the BAA and caving in to pressure, naively he sided with the Angling club. They still had to introduce rules of policing of their own. I was fuming and left to sweat until Roger returned, I just new it wouldn't happen.

Roger Mcbane was outraged of course, but fortunately an intervention from another source provided us with one final card left to play.

The stretch of river in question from Stanwick trough upstream to Haig Bridge is owned by The National Trust, who in turn leased it to the BAA. The Trust had by fair means or foul got wind of the current situation and been so concerned that a letter was sent to the club secretary threatening to terminate their lease if a fly only rule was not introduced. The letter apparently outlined the Trusts concern that these dubious fishing techniques were a threat to its good name. Bob Harmer broke the good news to me just before Christmas and more importantly before their AGM. He was almost as pleased as I was as we enjoyed a brew in my back kitchen.

"That should cap em Jack, thall not be many fish caught on fly in yon troughs, and I'm going to recommend a restriction, twenty yards below and above the neck of each trough as well".

I couldn't wait to break the news to Roger Mcbane. The AGM which I always attended was notable for the absence of the normally vociferous Reg Daly and his cronies. The twenty yard limit was voted in with ease amid resigned silence and is still in place to this day. Over eleven hundred salmon were caught on rod and line that year on the R Brock and its tributaries, not to mention all the hundreds of sea trout. A fair proportion probably 40% would come from those troughs alone.

26

GLUE AND GUNS

1988 was notable for a few more firsts in my career, a new MG Metro for myself for starters, I had never actually had a brand new car before although strictly speaking it was an ex demo model from the showroom with just a few miles on the clock. I thought it was a bit flash for a humble Beck watcher especially being white; Maggie talked me into it of course which didn't take much doing to be fair.

A new enterprise in propagation, namely char rearing was another first in February. This was implemented in Coniston using fine gill nets just off Brantwood. The idea being to catch char close to spawning and either strip the eggs out on site or keep the hen fish on until ripe. This process was not one I felt comfortable with because the mortality rate whilst handling these fish was very high. We did obtain many thousand eggs during this operation however, but the amount of fry eventually produced at the hatchery was in my opinion not justifiable. It was considered that natural stocks of these fine fish were so much in decline that propagation was necessary. I have always been of the opinion however that the change in close season and successful prosecution of offenders had a much greater influence on the eventual recovery of char stocks in Coniston. It must also be said that improvements in water quality especially in Windermere during the nineteen nineties has also helped immensely. The practical side of char netting was a ball ache of a job and very labour intensive. I spent many hours with Hank and Danny setting nets from a boat just off the shore to be then left to fish overnight and lifted at dawn. Much mortality occurred at this stage due to handling and the effects that shallow water had on these fish dragged up out of a net. It wasn't unusual for the swim bladder to pop like a balloon when a fish was removed; the fish was obviously doomed from that point on. The cold freezing mornings also created other problems when working in a wet environment, spending a penny when numb fingers were dropping off with cold was quite a challenge. I remember one particular morning when the temperature was about minus five, I had to help poor old Danny by pulling his fly zip up for him, and thankfully he had just about managed the previous part of the operation himself.

The spring period saw Char once again the main target for exploitation, some anglers were still prepared to risk capture by taking and selling on the fish. One weekend in April I had completed a fairly uneventful early patrol on Windermere with Hank, to which end I left him at his home at about half eleven. I arrived home myself in Brockley at ten to twelve anticipating a nice fry up, only to have Hank on the phone at midday.

"Jack my missus has just phoned me here int club, the Police have got three buggers at Windermere Nick with a load of Char, they were trying to sell em tut White Hart. I've had a drink! So I think to be on the safe side could you come and deal with it?"

I was stunned, Hank was telling me that in the space of half an hour since I left him he was already under the influence. I was dropped right in it, and more significantly he was the Boss on the day, what could I do?

"Aye OK Albert I suppose so, are you coming down"?

"No I'll gan back home and wait"

This was Hank at his best, in full control yet sat at home.

I retraced the journey to Windermere Police station to be confronted by three enthusiastic Bobbies very keen to sort out these latest Wiganites. The culprits had a bag of about one hundred char complete with the usual tell tale signs of maggot use. They openly admitted everything so quite a decent case was developing, possession of fish during the close season, and use of illegal bait. I took over the formalities of booking each man plus seizure of the big sack full of char. I had a brew with the Police during which Hank predictably phoned.

"Call in on thee way home Jack"

We all laughed together before I left, Hank's maneuvers were well known by all.

During May I planned a patrol on Coniston with Paul Nugent the Bailiff on the R Duddon. Paul was a smashing lad and another ex policeman. He did regrettably however have rather a drink problem that would inevitably be his eventual downfall. It was the classic state of affairs when he couldn't see his own problem, but everyone else did of course, he would put orange juice in his flask and be forever swigging at it. His breath was a fire hazard to anyone that smoked. I think the fact that he was single and living alone in an isolated cottage in the Duddon valley contributed to his dilemma. He hadn't proved a problem to me up until that particular day; however on this particular occasion when I met him at the boating centre it was obvious he was a bit worse for wear. I just tried to work round him as I maneuvered our boat down to the shore. Paul was rather quiet on the day, but the sickly sweet smell of stale booze hung on his every laboured word.

"Must have a bit of flu Jack, I'm feelin in poor fettle"

I nodded in reluctant agreement trying to ignore the situation when in reality He should have been sent packing. We eventually set sail at which point Paul perked up a bit. The first boat we came to had two anglers aboard and Paul took the oars with considerable difficulty much to my concern. I checked the first angler while they both looked on with obvious trepidations. Paul's boat handling skills left a lot to be desired at the best of times, so it was no surprise when he caused a clumsy and noisy docking procedure, luckily no damaged occurred. The first angler reluctantly admitted not having a licence, a fact that prompted Paul into an immediate prognosis and a fit of giggles.

"Who's a naughty boy then?"

This was said whilst demonstrably and sarcastically smacking the back of his hand before finally slumping forward across the oars.

I couldn't believe what I was seeing in front of my very eyes; it was a worst nightmare, while the two anglers gaped in open mouthed silence. I had never experienced anything quite like it before or since thank goodness. I managed to book the guy with no licence fairly quickly whilst bluffing Paul's behaviour as just his sense of humour. I was telling myself all the while that I would sadly have to report the incidence. I informed Paul we were heading back to shore making certain I alone handled the outboard; nevertheless he still managed to go arse over tit across the oars as we beached.

I informed the powers that be with some regret about Paul; I had to take responsibility for the situation not just for his sake, but to cover my own back as well. Ironically Paul fell over in his own kitchen a few days later breaking an arm in the process. Paul took a long period off sick and moved out of his lovely house. I looked in one day whilst up the Duddon valley only to be shocked by the state of the house and garden. Total mess and neglect are the only words to describe what I saw. That was eventually the end for Paul; he had little choice but to leave before he was pushed. I never saw him again after that day, but tales of his drunken exploits around Ulverston where he now lives occasionally come to light. The house was later sold off for a song as part of the privatisation process within the Water Authorities.

My next visit to Coniston was with Big Don in mid May, the day after seeing Liverpool remarkably beaten by Wimbledon in the FA cup final. This of course had put me in good spirits, however this particular patrol brought about a run in with two anglers who would make another mark on my career. I had laid a trap in the narrow section of Coniston between Brown Howe on the west shore and Nibthwaite to the east. I hid at Brown Howe amongst the trees to observe a small boat mid stream. I was being entertained meanwhile by a small group of bullfinches acrobatically combing every branch and twig of my surrounding foliage, I realised after a short time that the two men in the boat were bang at it with swim feeders, ground bait, and maggots. The plan was to see the crime then call in Don by radio, he would quickly motor round in the boat, pick me up and we could then do the business. This subsequently worked a treat; I climbed aboard and set off in a b-line for the two men. The heavens opened at this point which didn't help matters, I successfully caught both men red handed. I booked the older man of the two amidst some abuse despite him being in possession of a valid licence, It was raining so hard I had to use a pencil because the splattered pages of my notebook wouldn't take ink, I had learned this pitfall once before booking Sam Magowan in a thunder storm. The gist of his argument was that this guy hadn't been ground baiting or using maggot at all. The second younger bloke gave the same tale arguing just as vehemently. I seized a bucket full of bran and maggots before leaving hastily. The older man was Brian Kendal from Ince near Wigan, the second younger man as it turned out gave me a Joey, all I remember about him was a Liverpool FC tattoo on his forearm, tempting though it was at the time I decided not to go there. I was of course bitterly disappointed at losing one of my culprits; the legal department couldn't trace Michael Brown as he had put himself forward. The torrential rain had certainly clouded my judgment on that day.

Brian Kendal was found guilty at Hawkshead in November the same year despite a long and petty argument in court. He obviously got up the noses of the magistrates as well as everyone else because they fined him £200 with £50 costs. I was made up and chuckled to myself when Kendal left still rabbiting on about an appeal. The other guy of course was nowhere to be seen.

During the summer that year I continued to work with Reserves Billy Ferguson and Malcolm Spedding, also another helper was on board namely Tony Frobisher a factory worker from Ulverston. He was used quite a bit across on the Duddon, but sometimes came over my way to be used on the R leven catchment. Tony was a right old woman; he worried about almost everything and moaned about almost everything else. A patrol with Tony usually left me weary; worn down by his pessimism over fish stocks, river conditions, and general world affairs. In fact he bored the pants off everyone and we actually drew straws to see who got him next. Don christened him "Mr. twenty questions" due to the incessant grilling he imposed. Tony was also a bit nervous when it came to confrontation, so consequently I was rather worried as to what his reaction would be if we did get into anything tasty. He was for ever quizzing me about on going cases, or how well the other Reserve Bailiffs performed. I had heard just about enough one night, so a wicked idea I had been toying with was put into action. I innocently suggested a trip up Troutbeck and sure enough Tony immediately started his inquisition that lasted the whole journey.

"What's goin on up there then Jack? Does it get poached much? Who generally goes up there?"

I fed him with all sorts of bullshit about the likes of Cranston and Jez Bergerac, until I was even making myself nervous never mind Tony,

Cranston however was the one person that made Tony quake in his size tens, seemingly he had dished out a black eye on our Tony way back in his teens at Brockley Town hall dance. The memory was still very much alive, but what I deliberately failed to enlighten Tony with was the fact I myself had suffered the very same fate in the same place back in the late sixties, still that was life back then.

On arrival at Troutbeck I parked at Limefit Caravan Park just after eight-o-clock on a fine August evening knowing full well that nothing much occurred up this valley until at least the backend. I togged up in camo gear armed with a McLennan night sight and dragon torch.

"Follow me Tony and you take the scope"

One thing all Reserves loved was using the night vision equipment and Tony was no exception.

We set off up the road then cut through on an ancient footpath that gives an excellent view down to the river and up the valley. This is when I put plan X into operation,

"We need to be careful now Tony, I have it on good authority that there's been some action down here"

I could feel him stiffen as I spoke,

"What do you mean Jack? What sort of action"

"Your mate apparently"

"What mate? ...Who Jack...who?"

"Cranston and his Cronies I reckon"

I grinned mischievously to myself in the dark, while poor old Tony gasped almost falling over in the process.

"Don't worry though Tony, unless there's a white Granada parked at the bottom of this path we should be OK"

I was creasing myself as I crept quietly down the path desperately trying to keep control. Tony was stumbling perilously behind me. There was of course unbeknown to my companion an abandoned vehicle matching the very description positioned exactly as I had described it. Furthermore it had been there for at least twelve months. I stopped in dramatic fashion!

"Hear something Tony?"

"What Jack? ...What...where?

"Tony why don't you put the scope down the path, tell me what you see"

I watched gleefully whilst Tony clumsily arranged himself making more noise than a ratching hedgehog, I couldn't wait. Eventually he raised the scope; I could feel the tension in his body whilst he panned round. Suddenly he gave a sharp jerk and a squeak, Bingo he was on, hook line and sinker. He tried to tell me, his arm was waving, but his voice wouldn't go into gear, I pretended not to notice,

"See out Tony? What's to do? See out there or what like?"

"J-J-Jack ...It's... It's,"

"It's what Tony, what you seen mate?"

Tony was really struggling, I was just wishing Don was there, it was priceless, and eventually he managed to spit it out.

"Its...its...It's a fuckin Granada, yes a white one"

"You are joking aren't you Tony"

"No No have a look, see, see for yourself,"

I took the night- sight from him and peered at the offending vehicle.

"Well well Tony we had better move a bit canny"

I turned to my companion but he was nowhere to be seen, I was alone, he was away back, off up the same route we had come. I had chance of a good laugh to myself before following him back. I arrived back at the car to find Tony firmly sitting on a rock by the caravan park gate.

"What's to do Tony? Where did yu gan to"

"Jack, Jack, oh I am sorry, but I can't do this anymore"

"What on earth do you mean Tony?"

I was milking the situation to its limit, but I hadn't really expected such a dramatic reaction that actually made him run away. I started to feel a bit guilty because Tony basically threw the towel in there and then.

I took the poor bloke back home; the journey was conducted in total silence until we reached his house.

"Please don't tell any one Jack, please".

"Aye Tony don't worry yourself, we all get a bit scared sometime"

I didn't enlighten him about the old car and my prank; I think it might have made him feel even worse. I did relay it to Don however; none of us ever used Tony again after that. I felt very guilty, but Don assured me I had done the right thing because he for one wouldn't miss listening to Tony's endless whinging.

The summer was notable for one thing that year, the demise of Tom Thumb into the sordid world of drug abuse. He began with glue sniffing which not surprisingly he used to practice whilst out on the river bank with other like minded children and youths. There seemed to be a period up until around 1990 when the area around Brockley was littered with the tell tale plastic bags smeared with Evo-stick or similar substances. I came across Tom several times totally spaced out on glue, God only knows what it was doing to him. His long suffering parents were at their wits end, I met them one day at Railway dub worried sick about the whereabouts of number one son. The only consolation was, Tom spent less time fishing and more time experimenting with new substances. By the summer of 1989 he was hooked completely on Heroin, he was sixteen years old, getting bigger and nastier by the day. Fortunately for me he didn't bother with fishing anymore, but instead graduated to violence and burglary, then inevitably a young offender's institution. I only saw him on odd occasions after that as he disappeared off our radar for good. I have no doubt he will have a short sad life unless somebody in society gets to grips with him.

I carried on for the rest of the summer with Billy Ferguson and Malcolm Spedding sharing the load with Big Don. When the backend came Big Don became troubled with a serious back problem, he spent many weeks off work and out of the game. During November I ended up doing most of the redd counting on my own, this didn't bother me one bit, I could set off on fine frosty mornings with my two dogs as happy as Larry. It was one such day a Saturday, I had been working on the R Brant with many new redds recorded safely in my book, by Three fifteen I was parked up on the main road looking down the valley at the very top of this river. I was comfortably sat with a stale cup of coffee from my flask listening to the progress of the day's soccer. I often used this particular lay-by for observations both day and night. I had only been there ten minutes when I noticed a Black Land rover traveling down the lane crossing the beck. I put my binnocs on the vehicle and easily identified it as belonging to none other than our own Malcolm Spedding. The vehicle traveled up to Black Moss farm about three hundred yards past the beck. I wondered what Malcolm was on with in this neck of the woods, but I wasn't concerned, after all why should I be?

The Land rover was out of sight by now, but hadn't kept on going down the valley.

Then something odd happened, two men emerged from the farm buildings walking towards the beck in the valley bottom. This wasn't right, I couldn't explain it, I decided that further investigation was needed, so proceeded in my glaringly white MG Metro rather perplexed at the events unfolding. I had no choice but to follow the same route as the Land rover, I must have been visible to the two men as I approached.

On reaching the farm yard I parked right behind Malcolm's Land rover. I still believed that nothing untoward was happening, however my instincts were telling me different. These were soon justified when I walked circumspectly across the yard to a barn. I peered cautiously round to get a view down the steep field to the narrow head water. The sight before me was totally unexpected, aided by my trusty binnocs I saw Malcolm and another man stalking along the beck edge prodding and poking with a stick. I knew how many sea trout were spawning there because I had walked it myself that very same morning, I Looked again and to my amazement saw Malcolm kneel down on the bank holding a rifle, he actually had a gun. I withdrew for a brief moment breathing heavily to take it all in. I looked again just in time to see Malcolm fire the gun into the water. His mate then poked several times with the stick before Malcolm took very careful aim, again in a kneeling position, this time he fired and almost at once the second man pulled out a decent size fish. They put it on the bank to admire before Malcolm shot it again prompting them both to laugh. I watched in amazement whilst they then casually picked up the fish and headed slowly back up the field. I dashed to my car where fortunately the radio signal was strength five. I related the events quickly to our control centre and requested Police assistance immediately. I then dashed back to the sanctuary of the barn; my head was assimilating all the possibilities that could happen hear. What would he do? How will he react? He could shoot me for Christ's sake. I was stood by the barn just as the two men reached the gate from the field, our eyes met and Malcolm immediately dropped the fish behind the dry stone wall, but I saw it, they kept coming, my heart was pounding.

"Now then Malcolm, what you on with?"

"Nowt to bother you with Jack Carter"

His tone was civilised with a hint of menace, I brushed firmly passed them to pick up the fish.

"I saw it all Malcolm so you may as well stay where you are"

I held the fish aloft with mixed feelings of triumph and apprehension; both men kept walking until they reached the Land rover. Malcolm glanced back, just before he threw the rifle into the vehicle and shut the door. His companion who was unknown to me was an evil looking bastard, tall, scruffy, with dark angry features, and he stood his ground arms folded. "Where were the police?" I asked myself, and then right on queue in the distance on the wrong side of the valley I could see a white Panda. They were obviously lost, I was worried, and I desperately wanted possession of that gun.

I decided to book them both hoping this would give the Panda car a chance to locate us all. Malcolm's mate was Bill Cranston, brother of the notorious Paul Cranston. He actually said very little, it turned out that he worked for Malcolm and in fact they had been working at this very farm doing alterations in the house. I got Malcolm in my book successfully, cautioned them both, but still saw no sign of the Police. I decided that I had to have the gun come what may.

"I'm seizing yon rifle Malcolm, you know that don't you?"

"Aye whatever Jack if you must like"

This was my signal to go for it; I stepped up to the Land rover carefully opening the passenger side door. The rifle a 2.2 lay threateningly across the seat, I reached down and picked it up with considerable care. Guns have never been my thing so I wasn't sure what to expect. God knows what I thought was going to happen; I handled it like a bomb, nevertheless I did get it successfully into my car without any physical resistance although eyed intensely all the while by the two culprits.

It was at this juncture that Jonty Jones finally arrived looking more than a bit perplexed.

"Sorry Jack, I couldn't find the bloody place"

"Not to worry its all done"

Everyone seemed to relax a bit at this point not least of all me. I had actually pulled off the seizure of a rifle, an action never done before or since. Small banter was swapped for a few minutes and fags were smoked to calm things down, I pointed out to Malcolm that his days as a reserve Bailiff were well and truly numbered. Malcolm shrugged his shoulders indifferently, then as if trying to change the subject moved across to the Panda car obviously interested in its contents. I also looked in to see what on earth had attracted such attention. I could see a military helmet complete with artificial camouflaged foliage laid on the passenger seat. Malcolm pointed grinning, Jonty shuffled awkwardly.

"What's this then? New police uniform"

Everyone laughed except Jonty.

"I collect the stuff don't I? Military stuff, you know what's the word? Oh Aye memorabilia, Aye that's it memorabilia".

27

TWO WEDDINGS AND A FUNERAL

In February 1989 my old Boss and very good friend Joe Marwood had a severe stroke and died three days later. He was seventy four years old, still full of life and had just sown his plant seeds for the coming year. Poor Hannah steadfast as ever swore to grow them on just for Joe. I had the strangest feeling when I called round that day and inspected his creation set out meticulously in the back porch, just waiting for his ubiquitous TLC on returning from what turned out to be his final cup of tea. Joe had loved his retirement, doted on faithfully by Hannah. The garden was his treasure and main love in life not forgetting his pursuit of sea trout of course, so it was fitting he enjoyed his final contribution.

The funeral was attended by over one hundred and fifty people; I was one of the bearers with Big Don. I occasionally visit the grave to mull over old times and conquests with Joe. I tell him about the cut backs and changes in Fisheries and moan that they are all in the name of progress.

Later the same year Maggie and I tied the knot although we had been living together for several years; our big day was on April 8th which went without

a hitch, followed by a short honeymoon in Whitby. Danny got remarried
as well soon after, I only hope we didn't influence him. Danny had lived
alone since the untimely early death of Delia, but had coped well especially
as "a boy named Sue" only visited once in a blue moon. Don had christened
the lad so because he was obviously not the sex he wanted to be, we had
suspected for some time that Danny was troubled by his lads feminine traits.
Young Andrew had since moved away to Manchester and Danny confided
in me during a night patrol, apparently the lad was seriously considering a
sex change. Despite this burden I had noticed that Danny's demeanour was
on the up that spring and sure enough he informed me of his actions one
day whilst patrolling Windermere. Danny had joined a dating agency in the
New Year with immediate results. The first contact had been a local woman
from Carnforth, who by all accounts was a cleaner in her mid thirties.
Danny told me he had arranged to meet her in Lancaster for coffee.

"That's not very romantic Dan"

"Yes well I just wanted to suss her out before going any further"

What's she like then Dan?"

"Oh well…not my type actually"

"Why what happened?"

"Well, we were getting on fine, so I asked her back to my house the
following evening"

"Yes so how did it go Dan?"

This was starting to sound interesting, Danny Casanova on the loose!
Danny hesitated though giving a little embarrassed chuckle.

"Well, you'll never guess, I left her in the house while I went for some
fish and chips"

He sighed during a brief silence.

"And? Then what? Come on Dan you've started so you'd better finish"

Danny laughed again nervously.

"When I got back she was in the bedroom"

"Yes …and… C'mon Danny"

"Completely undressed"

"What!"

I clapped in amazement,

"Yahoo, never….Danny you old bugger, you old devil"

"No no no, not at all Jack, I sent her packing, can't be having any of all that nonsense"

"You are joking Dan, was she ugly or something?"

"No very nice actually, but that's not what I'm after Jack.

I couldn't wait to return home and relay the story to Maggie.

Danny's luck changed for the better or so it seemed soon after, because he met a widow from Cockermouth, none of us ever actually clapped eyes on the lady, but we new it was serious and a whirlwind romance quickly developed. Danny was a new man, smart, perky, and he even bought a new beret. In late May they eloped to Fort William only a month after first meeting. This was typical Danny, a living, breathing, walking cock up; he was gossip subject number one. Two weeks later however his world fell apart once again. I called round as soon as I found out, only to find a broken man sat alone in his cottage. Danny relayed how the pair hadn't hit it off at all well right from the day of the wedding, apparently she wouldn't let him smoke his pipe or wear his various items of head gear. He explained that she wouldn't let him do just about anything at all. Why hadn't he seen this coming?

Their return was even more dramatic when she insisted that she couldn't live with dogs, and issued an ultimatum, either they went or she did. I was stunned when Danny explained how he submissively took his beloved cocker spaniel and Delia's King Charles to the vet to have them put down, what on earth was he thinking about?

Knowing Danny like I did nothing usually surprised me, but this took the biscuit even by his eccentric standards. The tragic part was that she left anyway so the sacrifice was in vain.

I made Danny a cuppa, trying to convince him that he was best rid of the bitch. Later when I left the silence was eerie, I was so used to his little dogs yapping annoyingly when visitors came or left, and I would have given anything to be nipped on the ankle amid the din. Life went on for Danny despite one disaster following another; his resilience was as good as the next man and better than most.

Around the time of Danny's misfortunes the very mouthy Brian Kendal had appealed against the sentence handed out the previous year, to which ends a hearing was due in Lancaster Crown court. Lancaster courts are held in the Castle which is a formidable setting for any trial, so on arrival I was pleased to be on the right side of the law. We had a long wait that day until the hearing commenced, during which time Mr. Kendal was as bullish as ever. To rub salt in the wounds the guy with him in the boat was also there. Yes the same bloke that gave me a false ID complete with tatoo. It was none other than his son John Kendal. He turned out to be even cockier than his father. They both spent the morning bragging about a trip to Tenerife they were embarking on later that same day, following the inconvenience of this hearing of course. They greedily relayed how much benefit monies they had coming in. Of course all their previous exploits in the lakes were meticulously explained for mine and Don's benefit, they just never shut up! Other trials through the day meant we didn't get on until Three- o- clock, which only aloud time for the prosecution to outline the facts all over again. The Judge ordered an adjournment until the following day; this was the first ray of sunshine in an otherwise dreadful and tedious day. That now meant that those two scroats would not make their flight at Manchester. They protested of course, but a rebuke from the Judge did not help their cause one bit, I looked first at Don and then at Victor Bailey, it was difficult to keep a straight face.

The next day was a different kettle of fish because we went straight on to give our evidence. Both Don and I went back over events before the Kendal's took the stand. Brian Kendal defended himself inventing a bizarre tale that it was in fact his son that committed the offences and not himself on the fateful day. The idea behind this ploy was the fact that his son John could not be tried after the event, but all this hinged on whether he himself could get off. He even called his son in to the witness box to admit everything, it was quite extraordinary.

It was just before lunch that the Judge reconvened the court, I waited on baited breath.

The Kendal's looked confident, but I thought, surely not he won't buy such a load of bollocks will he?

I needn't have worried the Judge chastised them as the criminals they were; he gave Brian Kendal another £100 fine with £50 costs as well. The coup de grace that followed was unprecedented. He told the Authority to charge John Kendal for fishing without a licence and failing to state his correct name and address. I was asked to caution him there and then in the court. I did so with glee even though it was a bit nerve racking. John Kendal's face was a sight for sore eyes, I don't know if they ever got to Tenerife, but they never spoke another word or looked me in the face when we left the court.

The year of 1989 was time for more change, Big Don was suffering with back problems that still kept him off work for long periods and during these times he became miserable and depressed, where was the good humoured bloke I knew and loved?

Dick Myers was also in poor health, his chain smoking and lack of exercise was taking its toll. His patrols became less frequent, I relied more and more on Billy Ferguson and of course faithful old Danny, remarkably he was just as keen as ever.

The Privatisation of the water Authorities was a major event that year and Fisheries was farmed off into a newly formed National Rivers Authority (NRA) completely separated from North West water PLC. This kept us still within the umbrella of the Government funded by MAFF, and consequently turning into a powerful and effective organisation. Once again our own s section thankfully remained in tact; our corner was well fought as usual by Roger Mcbane resulting in all jobs being retained. Other functions within the NRA didn't fair as well as fisheries so I had a lot to be thankful for. Vesting day was September 1st and the first major change turned out to be Hanks installation as temporary Fisheries Inspector due entirely to the on going deterioration of Dick Myers. I was watching the situation very carefully, my main ambition in life had been for quite sometime to have Dick Myers job when he retired or left. I was sensing now that such a time was fast approaching. Hank was also keen of course, but I sensed complacency within, unwisely his belief was that the job was his by right.

In late summer Malcolm Spedding and Bill Cranston came to court both pleading guilty, which was no surprise. Long lists of charges were put forward including using a firearm to take fish, taking a sea trout in the close season, unclean fish, and unlicensed fishing.

They were each fined £50 for each charge with the exception of Spedding who was fined £100 for using the gun. The court clerk was absolutely made up with the rifle and paraded it in front of the magistrates held aloft in a dramatic western style pose; this produced a glare from Olivia Briggs that could have stripped paint.

My everlasting memory of that day however was the list of previous convictions held by my former colleague Malcolm Spedding. The list was the most disparate I ever heard read out, it included every kind of vehicle crime one could imagine, numerous acts of violence and grievous bodily harm, mostly directed at bad payers for work he had undertaken. He had even beaten up his wife and the most astonishing of all was cruelty to a parrot, I didn't dare to imagine what this must have entailed. He also had drug handling crimes to his name and most significantly other fire arms offences. I couldn't imagine why Bob Harmer thought he was such a sound bloke never mind the fact that I had worked along side him on numerous occasions. I think it is fortunate that no actual poaching incidents arose while out with Malcolm, I'm absolutely sure he would just have sorted them out on the spot.

I didn't have any dealings with Malcolm after that, but a curious and alarming incident just before Christmas that year may or may not have been down to him, I have never been able to confirm this one way or the other. A Saturday evening at home in December was uneventful until Midnight when we were all tucked up in bed. Firstly a taxi stopped outside the house, followed by a bemused driver hammering on the door.

"Taxi for a Mr. Carter?"

"No not mine mate sorry"

I just assumed it was a simple mistake, by twenty past twelve two more had turned up.

I had three taxi firms on the phone by half past. The door bell went again at 00.40 and standing there with his hat in hand was none other than a real life undertaker,

"Sorry Sir I have come for the body of a Mr. Jack Carter, who I believe has passed away, please except my condolences"

I looked in astonishment!

"Well I'm sorry to disappoint you pal, but I'm still alive"

The poor man was confused to say the least as indeed was I. He left empty handed thank God. Maggie was chain smoking by now and who could blame her. The door bell went again at 00.55, this time it was a Bobby with helmet in hand, I saved him the trouble

"I'm alive, and definitely still here, alright?"

28

MY BIG BREAK

Early in 1990 I changed my car after being persuaded far too easily by Maggie to buy a Blue Ford Capri, I was convinced back then every bloke should have had one. This particular car had only a sixteen hundred engine, as opposed to more powerful models around of two and three litres. I called it my sheep in wolfs clothing due to the iconic shape and sleek lines, but general lack of whumph!

I treasured the car nevertheless despite its poor handling, general impracticality, and my anxiety when negotiating any kind of hump back bridge.

Changes in the hierarchy at our Brockley Office since the NRA investiture meant that Roger Mcbane transferred up to Carlisle to greater things, which was no more than he deserved. He was still our main and general boss however, but with all of Cumbria to supervise as well. Our new Principal Fisheries officer was a woman would you believe. This caused general unease amongst the south Lakes team in what had always been generally accepted as a male preserve. Jean Slater was a thirty something red head who Danny took a shine to from day one, she was qualified up to the eyeballs, but very naïve about river and lake life per se. Personally I never had a problem, she respected Everyone's knowledge, let them get on with it and wasn't afraid to ask advice on the more practical aspects of day to day life. Jean Slater did not meet Hanks approval however, which predictably was no surprise to anyone. Hank would belittle the poor woman at every opportunity as only he could, and believe me he could. I'm sure she found this one of her greatest challenges at the time.

I monitored the situation carefully, after all he was doing the job that I desperately wanted and the present situation was bound to be working in my favour.

The NRA in its wisdom started to introduce more rigorous training as well as new health and safety measures. This now encompassed Bailiffs fitness and general health, which would then have to be checked and monitored on a fairly regular basis, as a result fitness classes were organised at Preston during January, February, and March to make sure we all stayed fit enough to do the job. I personally thought this was brilliant; I actually got paid for using a gym. We had swimming, circuit training, and even played five a side football, and then afterwards we could catch up on all the gossip with the Ribble lads. It was during the first session that I heard about the recent death of poor Len Ibbotson of "no hope" fame, he had apparently been suffering with cancer for quite some time. The usual cheerful banter from those lads was missing that day, not least without Lens contribution of jokes and wit.

Fitness training didn't bode well with everyone however, Danny strained his back the first week so gave up there and then, and fair enough he was well over sixty. Big Don and Hank however blatantly refused to participate claiming that it infringed their terms of employment. Personally I knew that Dons back was not up to it, but he just wouldn't admit it. Hank I suspect just thought it was all beneath him like all physical exertion. The biggest fuss revolved around a one off health check scheduled at Barrow. A private firm was engaged to do a sort of MOT on all staff. This required all the Bailiffs making a trip together on our allotted day. This was carried out amongst the usual grumblings and unrest from certain people. I went along and took the test with good results, which I actually found very reassuring. Danny, who would never dream of not doing what was asked, was Okay too. Hank and Don strutted around the place finding fault with everything and everybody until the inevitable happened. Hank lost his rag, they both spat out their dummies, Hank rounded everyone up and we all traveled home in silence. I think they both suspected some ulterior motive by the company to get rid of anyone who didn't come up to scratch. The trade union hat was worn firmly by both men that day. Don was also becoming awkward about many other things, which I put down to his on going health problems. He even took umbrage with reserve bailiffs being deployed on the lakes claiming they were doing the work that full time staff should be designated. It was in his eyes another threat. I never believed this train of thought personally, preferring to have more men on the ground to catch more offenders. To me it was that simple and didn't need complicating by over zealous union representatives.

The world was changing however, I could feel it in my bones, Dick Myers was laid up in hospital awaiting a by-pass operation, and I went with Don to pay him a visit. Dick was very philosophical that day and admitted his working days were probably over at fifty five. I left feeling decidedly upbeat, a state of mind I didn't share with Don. I was rather selfish I suppose, but Dick was fed up anyway, early retirement was what he really wanted all along.

That weekend I watched a classic cup final with United drawing three all with Crystal palace, but my main thoughts were on what lay ahead. The following Monday Dick Myers was officially retired after a successful heart operation. I knew then the time had arrived, I needed to prepare myself for the position I craved. It was my big chance, probably my only chance; it would be as far as I could go in the new organisation.

Sods law of course intervened in untimely fashion when my 90 year old Grandfather living alone at Knaresborough in Yorkshire became a concern. I didn't need distractions at this time, but when a complete stranger phoned to tell me that Grandpa Fred had bumped his car in the CO-OP Supermarket car park and what was I going to do about it. I obviously had to act in some way or at least do something. I was his closest living relative, usually visiting every couple of months or so. Fred was fiercely independent refusing most offers of help despite the fact that his beloved bungalow was falling down around him. I liaised with social services and his home help on a regular basis, so the situation was well monitored. Both Maggie and I would have preferred him settled in a home out of harms way, but he was having none of that. I made arrangements and visited him the following day after the phone call only to find him as defiant as ever. The offending vehicle was a Datsun Cherry, which despite its age only had seven thousand miles on the clock. The inside was like new apart from the mucky passenger seat where Fred's cat slept most days. The big shock came when I examined the exterior paintwork. Every corner of that car was slightly bent and each adorned with a different colour paint mark. The only journeys he attempted were trips to the CO-OP supermarket or the fish and chip shop. Parking at these venues was obviously now becoming beyond his years. These trips clearly weren't being achieved without some minor collision with the nearest vehicle. I suppose many a frustrated owner must have suffered as a consequence of Fred's parking technique.

I had no choice other than to confiscate his car keys; but when I put this to him he acted like a naughty child. He complained and sulked, making me feel quite awful. I was united with his home help who backed me up steadfastly. I took the keys anyway, and then left convinced that Grandpa Fred was off the road for good. This was the man who won Knaresborough Conservative club singles snooker championship at the age of 86, the very same man who won his crown green bowls title the year previously, Mr. super sportsman himself, it was distressing to witness his demise in this way.

I had decided the previous year to try and bolster my career chances by making some effort at gaining a further qualification in Fisheries work. I thought this was vital, but as time would tell I probably needn't have bothered. I began the Institute of Fisheries Management (IFM) certificate course in 1989. This was a correspondence course and by the end of May That year I had to sit an exam in Liverpool. I hadn't done any sort of academic work for years, since my O-levels in fact, so I was a bit apprehensive to say the least. I had managed the main correspondence work alright; in fact I had relished the information learned. On the day I traveled down with John Watson, he was the only other Bailiff taking the course; he was a big lad from Lancaster about thirty something and worked on the River Lune. I took to him right away and it was obvious that he was a keen enthusiastic Bailiff; this made the day pass much more easily as we exchanged stories and banter. The exam was routine enough, both of us leaving with good vibes.

A week later Grandpa Fred's home help phoned

"You'd better do something yon old buggers only gone down tut garage and got another key"

I couldn't believe what I was hearing, how had they not seen through him. I really had to do something this time. The vision conjured up in my mind of my ninety years old Grandad driving around Knaresborough was frightening.

I cleared it with Hank for a day off, I managed to hire a vehicle recovery lorry that was delivering to York the following day and they agreed to take me along.

On our arrival Grandpa Fred was not happy about what was happening, putting me through emotional hell while the driver hoisted his beloved Datsun on to the lorry, even his faithful cat was gazing into an empty garage. I have never felt so cruel taking his car the way I did that day, but needs must in the situation. I knew then that he couldn't go on much longer living as he did, it was a classic family state of affairs, an imminent day of reckoning that the majority of us will face one day or another. By the end of the day one lonely Datsun Cherry sat forlornly outside my house, I hadn't even thought about what I was going to do with it.

The position of Fisheries Inspector finally became advertised in early June and my interview date was down for the thirtieth. My main rivals were Hank obviously and a lad from South west Cumbria called Barry Gowans. Barry was the dark horse, a whiz kid with a degree, probably overqualified if anything, and a bit of an unknown force from my point of view. My advantage I hoped was experience, fourteen years opposed to his four. I couldn't afford to think about him too much, I just had to focus on my own quest. Hank of course believed the job was his for the taking and I couldn't help but feel for him slightly, after all he started back in 1956, surely he deserved a lift. His unpopularity was my main gain or so I hoped, not to mention his total disregard for any serious preparation.

My associate and very good friend Bob Harmer became my mentor leading up to the interview day, he coached me in presentation skills, management requirements, and not least he boosted my moral. I have a lot to thank Bob for to this day.

The time leading up to the interview was fairly uneventful; I continued with my one man quest against maggoters on the lakes and also spent some time down at the estuary. The time of year was just right for an influx of sea trout. Bob called frequently to check my list of questions for the interview and generally build me up. A presentation was required on what each candidate thought were the main requirements for the role of a Fishery Inspector. I was dreading this part, presentations never were and still aren't my cup of tea. I would much rather face a couple of hairy poachers, or be grilled in the witness box than stand up and spout expertise to a room full of people. I know plenty of experts in this particular exercise and each to their own I say.

The day of the interview was blessed with sunshine and warmth, spring was touching on to summer, my allotted time was eleven-o-clock, I was first on. I went over my notes before and after a meager breakfast; both dogs looked on with the usual expectancy of an early walk. I checked my presentation one last time placing each piece in order ready to be displayed on the overhead projector, which was the height of my technical skills back then.

I was greeted at the office with good luck wishes from just about everyone, I was very nervous, but totally focused and utterly determined to do well.

I first had to complete a type of written intelligence test that was all the rage at the time in such situations, full of silly puzzles and symbols designed to establish if you were a possible axe murderer in disguise. I never did find out how I got on. I then stood for ten long minutes in a lonely corridor waiting my fate; my heart was thumping in a manner I usually reserved for poaching incidents. I was soon put out of my misery and ushered in. The interviewers consisted of Roger Mcbane, Jean Slater, and a smart woman in a very distracting mini skirt who represented the personnel department at head office. I soon got into the way of things and threw everything I had at them including a faultless presentation; I think in hindsight I really enjoyed it. I left them with no doubt how much I wanted that particular job. I let them know that my crusade against crime for the past fourteen years was on the line, it was, I hoped payback time.

Normal service was resumed straight after the interviews, it usually took a while for decisions to be made in such matters and Hank was bragging how he had baffled them all with his superior knowledge and expertise of course.

The first signs of poaching up river were already showing with pristine sparkling sea trout recent arrivals into Brockley, my old adversary Sam McGowan was the year's first victim in a strange incident one night in July. I was on the second night patrol of the year with Billy Ferguson crossing The Iron Bridge at the top end of Brockley, It was about eleven thirty, when I casually glanced upstream only to see a light flash briefly across the river in Railway dub.

"Christ what the hells that Billy?"

He nodded in agreement,

"Yep saw summat"

I swung my old Capri into the car park conveniently positioned just after the bridge, quickly we togged up before heading warily back across the bridge on all fours. I stopped mid way, carefully glancing upstream, not a soul moved; even the mallards were dotted silently like dummies, heads within wings in peaceful summer slumber.

Suddenly there it was again only more obvious this time. A distinctive arc of light across the shimmering water, a few ducks fluttered away in protesting flight. I turned to Billy.

"We're in here lad, that's definitely a lamp"

We now had to pick our way quietly up to intercept our prey. It took a good ten minutes before we reached the cover of rhododendrons about half way up the path. This gave us chance to observe the action with ease. There was two men heading down toward us, the lamp was powerful and used sparingly. Within five minutes they stood precious little more than ten feet away … they were ours!

"Now then lads, Water Bailiffs"

I immediately recognised the distinctive Troll like features of Sam McGowan squinting under the dim footpath lighting; he spun round in frustrated anger, Quasimodo personified.

HN FOSTER

"Oh no not you fuckers again"

The second body was huddled with his back to us in a hooded fleece, he was attempting a fruitless act of non identity, and I peered round just enough to see the wispy ginger locks of Lesley Gaunt.

"How do Lesley what's going on then?"

He reluctantly lowered the hood and gave me a coy smirk.

"Dint thinks you lads were about yet like"

I began to fill my notebook with the necessities, it was all going nicely until I informed Sam that using a light was an offence and therefore I was seizing it. Sam had that spooky vacant zombie stare that I had learned over time to become very wary of, he was mumbling under his breath. I moved circumspectly to take the lamp from his right hand, but Sam was ready and turned sharply glaring in anger, I could see something dramatic was about to happen.

"Yur not havin my fuckin lamp, I never get owt back from you bastards"

I could only stare in astonishment this was obviously a reference to many items I had relieved Sam of over the years.

Sam violently lifted his lamp high enough to yank it violently from the motor bike battery nestled in a ladies hold all strapped across his shoulder. Sam held it aloft, and then in a wild act of triumph smashed it repeatedly on the iron railings. The light disintegrated disappearing noisily into the chilly waters of the River Stock, Sam wasn't done yet though, he also flung the bag complete with battery into the water as well amid another verbal onslaught.

Lesley Gaunt stood frozen to the spot seemingly just as shocked as we were.

It was such a bizarre act. I simply had to laugh at Sam, which of course didn't help the situation. I proceeded with booking both men, but kept a careful eye on Sam well aware he had numerous convictions for domestic and drink related violence. I think it was fair to assume Sam had been on the booze that night, so I wasn't taking any chances. I signaled to both men that I wanted to conduct a search. Billy did Les whilst I turned to Sam. I could see something climatic was about to kick off, but I didn't anticipate Sam's final contribution to the nights events. I faced him only to see Sam move back several paces still giving me the very evil eye and clenching grubby fists.

"Search…search, come on then"

His hands beckoned me in true football hooligan style, until Sam violently turned the pockets in his shabby jeans inside out, to which ends I tried to stop him going any further, it was by now blatantly obvious he possessed nothing further that could be deemed incriminating. Instead he began frantically throwing his clothes in all directions across the path, he was a man on a mission and nothing I said could placate him. Finally he stood there triumphantly, bollock naked on a public footpath in the middle of Brockley.

A pregnant pause of some magnitude led me to decide that leaving was our best course of action; after all we could retrieve the remains of Sam's lamp later. I turned towards our strange adversary

"That's fine Sam, if that's how you want to play it? But you'll both still be reported for using a light to facilitate the taking of fish"

I issued the caution before leaving, but neither man uttered another word. Sam leaned on the railings to light a joint, finally giving me a v-sign as we walked away. He was still totally naked.

I managed to recover the battery and green ladies hold all the following day, but never did find the bits of lamp. I knew it wouldn't matter in court, as was proven on the day some months later. I certainly got the attention of the bench when I related the events of that particular night. Sam got a fine and community service for his antics whereas Lesley Gaunt only got fined!

During those first two weeks in July various false rumours about the Fisheries Inspectors job were banded about as was the norm in such situations, but the Holy Grail finally came my way through a phone call from Roger Mcbane. I had finally cracked it the job was mine. I may have had a lucky break when I started out as a Water Bailiff, but this was all down to hard work, dedication and the general love of doing the job. Roger's exact words were:

"I could hardly give it to anybody else Jack could I",

That was music to my ears.

It took me a while to adjust the role; man management was all new to me. The first team brief was a nervy affair; Big Don was off again with back trouble which helped. My real concern though was Hank; after all I had been taking orders from him for fourteen years. It turned out fine in the end; he developed an air of inevitability emphasising the fact that he was winding down to retirement just pedaling his bike softer than ever.

I relished my new role with pride and tried to keep the team's momentum going, this was helped when another old adversary once again loomed back into view. It was September, very warm and calm, which is ideal estuary weather. I had myself spent quite a bit of time on the estuary. I had noticed my old friend Freddy Blencarn ratching about on several occasions obviously looking for netting holes. The salmon lave netting season finishes at the end of August, so I was concerned about the presence of Freddie especially as low flows prevented many salmon pushing on into fresh water. Freddie was following low water around the clock. He would be netting Flukes, but did he have a by-catch of salmon? That was the burning question. Danny had expressed concerns about Freddie and actually warned him the week previously during a "flue netting" sortie at Leighton viaduct. It was legal to operate a flue net; a method entirely designed for catching flukes, but did require the net to be attended throughout the operation. The fish had to be actively driven into the net using a method known as "possing". This involved a special piece of equipment that resembled the apparatus once used in washing clothes. It was basically a pole with a round flat end, which was smacked repeatedly hard down on the water to frighten any fish towards the net; it was a very knackering exercise. Of course had Danny seen any salmon on the day that would have been that?

I sent Danny with Paul Nugent's replacement Ken Davidson from Broughton to check things out at night. Ken was an ex postman and a big strong lad, just the type you need stood behind you when the going gets tough. Danny reported back the next day and explained how Freddie had been driving around the estuary most of the night without lights on. Freddie had a lifetime's experience of working out on the sands, I can't think of anyone who knew their way around like he did. Driving about in the dark would have been a risky business, quicksand's and hidden channels make Morecambe bay the most dangerous environment that we have to work in.

I met Danny and Ken the following day to discuss events, Danny's main observation of the night was a period spanning over an hour when Freddie was untraceable, mysteriously driving off into the night only to return some considerable time later without lights.

I planned an operation for that same night, it seemed fairly obvious Freddie was netting the viaduct then buggering off elsewhere for a while.

We were in position at 21.30; Ken was on the right bank side of the viaduct and Danny on the left, using the railway line for cover. I was downstream watching another hole within the channel. I got as comfortable as possible amongst drift wood, pebbles, and some scrub; it was a very dark night. There wasn't a breath of wind just the enervated tones of oystercatchers, redshanks, and the occasional lazy croak of a heron. The conditions were humid like summer, all in all quite pleasant; I wasn't even wearing a coat. I eventually heard the familiar faint and distant drone of a Nuffield at about 22.30. Stirring from my cramp I alerted my colleagues by radio. The noise came and went as our Nomad combed his vast desert. Occasionally a headlight could be seen to flash frustratingly in the wilderness. I heard the distant church clock strike midnight after which the tractor suddenly loomed out of the darkness like a dinosaur. I quickly fixed the night sight across the channel. Visibility wasn't good although I could just make out a man unhitch his boat and trailer and very soon he was afloat. My radio clicked twice, that would be Ken indicating that it was game on. My other concern at this point of course was Danny, would he be still awake?

I soon put these thoughts to the back of my mind to continue observing our man. He set a net parallel with the shore close to Ken's position, then rowed across to Danny's side and set another at right angles, he was no mug, and he had been there before. Half an hour after its arrival the old Nuffield exploded into life, belching away into the darkness, leaving a calm yet fragile peace. I rallied the troops quickly reconvening at the viaduct. Danny was awake fortunately and about to light up his pipe before I intervened. We had a brief discussion come argument as to what to do next, but my position as Boss carried the day. It wasn't difficult; all that was required was to sit it out until he returned. The tractor could be heard in the distance just as before amongst the night noises. I treated myself to a sandwich and drink while the time dragged. Eventually at 01.30 our man returned in similar ethereal fashion. The old Nuffield coughed and then fell silent and soon I could clearly make out the noisy wooden oars as he rowed gracefully across, nearer and nearer to my trap. On making the shore there was an exaggerated clank of metal on rock as he lifted the anchor on his net. I watched through the scope as he fished and hauled the first net, he was totally oblivious to our presence, confident even; he whistled God Save the Queen and went busily about his task. The net was recovered; he sat down to rest briefly probably feeling contented before letting his boat drift gently down towards his second apparatus allowing him a little respite. I held my hand up ready to give the signal, Danny was perched like a cocked gun, sixty odd and keen as mustard.

I dropped my hand as our man arrived at the second net. We covered the fifty yards in Olympic style. It was no surprise to see Freddie Blencarn at out mercy.

"Water Bailiffs Stop!"

Freddie feigned a heart attack as many had before him.

"What...what yu doin?"

"You're using an unauthorised fixed engine Mr. Blencarn"

"What's that like"?

Danny was straight at him by now.

"Come on Fred I only told you about it last week"

It was dawning on Freddie by now that he was in trouble.

"Aye whatever"

He moved towards his boat.

"I needs to fish yon net afore she ebbs off anymore"

I certainly wasn't going to let him in that boat alone, so I jumped in along side to fish the net.

A somewhat subdued Freddie Blencarn slowly pulled the monofilament net into the boat. The momentum steadily pulled us across, the amazing bioluminescence of algae flickered on the net and oars, this "living light" or "foxfire" as it can be known locally is the eighth wonder of the world in my book. I have only witnessed the phenomena on a few occasions; algal growths emit a surreal cartoon like flash or glow in the night when disturbed by any form of movement.

Freddie's net had a good haul of flukes and just for a minute I thought that would be it, then low and behold two salmon gleamed in the torchlight. Freddie stopped pulling immediately.

"Well bugger me thems fust yans as sin in o,er a month"

I ignored his remark by removing both fish, which fortunately were still alive, so I released them back to the water. Freddie hauled in the rest of the net which contained another salmon and even a sea trout, which I also released.

On our return to shore Danny and Ken brought a bag containing two more salmon and many flukes from the first net, which of course by now were all dead. I offered to give Freddie all the flukes totaling about seventy fish, but he spat the dummy out when I confiscated his nets.

"You've buggered my night up Carter, I don't want nowt from you buggers".

Freddie rowed back across the channel utterly dejected; we however left feeling very pleased with ourselves.

Freddie was prosecuted for using an illegal fixed engine, and taking salmon with an unlicensed instrument. He defended himself on the day and made a good account of the nights events. He was fined £200 nonetheless plus a further £200 costs. Freddie retired that year to become one of the most respected citizens of Flixton where he still remains to this day.

The year ended in style as Hank finally got an offer of retirement due to his long service. He was finally off his bike and put out to grass at sixty two years old, this meant that the hunt for a new senior Bailiff was now underway.

29

NEW BLOOD

1991 saw new blood in the team for the first time since Ken Davidson the previous year. The vacancy left by my own position on the upper Stock was filled by Billy Ferguson in January. The response to the rare advert for a Water Bailiff in the Cumbria Gazette was enormous; this was not unexpected of course. It was no surprise when the job went to Billy Ferguson. There were several good candidates apart from Billy, but enthusiasm on the scale he applied to his reserve Bailiff Duties was unprecedented. The decision made by myself and Jean Slater that day would prove both worthy and justified as time went by.

Grandpa Fred went back into hospital diagnosed with cancer in early February, this was a major blow. He had only recently been settled into Manor House nursing home Knaresborough complete with his beloved cat, so he remained a concern. I hadn't the heart to tell him I had just sold his beloved Datsun Cherry for £500 and the fact I was going to sell the bungalow to pay for his care.

Two "Springer's" were caught in Broxton Park during the second week in February by Johnny Jones; he was one of the straightest men on the river, even on a par with Bob Harmer. I was pleased for Johnny and it was good news for the river as these were becoming scarcer year by year. The sight of one of these pristine fish could brighten up and inspire a whole fishing season.

Danny to was becoming vulnerable and nearing retirement; not helped when he fell off his push bike during a return trip from Asda rendering himself unconscious in the process. He was off work two weeks providing a comical sight strutting about in a neck brace complete with pipe and beret. The boy named Sue visited him after having the sex change operation some months previously. Poor old Dan, no wonder he fell off his bike. Young Andrew now went by the name of Andrea, she or was it him paraded about in a mini skirt and had long blonde hair. Don recollected that from a distance he or she looked deceivingly attractive, but on closer inspection he'd severely told himself off for even thinking such thoughts.

The senior Bailiffs position vacated by Albert Hankey was filled in early March, this being another easy choice because the only serious contenders were Ken Davidson from the R Duddon and John Watson off the R Lune whom I knew from my IFM exam day. Ken was no way experienced enough, so the decision was straightforward. John Watson's reputation on the Lune was exemplary.

Tom Thumb was still around that year, but I gave him a wide berth when ever possible. I often saw him in Brockley skulking around looking for his next fix. I had him up in court during March for using a snare with Sam McGowan the previous year. I had created a scare of my own making on Court day because when I went to the Office to pick up the evidence for trial it was nowhere to be found. I just couldn't locate one sea trout together with a stick and snare, this was an absolute no no as far as I was concerned. Evidence is sacred, never to be shifted or removed once bagged and stored. I turned the place over, I had half the office girls running round, but time in the end beat me. I had no choice other than to dash into Court and proceed. I just made it in time to relay the morning's events to Victor Bailey. Victor of course was not impressed, he spoke without looking up.

"Let's hope they plead guilty then Jack"

My sentiments exactly!

I sat nervously through a long embezzlement trial before to my profound relief our men did indeed plead guilty. Victor loved it I could tell, I even thought he might have asked for the fish and snare just out of badness. Fortunately they were fined and I was off the hook. A lesson was learned that day though believe me, I had a team meeting to sort out the whole processing of evidence within days.

Grandpa Fred died in the last week in March, so obviously I took some time off to sort out his affairs, the bungalow was finally sold off and his beloved cat was fortunately allowed to live out its remaining days in Manor house.

Big Don was back in good spirits especially as we had purchased an ATV or Quad bike to enable better patrols out on the estuary. Don could cover miles out there whilst I kept radio contact back on shore. I had various observation points; from there I could watch until he was a mere red speck close to Morecambe. I was a bit worried about the safety aspect of these operations due to the nature of the environment he was in. I sometimes went with him as a pillion resulting in a couple of dodgy moments with quicksand, present day health and safety regulations now require two bikes together and definitely no pillions. This was and still is the most dangerous area to work in; people like Freddie Blencarn knew those sands like the back of their hand, that's something I will never have.

I traded in the Capri for a Ford Sierra estate because of the practical benefits really, plus we had bought a caravan, so it made good sense.

Training was coming thick and fast as the NRA endeavoured to hone our skills; we all attended power boat training at Knott end boating centre in May. This required us to participate in some team building in a wooden bunkhouse during an extremely stormy night. The following morning saw us enjoying bacon sarnies and debating how suicidal it would be to use a boat in the presiding conditions. Consequently the instructor took great delight in explaining that's exactly what we were going to do. I will always remember being kitted up in a dry suit, then climbing aboard a semi-rigid inflatable boat amongst cold giant waves and rain. In fact once we got going it turned out to be a thoroughly exhilarating experience enjoyed by all, subsequently followed by an excellent piss up.

In the backend that year I got a phone call from Barry Gowans in west Cumbria. Barry's father worked at the Paniclow Ltd dairy processing plant just north of Flixton. Barry relayed some alarming information. One of the security men had witnessed salmon coming and going through the factory gates on several occasions. We had a lengthy conversation in which I asked for more info. The very next evening Barry phoned again, apparently a well known poacher from Flixton one Simon Carradus a shift worker in the factory was supplying salmon to the canteen chef.

Barry was rightly very concerned about the safety of his father, who was at the time putting his neck very much on the line. I was exited about developments, but still needed more information, so I pressed Barry to deliver. I needed plenty to go at before taking on a big company like Paniclow. Several days past before Barry contacted me again, I was starting to think maybe the scent had cooled. It turned out to be quite the opposite; it was on a wet Monday evening in October around 19.00 when I got the call that finally set the ball rolling.

Carradus had brought in more fish, apparently from the R Leven, but the chef Eric Moffat had slipped one out on the QT and taken it home. This was the green light without a doubt. I considered it serious enough to inform Jean Slater. We soon agreed that the best course of action was to search Moffats house in Leighton for starters, then the Paniclow factory canteen and kitchens. The clock was ticking as I made out the information sheet required for my warrants. A quick call to Olivia Briggs alerted her to my pending arrival. My new senior Bailiff John Watson was on standby as well as new Reserve Bailiff Richard Teasdale the son of Hanks old mate Pete Teasdale. I called the Flixton police station where we all arranged to meet at 21.00.

I was a bit delayed due to Mrs Briggs's desire to know all the ins and outs of what was happening. The Sergeant at Flixton was also a bit of a worry because the first words he said to me were,

"I hope this wont affect anyone I know in Paniclow, jobs are hard to come by you know"

This was not what I wanted to hear; he was on our side, wasn't he?

God I hoped he hadn't alerted anyone. I jumped into John's jeep at 21.30 together with Richard Teasdale. Richard was also a private Bailiff on the R Leven having taken over from his father Pete. He was not only adopted, but also black. This was never a problem thank God. The only time it ever came up was when the joke about him working at night cropped up. This was inevitably a reoccurring yarn spoken many times by all those who thought it had never been said before. Of course everyone thought it was hilarious.

"They'll never spot you at night mate will they?"

Or

"I bet you don't even need to hide, they'll never see you coming?"

And many more along those lines, luckily he was a placid lad taking it all in good spirit.

We arrived at 21 Lumley Avenue, Leighton at 21.45; I knocked on the door armed with my warrant and two accomplices. The far from happy police Sergeant stayed in the background. The door was opened by

Mrs Moffat a timid woman in her forties. I asked for her husband who eventually peered distrustfully at us from the bowels of their hallway. I produced my warrant stepping smartly forward through the door in the process. Eric Moffat was also mid forties, he appeared harmless enough stepping into view. He was tall with dark wispy hair and had Dennis Healey eyebrows. Hands in pockets he scowled when I addressed him holding up my warrant, I then followed with the information and questions.

"Have you any salmon on the premises Mr. Moffat"

"Well yes, only one though"

I was then taken down into the cellar of his attractive Victorian terrace. The freezer was half buried under a mountain of household debris and what looked like a whole week's laundry. Moffat slowly edged over clearing a space and opened the lid revealing a salmon of about ten pounds laid conveniently near the surface. I guessed this was the one I had been informed about, probably a freebie for services rendered. I instructed John Watson to take notes of events before nodding Richard Teasdale in the direction of the fish. Richard held it aloft as I turned to Moffat,

"Where's this come from then?"

He was now looking rather more concerned and nervously wiped his brow, sweat was gently making an appearance.

"I got it at work, a lad fetches em like"

"Who?"

He was shaking now,

"Just a bloke, I don't know his name, I give him £2 a pound like"

He laughed nervously and wiped his brow again. I outlined the offences he could be committing as I examined the fish.

"Look at these Mr. Moffat, these are net marks"

This brought another nervous smile and shuffle. He was breathing heavily, but I continued.

"Have you anymore"?

He sighed again deeply before announcing profoundly

"Yes......I'm afraid there's another thirty over at the factory"

Now we were getting somewhere, all the information was proving correct, we moved back up to his living room and greeted by his smiling wife.

"Can I get you all a cup of tea?"

Poor woman, she hadn't yet grasped what was happening. It was at this juncture that Mr. Moffat took a turn for the worse. Dramatically he flopped back heavily into a chair clutching his chest. Mrs Moffat realised it wasn't a social call now alright.

Moffat was panting like a winded dog.

"It's my heart, fetch the pills"

He gestured to his now horrified wife who quickly obliged, I was in limbo for a minute, the three of us looked up each asking ourselves the same question, was this for real or a desperate ploy to either put us off or gain the sympathy vote. I didn't panic, instead I asked Mrs Moffat to fix that cup of tea, and then we all sat down. The last thing we needed was a dead witness.

"Just take it easy sir we can wait, do you need a doctor"?

Moffat shook his head and gradually became more at ease, so I gave him ten minutes before moving to the next phase. I produced my warrant for the factory,

"I will need to see the fish at the factory Mr. Moffat"

He seemed somewhat composed by now nodding compliantly.

"I'll have to tell the lad at the gate, for security like, Ill have to phone him, tell him we're coming."

I argued the point for a few minutes, I didn't want to let the cat out of the bag yet, but he remained adamant. I gave up in the end. I would just have to hope security was indeed just that. When we left the premises a very worried wife nervously stood on the doorstep while we headed off following Mr. Moffat, I put Richard in the car to accompany Moffat just in case he went funny again, or considered doing a runner.

Paniclow Factory loomed into view just before 23.00; we parked up next to Moffat before walking across the massive car park and entering the gatehouse. Everything looked normal; I half expected to see people dashing round with bags of fish like something out of Benny Hill, instead the noise and workings of a busy factory night shift seemed undisturbed. We were processed like any other visitors complete with name badges. The security guy either new nothing, or more like wanted it to appear so.

The walk to Moffats Kitchen was quite a distance and made in silence, eventually we arrived amid gleaming stainless steel sinks and cupboards. The room was large enough to feed a substantial workforce, Moffat went straight to three walk in freezers down the left side not unlike those of John Barker searched at Windermere.

The doors were flung open and thirty or so salmon as described lay neatly on one side in the first freezer. I pointed out to Moffat that those were fresh river fish, some had vegetation still attached, several had snare marks, some had net marks. Moffat even had them entered in his books all paid for with cash, no name of course. I dropped the name Carradus into my questioning, which made Moffat wince and sweat all over again. Fearing another heart do I helped the other lads load up all the fish before having another go.

"Did these fish come from a lad called Carradus"?

Moffat shuffled and coughed,

"No no Bert gets them from him"

I was becoming confused.

"Bert? Who the hells he like?"

Moffat sighed heavily and explained.

"Carradus gets em I guess, and then gives em…well sells em to Bert, Bert Partridge from out of Flixton Hall. Bert sells em on to me, do you see?

I was certainly getting the picture, I gathered from all this that Bert Partridge was some sort of fence; he probably had fish in his house as well. The last thing I managed to do was get the security guard to photocopy the invoices and indeed Bert's name was there for all to see. It was 03.00 by the time I got home; I was too knackered to think about my next move. I was soon asleep that night; I dreamt about freezers and salmon, what else?

The following day was to be another packed with action, by nine o clock I had phoned the courts to apply for more warrants. I needed to be at these premises hopefully before anyone got wind of last nights events, although this would be a tall order. I had no way of knowing whether any of the main players were in each others pockets, or just business acquaintances. Barry Gowans phoned with details of two poachers Carradus and an accomplice called Steve "stinky" Shepherd and both lived in Flixton, he also volunteered some of his Bailiffs to help out. I organised a rendezvous at Flixton nick at 13.00, frustratingly it took me all morning to sort everyone out. Mrs Briggs was unavailable, so I had been given an address in Flixton of another JP who would sign the warrants. I arrived at the nick an hour ahead of rendezvous time so that an officer could accompany me to the isolated home of this particular JP, apparently a farmer.

I traveled with Ann Black a pleasant WPC to a remote farm cottage between the shore and railway line. I knocked on the door amid numerous chickens and an enormous ginger cat waiting for any opportunity to sneak in as soon as the door opened. I turned to my companion taking in various noises faintly coming from within.

"What's he like this chap then?"

She forced a wry smile.

"He's very nice actually, lived here all his life, he does like a bit of fish though!"

I was naturally disturbed by that remark it was not what I wanted to hear. There wasn't time to dwell on it fortunately. The door opened and I was invited in just as the cat shot passed me. The JP in question was indeed very pleasant if a bit rustic giving no indication of any fish related bias, consequently I was soon leaving armed with three new search Warrants.

We all gathered for a briefing back at the nick amply supplied with tea and biscuits.

The plan was for me, John Watson, and Richard Teasdale to search the home of Carradus, while Billy Ferguson together with Barry and one of his Bailiffs would go and do Stinky's. I decided that Bert Partridge could be done last.

We left in a four vehicle convoy in the direction of Oak tree Crescent, Flixton eventually arriving outside number thirty four at 14.15. I parked my Sierra directly outside the house. WPC Black pulled up behind and everything seemed quiet enough. Barry's land rover drove slowly past on their way down to Stinky's. I assembled my group, then approached a smart semi-detached complete with normal tidy looking flower garden.

The door was already opened by a small plain harassed looking woman holding a snotty nosed kid about a year old. I tried unsuccessfully to put her at ease with small talk before dropping the warrant bomb shell on her. I thought about Len Dixon's wife back during those similar circumstances in Brockley, a similar result right now would do nicely.

The sight of the warrant prompted a shriek by this beleaguered woman; she immediately put down the now blubbering child.

"Simons out but if he does come back you'll have to take care"

The words were a timely warning spoken with more steel than before; I knew Carradus had a reputation of being a bit handy. I was more than a bit worried at this point, nevertheless in we jolly well went. The downstairs like the garden was immaculate, not a sign of fish anywhere. The only freezer was with the fridge, I made a quick search upstairs with Richard where it was obvious no fish had been stashed away. I certainly wasn't into going through all their personal stuff like knicker draws and the like, so I quickly retreated. A warrant is a serious and powerful tool, but needn't be unnecessarily abused.

Ten minutes after arriving I joined John Watson with Ann Black in the warm sunny back Garden, John was busy in the shed where some fishing nets had been found. The next events unfolded in fast and furious action. I watched John sorting through a box of nets suddenly to be accompanied by the sound of a car screeching to a halt in the street, followed by a severely slammed door. A man who could only be Carradus flung open a wicket gate and stormed into the garden. This was the first time I had ever clapped eyes on him, he was indeed formidable, tall, very well built, and exceptionally angry. His face was like a furnace, completely wild and out of control. I was temporarily frozen to the spot. The actions of Carradus seemed to proceed in slow animation propelled by adrenalin.

By now he'd reached the shed grabbing a fence post conveniently leaning on the door, before anyone new it he had it aimed and ready to swing at Johns head. I was awakened from my trance by the violent screams of Mrs Carradus,

"No No.........Simon.......NO!"

She saved the day that's for certain; Carradus certainly would not have pulled back for anyone else. He was still holding the post when I nodded to Ann Black. I stepped quickly forward and placed my hand on the trembling shoulder of Simon Carradus, I could smell the anxiety.

"Simon Carradus, I'm arresting you under section 25 of P.A.C.E."

He glared at me for a second; I stood there on red alert bracing myself expecting a bunch of fives or maybe a clout from the fence post at the very least, once again Joe Marwoods prognosis of old flashed through my mind. I had made my commitment the rest was up to Carradus, I noticed WPC Black edging forwards out of the corner of my eye, it was then Carradus let his head drop with a deep sigh before speaking.

"Aye alright mate"

I was able to breathe again and we marched him off.

14.40pm saw us all back at the nick, Carradus was placed in the cells, I was placed in the canteen savouring a well earned brew. The lads from Stinky's came in led by Barry; he came purposefully to my table.

"We've hit the bleadin jackpot at Stinky's"

Barry was bursting to tell all.

"He's only gotta a frigging freezer upstairs hasn't he? And guess what? Right there int front bedroom, it had seven bloody fish in, all salmon at that, what du yu think about that then Jack?"

I was naturally well pleased, the whole case was building up, and a very relieved John Watson came across to inform me that five nets and a wetsuit had been seized from the shed.

I conducted a tape recorded interview on Carradus with John and Ann Black. He was pretty civilised under the circumstances and admitted poaching the fish recovered from Stinky's as well as laundering the factory fish through Bert Partridge. I decided to let Barry interview Stinky Shepherd because I still had the warrant to serve on Partridge; he was the final piece in the puzzle

John and I arrived at Bert's cottage dead on 16.30; he was just preparing to leave for the next shift at the factory. Bert was a nervous plump sixty year old. I knew we were expected because the look on his face was more of relief than anything. I guess so much had happened he would almost certainly have been tipped off probably by Eric Moffat, if not, then the security man maybe.

I was feeling sorry for Bert even before I produced the warrant or the canteen receipt book with his name clearly documented, he showed little emotion on reading it, so in we went. The inside of Bert's little cottage was quite unique; firstly we were confronted by his son sat in a wheelchair deep in the kitchen. This stopped me right in my tracks, the poor lad was obviously retarded, he smiled gently, and bits of his last meal left a trail from lips to shirt. His head was cocked to one side in blissful ignorance.

Bert was reading my thoughts and broke the silence,

"Mi sister cuz down while I's at work and sits wid him"

I was starting to feel uncomfortable by now, warrants aren't supposed to be for unfortunate souls such as this, why had this happened?

The contents of the house were amazing, Bert must have been a compulsive hoarder, and every room was full to brimming with boxes containing every conceivable household item imaginable, including huge quantities of bedding, numerous dilapidated Hoovers, washers, dryers and furniture items. I have never witnessed anything like it before or since. His poor son could hardly turn round, needless to say we never discovered a thing, and neither did we look very far come to that. We couldn't even get through the door in two of the bedrooms. There was a freezer in the garage, but only withered up peas and fish fingers looked up at me. It was a hopeless pointless exercise, even embarrassing; I was on the point of leaving when Bert pulled me to one side.

Poor old Bert confessed to handling the fish from Carradus, then selling them on in the factory, he literally dropped himself right in it, clearly the game was up. The ramifications following our raid on Paniclow Ltd rumbled on for weeks, rumours abounded about sackings together with fish dumped left right and centre by Tom Dick or Harry. The number of fish seized rose daily with every bit of gossip on the grapevine until it was well over a hundred. The truth however would of course have to wait for our day in court.

30

THE NEXT GENERATION

The trial of the Simon Carradus took place at Flixton Crown court one day in April 92 just after all Bailiffs had been issued with uniform for the first time. I turned up on the day dressed in green from head to foot. I felt as if I had just popped out of Sherwood Forest. I was convinced everyone was staring at me, when of course they weren't. It would be several months before this particular phobia subsided.

Victor Bailey had done a deal with the defence solicitor one Mr. Fish would you believe. He suggested all the poaching offences be dropped if his man pleaded guilty to the public order offence and obstructing a Water Bailiff. This type of bargaining was not unusual and in any case the Judge would hopefully get the full picture as the case unfolded. The other three defendants pleaded not guilty and their proceedings were adjourned.

Carradus was fined £150 on each charge plus costs of £75, so not a bad result really; we got the case reported in the Flixton evening mail, with the headline *"Bailiff threatened with wooden post"*.

The trial date for the others was exactly a month later in May, this proved to be a long tedious day. The venue was changed to start with due to alteration work in the main courts. We all assembled in a very small makeshift Magistrates court down a creepy backstreet in Flixton. The fish stood humming in the corner much to the usher's displeasure. The evidence from our end was put forward during constant interruptions and nit picking by the defence. Victor once told me that this is a sign that the defence doesn't in fact have much of a defence at all. Instead they try and pick holes in procedure, prosecution evidence, or even weather conditions and visibility. We had all these on the day, so I assumed we must be on a winner. Mr. Fish then argued that we hadn't even got a prima facia case at all for most if not all the charges. The bench retired on this one and the mood at our end changed, surely they couldn't throw it out... could they?

Half an hour later we were sent for lunch. I returned to the court room as instructed at 1pm, the room was now being warmed by full sun. The bench appeared at half past to announce that there was indeed a case to answer and I breathed a sigh of relief. Bert Partridge got away with the charges in the receipt book and Moffat had a charge wrongly worded by our legal department, so that also went out of the window. The usher opened the windows as time went on; the fish were just about cooking. The final hour of the proceedings was spent trying to organise a trial date, but unfortunately every time a day was mentioned someone or other popped a hand up to say he or she couldn't make it. This was bizarre, I have never seen the like since and it was August before a date was finally agreed by all.

In 1993 I had been long enough at my career for one generation of poacher to be replaced by another including siblings. One such character was Len Dickson's lad Ian.

He had left school over a year previously and had unfortunately in 1992 teamed up with Sergio Ferrari's youngest lad Sammy. The pair had been brought to my attention in July by the now fading Timmy Dunne.

Timmy was not the man I once knew and avoided, he was rarely seen patrolling the town apart from the odd stroll around Brockley weir, time as they say was catching him up. I chatted with him one afternoon while he sat watching the beck like some ancient Heron. It turned out that Timmy lived close to the Dixon household on Cinderbarrow estate and the comings and goings of these lads had not escaped his notice.

During August I received further confirmed reports of fish changing hands at the premises and was of the opinion that a search warrant may be needed to turn the place over. The event that happened next was the catalyst for such action. I was on a night shift with Danny approaching the stretch of the Stock just above Brockley town water. It was early August on a fine balmy night just prior to midnight. We spotted some lamping in progress at Stoneybase pool, so crept onward in pursuit. Our adversaries were moving steadily upstream, we had to wade through the beck to enable any meaningful chance of gaining on them. Danny was right behind me as I felt my way carefully through the warm stream.

We hurried on until only yards separated us. The tell tale beam of light swept over a deep pool at Gilbertsfield, another of the most poached locations in Cumbria. I could clearly see through the night sight a stick with snare attached, I leaned across to Dan still perspiring from my excursions.

"Best thing we can do is jump em while we can"

Dan nodded his agreement, so we unburdened ourselves of heavy rucksacks, just retaining essentials needed, hopefully for an apprehension.

I gave the signal, and then we rushed in lights blazing

"Stop now Bailiffs!"

All hell broke loose; one went past me like a gazelle downstream and before I knew it the other lad fled in the opposite direction sending Danny flying in the process. The only consolation was their lamp stick and snare was lying on the ground in front of us. I rushed back to the rucksack for my phone. The first generation of mobiles would be laughed at today, but these heavy monsters were revolutionary back then, although very clumsy in such a situation. I was pretty sure that young Dixon and Sammy Simpson were our targets a fact I quickly relayed to Brockley Nick.

We took a much needed breather; Danny lit his pipe and chuckled."

"Too damn quick for me them lads Jack, must be getting old?"

"Aye and they're getting younger Dan"

We headed off downstream back toward the Sierra, but on crossing back through the river my phone rang. The exited voice of PC Tony Fleming relayed the news that our two miscreants were waiting for us in the nick.

The rest was a formality, they coughed the lot.

That was that or so I thought, but sometimes these things snowball out of control.

I was in a deep peaceful sleep at 7am when Maggie woke me.

"That weirdo Dunne's on the phone, says it's urgent"

I stumbled to the phone.

"Jack yon house as bin like bloody Blackpool all neet, folk coming and gaain all oert spot, I've sin some salmon an all. I reckon yon spots full a fish man!"

I calmed Timmy down and told him to keep his head down. I paced round the room for a minute ignoring a hot mug of tea lovingly provided. I made the decision to go for the search warrant. I quickly sorted myself out before phoning Big Don and Danny then Brockley Nick. It was 08.00 by the time I arrived at the home of Olivia Briggs, Warrants could still only be obtained from a justice of the peace and Mrs Briggs lived not too far from my own home. I presented her with my forms for the warrant explaining what grounds I had and relayed the previous night's events. Olivia Briggs was no fool and readily signed the papers. I left in a hurry for the Police station where I had arranged to meet up. It is always advisable to have a Bobby on side when executing a warrant, so Jonty Jones gave me a young Rookie WPC who looked about sixteen. I was not impressed, but who was I to argue. At 08.45 I knocked on the door of a tired looking council house I once knew in a previous life from back in Len Dixon's heyday. I stood clutching the precious warrant staring at the half rotten front door. The paintwork looked older than me. The sound of barking dogs was everywhere, from within the house, in the neighbours and down the street. The door was answered by Lens wife a bedraggled woman of well fed physique. She looked puzzled?

"Mr. Carter, haven't sin you for a few years, if tha wants Len love yuv no chance, he's long gone, left over a year ago"

I took all this in before explaining about young Ian and Sam, her face fell, and she looked beleaguered and very tired. I slowly displayed the warrant in front of her nose; two lurchers now silent pushed passed and sniffed me all over. Lens wife looked up with a tear trickling from one eye.

"Nay has it come to this, he's no better than his rotten old man, a chip off the old block that one I'm afraid"

The mood had changed completely, there I was feeling very sorry for this poor woman, when number one son could be legging it out the back for all I knew. Big Don gave me a nudge and nodded towards the house.

Lens wife stepped aside and in we went, Ian was stood at the top of the stairs in his boxers holding a squawking brat. He was a father at seventeen, what could we possibly find next. The answer was in the back kitchen in the chest freezer. Seven salmon all with snare marks laid waiting for our inspection. We also found a gate net, a gaff, and several snares all in the wash house. I suspect these were left over from Lens days.

All in all it was a good result and significantly brought the biggest smile to Timmy Dunne's face I ever witnessed.

In late August we again assembled down the side street in Flixton for The final trial in the Paniclow saga. The fish were displayed one last time looking extremely worse for wear, filling the room with their own special aroma one more time. The trial went smoothly enough, Bert partridge flew away Scot free, which was no big loss, and his sister was stood at the back of the court resolutely clutching her bible. Steve "stinky" Shepherd was fined £100 for handling salmon in suspicious circumstances plus £50 costs. Finally Moffat got £300 for each of the two charges of handling salmon after August 31st plus a whopping £300 costs. He was naturally devastated; he alone had been singled out as the main player. Moffat hung his head when the verdict was read out. The Flixton evening news had the headline "Paniclow chef's fishy tale" and went on to describe in graphic detail a court room full of smelly fish that swayed the jury. Moffat had already been pensioned off before the final trial date despite his high standing as a supplier of top quality buffets. His speciality was of course wild salmon!

In October that year poor old Bob Harmer died suddenly from a heart attack, he was a very good friend not to mention his influence and guidance when I applied for the Inspectors job. His backing and support during the rough days with Brockley AA were paramount in bringing the psycho mafia to heel. The parish church in Brockley was full to bursting for Bob's funeral, he was a very nice man and hugely respected especially by me.

31

TO CATCH A ZULU

The year of 93 was about the time when the world of poaching became more and more influenced by economics. Salmon farming in Scotland and Ireland was now flooding the market with average quality fish which all looked the same. It was now possible to buy a salmon in Asda or Tesco's for just a few quid. The average housewife didn't care whether the fish was farmed or straight out of the R Stock, they looked near enough the same, even if the farmed fish did taste inferior to any self respecting palate. This of course affected the returns available to poachers, which then had to be weighed against the risks. Black market Fish that once fetched anything up to £7 or £8 a pound was now only worth a fraction of that maybe as little as £1 per pound. The south lakes team was very proficient at this time, most known poachers around Brockley had at least one if not several convictions stacked against them and most were now working for a living. Very few still plodded the benefit trail, instead preferring the steady reliable income provided by employment. New offences were also coming to light. The drift net fishery in Morecambe bay that primarily targeted the highly valued Sea Bass was allegedly picking up shoals of sea trout especially in the Duddon estuary or off Morecambe in the Stock channel. This problem was inevitably going to get worse during the next few years.

Live baiting was another growing concern, this is a method preferred by some pike rod anglers. Basically it entails using rod and line with a live fish impaled on a treble hook, then trawling it behind a boat or even just from a bank side rod and line. Windermere and Coniston were the main problem areas. The law at the time allowed fish to be taken from any specific water and then used as live bait, but only on that same water. The reason being to prevent the introduction of alien species. In reality certain individuals brought scabby specimens of live fish such as roach, bream, chub or Dace, usually removed from some anonymous backwater or canal in the depths of Lancashire. The problem was of course that any fish left over at the end of the days fishing would be tipped into the unfortunate water regardless of any risk of spreading disease, or the introduction of none indigenous species.

I had several successes with shore based anglers, but the real problem was in the boats. Certain pike anglers went to great lengths to deceive, having facilities for keeping live fish both at home and in transportation. Specimen pike weighing up to and in excess of thirty pounds are pursued by fanatical followers of this sport, they will quite happily sit in a small boat in the freezing cold for days on end. The fish are weighed, photographed and generally posed with before being returned to fight another day. Pike are awkward fish to handle, I have seen severe injuries to uneducated anglers who put hands either, in the mouth or near the gills of pike, both of which contain razor sharp teeth and gill filaments respectively. I used our own fibreglass boat to patrol the lakes more frequently in an effort to combat this type of fishing.

One particular rod and line incident on Good Friday concerned a venue near Carnforth. Whitebank Coarse fishery was a collection of small ponds attached to a big new house and owned by the eccentric Robin

Golightly. Golightly was a small ginger haired man in his late thirties; he had loads of money left from a family heirloom. He was really just playing at making a living, which I found quite annoying really. His income was primarily from selling permits for rod and line fishing. I had been on numerous occasions to check anglers without any problem until this particular day. I parked in the car park just as I had always done, proceeded down to the fishery and started to check what proved to be quite a good turn out of anglers. I had dealt with about ten compliant fishermen when I noticed Golightly heading my way in determined mood. He was often prone to contentious comments and unfortunately Authorities such as the NRA did not rest easily with him. The events of that particular morning however were well out of order. I waited to say good morning as he approached, but instead I was met face to face by a man who had definitely got out of the wrong side.

"I've told you Bastards before don't come here without telling me first"

He was finger pointing, very excited and egged on by a large black dog of ill-defined pedigree.

I was about to try and calm him when he raved on some more

"You're trespassing and what's more your cars in my fuckin car park without my fuckin permission".

His face was crimson I was quite shocked, but managed to stay just about composed enough to produce my warrant and point out my powers. He was having none of that though, instead continued until he completely lost his temper.

"That's it fuck off, go on just fuck off or I'll get my digger and tip your fuckin car over".

He now started to walk back towards the house where I noticed a JCB parked; somewhat concerned I followed watched by numerous gob smacked anglers. Surely he wouldn't carry out his threat...would he?

I knew decisive action was required, so I caught him up thrust my warrant in his face and shouted:

"I am reporting you for obstructing me in my duty, I have the powers and rights to enter this land and check the anglers!"

He stopped at once in his tracks, what now? I thought about the time I arrested Simon Carradus, would I get a right hook this time?

In fact quite remarkably the opposite occurred and he changed completely, after a short pause to reflect he actually started apologising.

"Mr. Carter I'm sorry can we start again, I was a bit out of order I'm sorry. I get sick of folk just wandering on here".

I was still shaking but stayed cool enough letting the adrenalin gently subside back under cover. I pointed out that I Wasn't just wandering on to his property; I had a right to be there. He talked in a much friendlier manner for several minutes and even shook my hand as I left. I assured him I would knock on his door in future before going round the anglers, providing it wasn't too early in the morning. This is not a requirement but in his case possibly not a bad idea. He was fine thereafter, so what rattled his cage that day? I'm not sure maybe he had a row with his wife. Big Don visited on a few occasions when he was not off sick; he christened him "Shagnasty"

I think maybe the threat of actually being reported had triggered the realisation that he could land himself in court, which saved the day I reckon.

Shortly after this incident Danny reached the age of 65 and retired, I think he would have carried on until he dropped if truth be known, his enthusiasm was as fresh as ever.

I was pleased to see him go on welfare grounds, Bailiff Duties are really for young men. Danny was not fit to be trailing around at night or crawling through the undergrowth. He was still active and fit so retirement it was, we gave him a good send off in the Blue Anchor. A boy named Sue made a brief appearance; she or he looked ever more ridiculous. Andrea as I carefully called her or him left soon after Don had engaged conversation.

"What have you said to her Don?"

He glanced mischievously at me,

"It was going well till I called it Shim"

We both laughed, trust Don.

In June the ever impressive Billy Ferguson nabbed some poachers in the estuary near Leighton. I had tasked him with some early morning patrols, which he pursued with his usual enthusiasm. He apparently dropped right on them returning to a vehicle hidden nearby. You make your own luck in this job, which starts by making the effort to be there went it matters. Billy phoned me at 04.30 in the morning to summon some help. I was with him in twenty minutes. He had caught a local lad from Carnforth together with another bloke from Morecambe. A net with six sea trout was already in the back of the Land rover. The case was straightforward enough and Billy was well pleased with himself.

Dip netters were increasing on the rivers in south lakes during the nineties. The dip net is an instrument licensed by the Authority specially for catching elvers. These young eels return to fresh water homing in to the streams of birth in the same manner as salmon or sea trout. The dip net is a hand held net with fine mesh literally dipped in the water and held against the oncoming night tide. The net is set to intercept the three to four inch elvers migrating upstream. The operative usually has a head torch to see what he is doing. A good haul would be several kilos worth around £30 a kilo at that time. The catch was then sent down to Gloucester for export possibly to Japan. The elver like most marine species was already in decline. Patrols to check this activity had to coincide with big spring tides and these in turn arrived with a full or new moon at or either side of midnight. This was usually a straightforward show of strength; two of us would turn up and check licenses and authorisations as well as observing the nets being fished. Once again the majority of these men were from Lancashire down as far as Preston, they would pop up the M6 to fish any of the tidal rivers in the area. Violations were rare, but useful information was gathered to monitor the health of each elver run. I inevitably came across the occasional offender. I had a case against one man who fitted a leader to his net; this was a piece of netting fixed to the opposite bank to divert all the elvers into his own dip net. I put this down to greed and the fact that this particular Gent was from Yorkshire. Another was Freddie Blencarn's son George, he constructed a square net which he threw into the water then pulled it in like a trawl, he caught nothing but did get fined £150 for using an unlicensed instrument.

In August the same man came to my attention again. I had been concerned about the pairing of George with Ronnie Macadam brother of the late Michael Macadam. Both men were full time fishermen out in the bay covering the whole spectrum of activities from shellfish to salmon. The pair also took out Lave net licenses annually. It wasn't too difficult for salmon caught in say a drift or draw net to be then brought off under the protection of a lave net license. I had reason to be suspicious about these two characters following a phone call from good old Mr. anonymous, who also not surprisingly just happened to be a fisherman from Flixton. I was told that the pair had been operating in a vast hole formed at the bottom of Red dyke weir. This so called weir was in actual fact a massive breakwater formed from tipped stone out of a nearby quarry in the village of Red dyke itself. I did go down and observe a couple of tides but saw nothing, I realised that they must be using tides that favoured fishing at dusk thus allowing them to make the trip back across the bay in semi-darkness, lessening the chance of being detected. I had to wait another two weeks before a likely tide occurred again. It was one Tuesday evening when I parked up under Leighton knot; the late summer sun was still warm a truly splendid evening. It was simply a pleasure just to be out and watching the numerous Scotch Argus butterflies drinking in the evening sun. I climbed the steep shale clad hill reaching my vantage point along side the trig point. Both dogs loved this terrain covering every inch in pursuit of rabbits and the odd squirrel. I was in position by 19.00 spanning the panorama with my binnocs. The point of entry for most fishermen was on the opposite side of the bay at Gillys head. This is at least four and a half miles away as the crow flies. Red dyke weir was about three miles from the Knott so I had the entire bay covered. The duo in question came into view at 19.30; the familiar form of a moving black speck emerged round the headland from Flixton. They made a b-line for Red dyke, the crucial point about this whole operation was whether or not they stopped to use a lave net, or just kept going until they reached the weir. I never took my eyes off them as they drove on. The setting sun made observation a painful process at times; prolonged use of binnocs in such situations was very uncomfortable.

The tractor was obviously towing a boat and trailer and as suspected never stopped until they reached the weir. Twenty minutes from my first sighting the pair launched a boat and started netting. I was sorely tempted to call in the troops at this point, instead I stuck with my original decision to observe and then plan a full scale operation for hopefully the following day. I noticed some nasty weather moving in at 20.30, a threatening black cloud appeared to be moving menacingly across the scene from the south west. I shivered when a hot breeze spun through the broom and gorse around me. I watched the two men at work, diligently launching and re launching the boat. The light was getting bad so I couldn't see exactly what was going on, I was thinking and planning all the while. One Bailiff would have to be on the weir itself to see the netting; another would have to be on Gillys head. The two men would have to be in view at all times to counter any claims to catching fish with a lave net. I lost sight of proceedings at 21.30

when thunder and lightning dramatically passed across Red dyke and Morecambe; I wondered how would the two men cope in such a storm? Should I call the coastguard? I didn't bother as this would scupper any chance of nabbing them. I stayed on the Knott until 22.10 when I could hear the tell tale drone of a Nuffield heading for home. I strained every sinew trying to make them out, until a quiet state of calm descended once again in the empty darkness. I was contemplating departure following a cup of stale tea, when I became aware of a remarkable sight. The surrounding undergrowth was lit up; even the dogs settled and gazed on warily. I was puzzled at first, then realised it was a large population of glow worms *Lampyris Noctilucia*, apparently the females start glowing around ten o clock. I marveled at the wonder of the display around me, it was rather comparable to seeing a town lit up at night from far off. Hundreds of small lights covering the surrounding area, right place right time I guess! needless to say I remained for some time

The following day was warm and settled once again, I rallied the troops at Croftgill for a briefing. I had worked out a cunning plan based on the previous night's events, I told John Watson that he would be on Red dyke weir to observe netting operations; he would be radio call sign Mike 2. I would direct operations from on the Knott and be Mike 1. The west side was to be covered by Richard Teasdale call sign Mike 3 on Gillys head, that should make sure we have continuity of evidence and ensuring visual contact was maintained throughout.

Billy Ferguson and Ken Davidson, call signs Mike 4 and 5 I tasked with lying in wait on the ATV's behind Gillys head and out of sight. They would be vital in actually ambushing the two fishermen on their return. We busied ourselves all morning checking radios and all the gear. The quads were fuelled up, started and run round the compound. The operation was named Zulu, a term used to describe a tractor on the sands. This was necessary due to radio traffic having been intercepted in the past. For some reason despite the NRA having its own dedicated waveband, taxi interchanges often interfered with our work. I was actually asked to do a pick up fare in Morecambe on one occasion. I was taking observations on the Knott when a voice chipped in

"Mike 1 can you collect Mrs Smith from 52 ford crescent going to Broadway"

This was a nuisance, but hugely entertaining at times.

That evening I instructed my team to be in position at 18.30, I climbed the hill on to the Knott once again, no dogs of course on this occasion. Once settled radio checks were conducted without fuss or unnecessary waffle, everyone new what was expected and I trusted them all. The weather was again perfect, I couldn't see any reason they shouldn't come. I was rewarded at 19.10 when Mike 3 confirmed our target Zulu had been sighted leaving Flixton; my heartbeat went up a notch, game on!

I confirmed a positive sighting ten minutes later when the tractor began the dash across from west to east. I checked with Mike 2, he was settled and in a good position. He then confirmed,

"Zulu approaching coming my way"

A repeat of the previous nights crossing confirmed the first vital piece of the jig saw, the tractor did not stop once until reaching Red dyke weir, no excursion to use lave nets had even been attempted. They must have felt very confident because they didn't even stop to walk about or even pretend to lave net, if they had I would have had great difficulty proving a case. Mike 2 confirmed the boat was launched and a net in the water at 20.00 hours. The light was good fortunately, none of the flash storms of the previous night, I could see the men operating but only as specks in the distance. I was thankful of John Watson's presence on the weir. Mike 2 confirmed three separate netting operations by 20.45 and they were now having a smoke. By 21.15 they were loaded up and ready to return, I was thankful because the light was now fading fast. I checked with Mike 3 instructing him not to take his eyes off the returning Zulu for one second. I then appraised Billy and Ken of what was happening, so far so good!

I could just about make out the tractor in the growing darkness as it headed back, Mike 2 was already in his van heading for Gillys head, now was the time to set the ambush, it was all going too well, I should have known when Mike 4 broke the silence;

"The bloody quads stuck in the sands Jack"

I couldn't believe what I was hearing

"What do you mean? What's happened?"

"The bikes stuck we can't move it"

I was pacing round in circles in the darkness, think, think!

"Mike 3 if it stays stuck both go on one bike, don't miss the interception whatever you do"

That course of action even back then had become a health and safety no no, but I wasn't about to let the chance slip away because of protocol.

The sound of panic in my voice must have been very none reassuring.

I was also on the move by that time, crashing and sliding down the shale hill to my vehicle, I slipped clumsily a couple of times before reaching my goal. Mike 5 called to say that the quad was now freed and they were about to head off and intercept the target, which was the good news at least. The bad news was Billy's radio had gone AWOL. I could live with that state of affairs providing they intercepted the Zulu. I was soon underway, foot hard down on what is a journey of over fifteen miles to reach Gillys head by road. The radios went silent; all I could do was hope as I raced round. I was only a couple of miles from Gillys head when a strange voice gave me a jolt.

"Hello, anyone receiving, anyone there?"

What on earth was that? The voice was female, I realised it was my radio, not a taxi though, just some strange woman's voice. It happened again!

"Hello, anyone there?"

I stopped the car, I had to! I looked down at the radio as if it was about to blow up, it certainly felt that way.

Eventually I gingerly picked it up off the car seat.

"Hello this is Jack Carter of the NRA, do you read?"

A frail high pitched voice replied almost at once.

"I've picked up this radio off the roadside"

I had to hand it to the woman, not only had she found the damn radio Billy had lost she actually had the common sense to speak into it. The radio was safe for now so I thanked her and hurriedly took down her address for Billy to collect it later. I apologised emphasising that now wasn't a good time to chat and sped onwards. This was a surreal intervention, but I needed to press on. I arrived on the beach below Gillys head at about 22.15 and immediately saw George Blencarn and Ronnie Macadam in the capable hands of the team.

John Watson met me all smiles.

"It worked a treat the buggers have six salmon on board, said they got em with the lave net"

"Right we'll see about that then"

I made my way over at once,

"Now then George what you been up to?"

"Nowt Mr. Carter I've gitten six fish with mi lave net and these buggers says I dint"

I walked slowly round the tractor to where a lave net was stashed neatly behind the seat. I examined it under George's attentive stare.

"It's as dry as a bone George, never moved I reckon"

He shuffled nervously

"Yes it has we got yon fish wid it"

I pointed out that we had all watched them, there and back across the sands, also pointing out the fact they hadn't stopped betwixt and between at anytime, both men denied the point in animated fashion, which was the norm in those situations especially with Flixton fishermen. I cautioned them both before seizing all the gear. They were not happy of course, but seize it we did. The boat was hitched on to Billy's Land rover complete with nets and fish. Billy was shit up to the eyeballs from his efforts at freeing his quad bike, although he didn't half smile when I revealed the whereabouts of his radio.

The boat with trailer and gear was stashed safely into Croftgill and the six salmon bagged into the freezers. I was safely home after mission accomplished just after midnight.

The following day I had a meeting with Jean Slater following animated complaints from Blencarn and Macadam about their loss of equipment. We decided to return the boat once forensic work had been completed due to its importance for his livelihood. The law suggests that although used in illegal activity the capability to pursue normal working practice should not be with held unnecessarily or just for badness despite my recommendation of just that. Personally I thought keeping it would have been a good deterrent, however arrangements were made for the two men to pick it up.

Big Don was now in a poor way health wise and even early retirement on the grounds of ill health was being considered. Don's heart was no longer in the job that was plain for all to see, his back problems had taken over. I visited him about once a week trying to lift his spirits, although I sensed an air of inevitability. I was already missing his humour and enthusiasm.

The void left by Danny's retirement was to be filled by a friend of John Watson's who wanted a life change from working in an office in Manchester. I thought about my own initiation to the world of the Water Bailiff and couldn't help but make a comparison. Phil was an

excellent choice from stiff competition. He was a pleasant bloke soon
getting the reputation as the nice boy from Cheshire. Yet another shake
up and change in the organisation meant the River Kleen disappeared
from my patch to the Lune team during the autumn. I was sorry to lose
this small but productive river where I had some good friends. I also lost
Whitebank Fishery and the inimitable Robin "Shagnasty" Golightly, still
never mind eh!

32

A MAYORS TALE

In February 94 Big Don finally gave up working, he was crippled by a bad back and only forty years old. He took the sick route into early retirement and hasn't been able to work since. We gave him the usual send off in the Blue Anchor, but the atmosphere was not brilliant. I presented him with a camera bought from the whip round and that was that really, not a memorable day at all.

The two culprits from operation Zulu came to court in March and pleaded not guilty. The NRA in its wisdom was now employing full time lawyers and solicitors in its own right, this meant that my good friend Victor Bailey had been put out to grass, I never got chance to thank the man, who for many years had fought my teams corner through many a court battle. Dorothy Squires was long gone too, all in the ever changing world.

Macadam and Blencarn now faced a fresh faced solicitor called Susan Morton, who hadn't much idea went it came to broad Cumbrian Fishermen. I struggled in the witness box while she came to terms with

the facts; thankfully the case was strong enough to win the day. The
Bench were not taken in by lies about lave netting to catch the salmon
on show in court, each man was fined a whopping £300 each, plus £250
costs. Magistrates were getting tough and in my opinion not before
time. The two defendants had been sent a clear message on the day,
don't lie and cheat in a courtroom. We as a team were absolutely made
up, especially as our new solicitor had not exactly lit the place up, Victor
would have loved laying into those two culprits that's for sure.

The chances of catching a poacher during the day time on the three
rivers of Brockley were now few and far between, however rumour had it
that Jez Bergerac was still performing. On the strength of this I settled in
a favourite hide just downstream from Brock mill one Sunday afternoon
in July. Cranston no longer manned the mill thank goodness, so no
siren to worry about. The sun shone and I settled in for a long stay, after
an hour I was in my state of torpor, lulled by the gentle rhythm of a
gurgling river and waiting hopefully. The change of noise that stirred
me was not that of any poacher, but a couple walking up the footpath,
nothing untoward there one would think. The man looked to be mid
forties whereas the woman was younger and blonde, the pair stopped by
the very pool I was guarding and began looking surreptitiously up and
down the footpath. I carefully had a closer look using my binnocs and
then easily recognised the man to be none other than Andrew Spiby, the
reigning Mayor of Brockley no less. I guessed the woman in question
was probably not his wife and mother of three kids. Next thing I knew
they were at it there and then on the riverbank, articles of clothing soon
littered the grass and naked flesh was on full view. I was trapped only
yards away and powerless to do anything, any movement on my part
would have been hugely embarrassing for all parties. I suppose I had a
good case for blackmail, but I was more concerned about looking like
a peeping Tom. Hiding in bushes has always been an excellent way to
catch poachers, but being compromised could lead to all sorts of the
wrong conclusions. I had no choice but to stay put and keep extremely

still, I remember they had a golden retriever sat looking on, which provided more reason to sit tight. Luckily a quickie seemed to be the order of the day because they were togged up and ready for the off in less than ten minutes. I never told a soul about that day and didn't use that hide ever again either.

The remainder of that year was largely uneventful apart from a strange incident one night in September whilst on a routine patrol with Billy Ferguson.

I had patrolled the full length of the R Stock from Leighton back up to Brockley and listened all night to Billy's whinging about various family matters. He never failed to get stuff off his chest, usually domestic or marital problems concerning his brother and three sisters. I didn't mind really it helped pass the time on a routine shift, but after six hours I sometimes just switched off. This particular night I pulled into the Brockley AA main car park just south of the town for a last cup of coffee before knocking off. I glanced at my watch, it was 03.30, I turned to Billy who was relating the state of his Fathers poor health in graphic detail,

"Lets just pop down and put the scope across yon meadows before we go home Bill"

I grabbed the thing before Billy could argue and wandered down to the gate. I spanned round until amazingly I spotted a person right by the river, but I just couldn't make out what was going on.

"You won't believe this, but there's a bloke on the river, just down the field"

I passed the scope to Billy,

"Aye your right, he's kneeling down now, looks as if he could be sorting a net"

I had another look and had to agree he did indeed look to be sorting a net, his arms were moving about busily.

"Right Bill lets get down there sharpish"

We stealthily crept along a stone wall until we were positioned twenty yards from our man, I couldn't see anyone or anything else near the bloke. I stood watching and listening until it became obvious that the guy was talking out loud, I couldn't weigh it up at all. I gave it five minutes then turned to Billy,

"Come on lets bounce him"

I scaled the wall and shot across to the mysterious man in the middle of a field in the dead of night. I got the shock of my life, stood before me was an old lad well in his eighties wearing pyjamas, dressing gown and carpet slippers. He was rambling and moaning out loud to himself.

Billy was first to speak,

"He's escaped Jack; I reckon he's just wandered off poor old lad"

This was a fair analysis, I called the Police and we escorted him up to the road. I couldn't get any sense out of him at all. The Police confirmed his ID after some gentle questioning. The old man was evidently from Silver Green old folks home, the Police took him back sat forlornly in a riot van. Billy and I went home wondering why he hadn't been missed at all? I never received a single word of feedback, or any thanks about the incident from either the Police or Silver Green, so that was that we are no wiser to this day.

33

PINK MULLET

The problems of drift netting out in Morecambe bay especially The Duddon estuary came to the forefront in 1995 when enormous sums of money could be made catching Bass. Martin Black the Fisheries chief from MAFF gave me a call in June to form a partnership with my team that would last a decade at least. He was and still is a sharp and very keen operator, stopping at nothing to control the hauls of Bass coming ashore. The by-catch of salmon and sea trout also came to the fore front, so it was for those reasons we started joint patrols. We decided to concentrate on stop and search operations at Flixton stone jetty. Things became quite hairy some nights, boats all returning laden with fish. Martin measured the Bass and I checked for any salmon or sea trout, most fishermen were quite put out. The offence regarding Bass was that of selling for profit whilst not being registered and licensed with MAFF, in fact it was a free for all, just about everyone had a boat and some nets. Various reports came in of large hauls of sea trout; these were famously known locally as pink mullet which was a cryptic comparison to a low value fish. No prosecutions came about from our efforts, but the pressure exerted on various individuals eventually paid dividends. Two overriding factors ruled the game, apart from actually catching the fish of course. Firstly when you catch a fish, then you need some where to sell it, preferably tax free. Bass could make £2 or even £3 per pound and a decent catch could be twenty stone or more, plus more than likely a cash only transaction. This was poaching with high financial gains to be had on a regular basis. The numbers of legitimate and not so legitimate dealers operating was growing as a result and had to be checked. Martin and I visited most and examined all records if there was any. The visit was followed up with a call to the Inland Revenue, the second or follow up route used to tackle the problem. The effect on fish dealers was devastating and in a lot of cases put them out of business altogether. That made life much more difficult for both netter and receiver. The continued effort and pressure we have exerted has eventually reduced the number of fishermen to a handful of fully registered and kosher individuals who actually make a decent living without wiping out both Bass and salmonids. The salmon and sea trout population returning to the River Duddon has now also recovered considerably, which more than justifies our efforts. 1995 was taken up almost entirely sorting this problem and unfortunately resulted in an in house situation that cost a Bailiff his job.

The frequent stop and search checks at Flixton produced a fairly accurate picture of who was operating more than others and one man in particular turned up at the jetty many times. This individual was called Eddie Lewis, another factory worker from Paniclow. Tales of pink mullet landed by this guy were rife on the grape vine; however I never got near a case as he always came in with sea fish. We set up lookouts at various points amid rumours of hauls of fish dropped off before his boat reached the jetty. The main source of information came not from the general public or other jealous fishermen, but from one of Frank Bells own Bailiffs up at Ravenglass. I received more and more calls from a lad called John Hawkins. He was by all accounts a tip top Bailiff with an exemplary record, but obviously Eddie Lewis was not on his Christmas card list. I actually got on alright with Eddie, so consequently tales of skulduggery up the west coast didn't sit well for me, it just didn't feel right somehow. Things took a turn for the worse when I was taking observations one day on Gillys Head and bumped into John just as I was leaving.

"Hey up John what the hell you doing down here?"

John was well wound up,

"As lookin for that Lewis bastard, I naa he's aboot Marra,

I was miffed that John was off his patch and on mine.

"Does Frank know you're down here like?"

"Naa but its okay as on mi day off Marra"

I couldn't believe what I was hearing and let it be known in no uncertain terms.

I had strong words for John and also Frank when I later filled him in. Frank had no inclination, although admitted that John was becoming more than a bit obsessed with trying to nail Eddie Lewis. I was assured that Hawkins would be brought back into line, but the situation went totally pear shaped a week later. The phone rang at 00.30 on the Saturday night and I wearily answered, it was Frank Bell.

"Jack, John Hawkins reports that Lewis has just finished drift netting up our end and is on his way back, we'll come round to Gillys head and meet you on site"

It took me a few minutes to digest the news before quickly leaving for the rendezvous; I also arranged to have Phil Lancaster meet me there too. I arrived at Gillys Head at 01.20, where Frank and John already stood waiting, Phil arrived a couple of minutes after me.

John Hawkins outlined how he had watched Eddie's boat netting up west, so a stop and search when he returned should take him nicely by surprise. Lewis could launch and recover a boat on the beach by Gillys Head, therefore all we had to do was wait.

Lewis returned on the top of the tide just after 02.00 right into our arms, John Hawkins had been very quiet all evening, a fact that had gone unnoticed up until then. Lewis was stopped as he returned up the beach by tractor; he was totally compliant if a bit cocky. Phil and John searched the boat contents thoroughly including all the nets, but only found a decent haul of Bass, plus a few cod. I was all for leaving until an amazing incident occurred, John Hawkins suddenly without warning dived across from God knows where and jumped on Eddie Lewis effing and blinding in the process.

"Yu bastard I naa thas gitten fish, where ave yu hidden the fuckin things"

We all jumped in to rescue Eddie at this point, who was ready to take John on by now and a more even match would have been hard to find in all probability. I used all my diplomatic powers to diffuse the situation ensuring Frank got John the hell out of there and away back to west Cumbria, which was the best place for him as far as I was concerned.

Needless to say an in house enquiry was soon implemented and John Hawkins was suspended. I had to eat humble pie with Eddie Lewis big style to stop him going for a prosecution, why he didn't in the end may have been down to the fact that he had got away Scot free from the incident. I think maybe we were unlucky that night and although Eddie hadn't caught any sea trout on that sortie he easily could have.

John Hawkins went on long term sick and generally lost the plot in the end, so six months later he was sacked. He was the only Bailiff to suffer this fate since Reg Smith and company all those years earlier, and also from the same area of course.

Eddie Lewis was searched again on several occasions, but apart from a warning about some of the mesh sizes in his nets from Martin Black no offence was ever detected. Lewis is still fishing to this day since retiring from Paniclow and is now fully registered with Defra.

Late in 1995 news came through that our fisheries world was to be turned upside down once again due to major reorganisation, apparently the NRA was to be disbanded altogether and become part of a new bigger organisation called the Environment Agency. The EA as it is usually known would take in the all Government run waste regulatory bodies and the Inspectorate of pollution alongside the present functions of the NRA. The process caused valuable staff time to be taken up adjusting to the new set up until inauguration day finally happened on April 1st 1996.

34

BAILIFF, POACHER, FARMER, SPY

Pat Garner was a Farmer from Brockdale bridge farm who in previous years had always kept an eye on the R Brock close to home and indeed tipped me off on several occasions; unfortunately Pat went and got caught poaching himself one Friday night in September 96. This was a huge disappointment to me and turned out to be a repeat of the Frankie Wilson case back in 1981, funny how history repeats itself, it also looked like Pat had probably been poaching his own farm over the years as well as grassing up others. Glen Bracken caught him red handed lamping during the back end up in Borrowdale, he had taken his teenage daughter of all people. Four stale looking sea trout were already in the bag when the pair felt the wrath of Glen.

The oddest thing about this case came about a week later, when out of the blue Pat phoned me in a bit of a state.

"Jack I needs tu see yu, can yu come up fairly soon like?"

He whispered down the phone in a sort of furtive manner, it was quite mysterious, yet intriguing at the same time. I was a bit concerned; after all I didn't want to tread on Glen's toes, nevertheless my curiosity got the better of me,

"Aye Pat I suppose I could, but I won't be able to help with what happened, you realise that don't you?"

Pat's reply was again said in a soft manner,

"Aye fair enough, but I must si thee"

I arranged to visit Pat's farm later the same afternoon, but before setting off I informed Glen about the latest turn of events and we both wondered what could possibly be on Pat's mind.

The beck had come up overnight so there was nothing taking any hurt and a quick visit to the weir in Brockley was part of my schedule when I set off. I arrived at the weir on a beautiful late September Saturday to find the usual group of spectators watching the salmon running. I spent five minutes with Johnny Jones from Stanwick admiring the fish on view when my attention was switched to an incident unfolding under the weir. Folk were shouting and pointing at the white water gushing under the weir from the previous night's rain. I recognised Ben "fingers" Jackson pointing in the water and feared the worst, his wife and kids were also there screaming at this point. The next thing I knew Fingers was actually trying to walk across the weir, which was obviously too high for such a manoeuvre, but why? That was the question I asked myself.

The answer came from Johnny,

"Looks yu Jack, his dogs int water"

Indeed he was correct, a golden retriever was desperately fighting to swim across the river at the top side of the weir, I watched in horror as the poor animal was easily swept over in the swift current. People screamed as events unfolded, but the dog vanished in the turbulent mass, Fingers came back and then urged on by the crowd started to wade across, only this time under the weir itself. I raced to the scene just in time to see Fingers loose his grip and flounder in the foam, a bystander hurled a life belt into the water, but Fingers couldn't reach it, I could see he was weakening. The same man tried again and this time he just about grabbed it, everyone piled in to pull him ashore. Ben Jackson was so exhausted when he finally landed safely ashore that an ambulance had to be called. Paramedics successfully sorted Fingers out, but alas the dog was a goner, I recovered the poor beast washed up at Mill Bridge. That was a dramatic start to my afternoon, when although a dog drowned a mans life was nearly lost as a consequence.

I had to leave the unhappy scene rather quickly to make Pat Garners farm by 15.00 and on arrival my newly cleaned car was subject to a very shitty farm yard. I walked tentatively across the yard in ankle deep manure, saturated by the previous night's rain. A grubby Springer spaniel accompanied me to Pat's front door, which just happened to be a brand new Everest white double glazed job. The door would have been very impressive if not for the blatant open holes in the wall next to the door frame, which totally defeated the object. I knocked hard on the glass; the spaniel vigorously wagged its ample tail expectantly. Pat answered and beckoned me in with a gesture to wipe my feet, while the dog left a trail of shit across to a blazing coal fire. None of the dog's actions fazed anyone in the room including Pat's formidable wife, however the clandestine actions of everyone concerned were starting to irritate me.

"What can I help you with Pat?"

He stared back at me with his finger to his mouth in a motion to remain silent, then whispered,

"Follow me Mr. Carter"

I was then taken back outside and led across to an out barn at the other side of the yard. Once inside Pat relaxed and we sat down on some hay bales.

"Mr. Carter you know obviously we was pulled tuther night, well what I wants to know is, how did they know, I mean how could they know we was up there?"

I was as bemused as he seemed to be,

"What do you mean Pat?, I don't get it"

Pat looked around and started to whisper once again,

"Mr. Carter I fetched us tut Barn cos I'm pretty sure the phone is bugged"

I stared back in disbelief; the man actually thought big brother was listening in...surely not?

I laughed out loud, I couldn't help myself,

"Come off it Pat, who the hells going to bug your bleadin farmhouse for Christ's sake?"

Pat was infuriated and stuck to his story,

"They must av, no other explanation for it; I've bin goin up yon valley fur years, never sin yon Becky once"

I gave him the answer he didn't want to hear,

"You've just got caught Pat, that's top and bottom of it, and whatsmore you've had it coming by all accounts"

I was in danger of losing my rag, but the thought of Pats family whispering their way around the house rather made up for the fact that he had blatantly admitted poaching Borrowdale for years undetected. I was about to leave when a wicked thought went across my mind.

"You had better check all your buildings Pat, I believe MAFF sometimes keep a check on folk, but you didn't hear it from me, alright"

Pat froze with open mouth; he was in no state to disbelieve me

I left him to it with something relevant to ponder.

35

THE SILLY SEASON

The type of poacher encountered over the years in south lakes had mostly been locals, or Lancashire based gangs and individuals, however in the ever changing world of crime nothing stays the same and one gang encountered on the River Leven proved a different breed altogether. In August 97 Richard Teasdale discovered a family outing with a difference while on his daily coverage on the lower beat. It was a very hot day with many people taking to the rivers to cool off. I always called it the silly season due to the shear number of people involved. My phone was always red hot during those conditions and usually most calls were false alarms, a group of innocent bathers could easily be mistaken for poachers by those who considered any bare flesh in the water to be involved in some form of illegal activity. Of course it worked both ways with some poachers actually mingling with bathers, so confusion usually reigned during those periods. The classic example had been Cliff Woof who hid a sea trout in his push chair in the course of a family picnic; the unfortunate fish had been tickled in the weeds at Gilbertsfield. I only got to know because a member of the public had witnessed the event and phoned the police.

Richard Teasdale was walking past a similar scene with women and kids picnicking on the bank, but alert as ever he spotted a net across the full width of the river close to two men already stripped off and swimming. Richard kept his cool and carried on walking back to his van, then called me up on his mobile.

I immediately called the police as everyone else was scattered round the county and half an hour later I was at the scene. Two Bobbies from Traffic arrived, followed soon afterwards by John Watson. The plan was simple; they were in a cul-de-sac so all we needed to do was wander down and hopefully catch them red handed. Inevitably it didn't pan out that way, the gang of three women, three men, and various toddlers were apprehended coming away from the river soon after we set off as a group. I stopped them assisted by the two Bobbies and then sent John Watson and Richard on ahead to hopefully find some evidence. A large white box van was the sanctuary awaiting our captives, but the police intervened just as the first man put his key in the lock. A thorough search then commenced as a ploy by us to buy the valuable time we needed. A mere ten minutes elapsed before the dulcet tones of John Watson spouted from my handset.

"Mike 1 from Mike 2 we have found the net and a sack with seven salmon in, not only that two face masks, and yep there are net marks on the fish"

I turned to the group who so far had remained very quiet, the first guy met me head on, and he was a handy looking lad with an Everton FC tattoo on his forearm and not to be messed with. It was obvious he put two and two together after overhearing the radio message.

"You're not blamin us for that lot, no fuckin way pal"

His scouse accent sent the usual alarm bells ringing, what was a bunch of scousers doing in the River Leven. The two police officers returned from the van, which was clean apparently, so I booked all three men amidst some abuse from the hard faced women keen to make my life as uncomfortable as possible. I am convinced those guys would have kicked off big style if the police hadn't been there, they looked the type to go to whatever length it took to evade being identified. It turned out Birkenhead was where they called home and the best place for them as far as I was concerned. The circumstantial evidence found was more than enough or so I thought, especially with Richard Teasdale's earlier sighting.

The group was up at Lancaster Magistrates court later that year in October, but a few days prior to the trial another incident occurred reflecting the disturbing change in society associated with the modern world.

The lower section of the River Leven was fished by a syndicate consisting almost entirely of worldly senior citizens who gathered daily purely to fish and enjoy each others company. They didn't catch a great deal as a rule, a fact that caused some grumpiness at times, although even if they didn't admit it the river was a second home and a welcome break from the nagging wife. The day in question had three of these Gentlemen in situe quietly fishing and minding their own business. It was 11.00 when a minibus pulled up by the fishing hut. In it was a group of individuals who disembarked and then went on to the river bank to confront our three Gents. The events that followed were despicable to say the least because a group of men in their twenties harassed and intimidated three old men all in their eighties culminating in physical abuse. One old lad had his rod snatched from his hands then snapped and thrown in the river. Why did this occur? Hunt saboteurs on the loose that's why! The group was a bunch originally on a day out to protest at a meet of the Lunesdale fox hounds, except the hunt had been cancelled so they were simply roaming around Lakeland looking for some innocent people to harass. The group eventually left leaving the three old men frightened and very pissed off. The police never did catch the culprits who were long gone before the alarm was raised.

The only good that resulted from the episode came via a local tackle shop who generously donated a new rod to the old guy whose own was smashed. It's a shame that hunt saboteurs and animal rights protesters are so misguided, anglers or any pursuer of game are nine times out of ten some of the best protectors of habitat and wildlife there is.

The trial of the Birkenhead three was a bad day at Black rock if ever there was one, not only did they defend themselves courtesy of a duty solicitor, they got off Scot free. The Magistrates decided in their favour that not enough evidence existed to link them conclusively with the fish and nets, matters were not helped by tactics of intimidation in the court waiting room before the trial. I have never understood why this is allowed in courts both then and today.

1997 also saw Danny O'Hare go down hill fast; he had been diagnosed with cancer in the spring and by the summer was so bad he was in a Hospice at Lancaster. I think he had some type of brain tumor. Luck had never shone down favourably on Danny, but even during his illness he stayed amazingly cheerful. I visited him several times in the Hospice and could only watch him fading away. Poor old Danny had bought a new bungalow in Brockley, where he moved into for his final weeks, he died a few days after Princess Diana, a boy named Sue came to the funeral looking like a transvestite and that's the last time I ever saw shim.

36

THE HOLE IN THE FENCE GANG

1998 Was uneventful regarding poaching, but remarkable for crime. In April Croftgill stores fell victim to a daring raid during the middle of the night, resulting in the theft of both our quad bikes, two electric fishing generators and our one and only water pump. A gang of thieves had parked a vehicle and trailer in a field opposite the store then smashed a way in to the building through the roof leaving a trail of mayhem behind them. The alarm had gone off but being in such an isolated spot nobody heard the damn thing until it was too late. I was roused at 5am by the police who had been tipped off by a milkman. On my arrival I could see that the gates had been forced open in the smash and grab raid. The Environment Agency like all its predecessors does not insure equipment due to very high premiums, so the loss was probably in excess of £12000, wiped off in one go. I made certain that the store was repaired and the doors fortified like Fort Knox. We had also recently acquired additional storage for our boat nearby at Bank House the main flood defence depot in Brockley, so I decided to switch the usage and keep the boat at Croftgill in future. Two brand new ATV bikes arrived in June just in time for the busy season out in the bay. Our storage at Bank House consisted of three shipping containers I had recently purchased at Liverpool and the security was much better, nevertheless I was becoming a bit nervous after the Croftgill attack. It then turned out that my fears were justified when Croftgill was raided a second time, but fortunately nicking the boat was either beyond them or they just didn't want it. The thieves broke in through the roof on that occasion also. I subsequently strengthened the locks on the containers at Bank House depot as well just in case, I really was becoming paranoid. The extra measures proved vital when the Bridge House depot also suffered a raid in early July. Once again small plant disappeared as well as a 4X4 and trailer, all being the property of our flood defence team; however no fisheries gear was taken thanks to the armoured locking arrangements on the containers. Visible signs of their efforts to do so could clearly be seen. The thieves had ram raided the main gate to gain entry, so from that day on a JCB was parked across the gate. This gang of thieves were rumoured to be from the Barrow area according to Police intelligence, they specialised in small plant mainly and ATV bikes obviously, which by all accounts are very desirable. Rumours were flying around all over concerning all aspects of the break ins, the favourite and most likely seemed to favour the Irish connection. Evidently a lot of stuff was dismantled or changed significantly, then shipped to the Emerald Isle, who knows? Personally I am no wiser to this day. The situation worsened when the Bridge House stores were robbed again the very next night, access was gained this time by driving through the next field and cutting a hole in the chain link fence. A very expensive power washer was taken from a brick building, which required considerable effort on the part of the thieves not least because it was bolted into solid concrete. Thankfully our quads remained safely within the containers which didn't prevent me worrying to such an extent I decided action was needed. The Police involvement in all this involved as many traffic car visits that could be permitted, which varied a great deal. The ease with which the thieves were gaining access without any hint of detection made me not only even more paranoid, but puzzled as well, could it be an inside job?

I had no one person in mind and still haven't to this day, however I went to Jean Slater's office and outlined a plan. I obtained her backing to use my team to stake out Bridge House depot through the night and catch these bastards before we lost any more quads or gear. I informed the Police of my plan and agreed to ring them immediately anyone showed up. I set up a Rota to stake out the depot from midnight to 06.00, Operation Kingfisher was launched at midnight on August 31st. I did six hours with Phil Lancaster, one of us hid in a copse close to the depot and the other cruised around or waited some distance away in a vehicle. We did two nights then swapped with John Watson and Billy Ferguson, a week went by and we never saw a thing. I decided to give it two more nights over the weekend, and then call it quits. On the evening of the Saturday John Watson phoned at 23.50.

"Guess what Jack?"

I waited on baited breath,

"We've been done over again; the bastards have come through the fence on the other side this time"

I couldn't believe what I was hearing, how could this be? I suspected then and I still do today that some sort of inside information was passed to who ever was responsible.

For me it was too much of a coincidence, after staking the place out like numbskulls for a week the buggers had nipped in prior to our shift commencing.

The only saving grace was the remarkable fact that the ATV bikes were once again still unscathed, however three outboard motors were missing from the first container. It was plain to see acetylene cutting gear had been used to cut the lock. I don't know why they didn't carry on; maybe and most likely they were disturbed. That was that, I was left totally frustrated and no nearer to this day of knowing who was responsible.

Thefts of quads and small plant has continued in south lakes since that time, mostly from Farmers or small businesses and to my knowledge very few convictions have occurred. The alarm systems now in place at both Croftgill and Bridge House are very sophisticated as is the new fencing around the perimeter.

37

JOHNNY JONES AND THE WILD WEST

Johnny Jones was and still is just about the nicest and straightest angler I have had dealings with on the river during my entire fisheries career. Johnny was as keen as anyone fishing at every opportunity using all methods; his specialty is fly fishing for salmon and sea trout at which he is the master. Johnny got divorced some years back and rumour has it his wife just couldn't compete with his passion for angling, not to mention the cost of all his ever changing fishing tackle. The only instance I can recall that Johnny broke the rules came during the Mafia years at Stanwick trough. It was one of those crazy days when fish were coming out left right and centre, I had been up river all day with Big Don and called in at the trough on the way home. It was October 17th one day after the start of the close season for sea trout. Don and I walked on to the bridge at Stanwick to look down at who was in attendance, when out of the undergrowth who should appear but Johnny holding a very dark coloured cock sea trout, which he proudly held aloft for inspection.

"Look yu here lads what does yu think of this beauty?"

I glanced at Don who like myself realised we had a situation here.

"Aye Johnny that's a decent cock fish alright, I take it you've just caught it yourself"

He was oblivious poor bloke; instead his grin was from ear to ear,

"Aye I have just gitten him on worm Jack"

He then started to wave the fish about for all to survey, so I quickly ushered him back into the bushes and out of sight.

"It's a flaming sea trout Johnny"

"Well I know that for Christ sake Jack don't I, what's up like?

Don intervened grinning broadly,

"Aren't they out of season now Johnny?"

Johnny took a sharp intake and gasped, the penny dropped more like a lead weight than anything,

"Oh shit, Oh bugger"

That was the best he could come up with at the time; he was in shock, poor old lad.

Johnny had never even had a parking fine and here he was nabbed red handed. Don looked at me reading my mind and obviously thinking what I was thinking.

"Take the bugger out of sight Johnny, get lost with the thing, we haven't seen it alright"

He didn't need telling twice and disappeared through the undergrowth in the blink of an eye.

Johnny Jones moved into a riverside cottage by the falls at Long dub, he rented the property from Broxton Hall and it was all very cosy. Johnny fished the long dub and became a volunteer warden in the park. His cottage became a pit stop for Bailiffs where a brew and a Tunnocks wafer were always on offer. Johnny was always first to know about anything happening on the river, whether it be who had caught what fish and how big, or just some scandal amongst anglers. Living on the river as he did was not unlike my own situation by The Green in Brockley, I was never quite off duty, a fact that eventually led me to move to another part of the town and well out of site of the beck.

The new millennium dawned and it was during that first year Johnny Jones played a blinder, I personally suffered a long bout of sickness due to a condition known as "Menieres disease" which started in 1999, originally and wrongly diagnosed as Labyrinthitis. I don't recommend this affliction to anyone and unfortunately I have suffered regularly since that year. In July 2000 however I was phoned up by Johnny on a red hot July afternoon just after 14.00, he sounded out of breath and very concerned,

"Jack lad you'd better get down here there's some blokes in Long dub poaching, I've told em to bugger off, but they reckon they're only swimming. One said that they've walked up through the Park Jack. I really think you need to get down here"

"Right Johnny keep your head down and Ill have a look",

Now grand bloke as he was, Johnny often phoned with bits of info, usually car numbers or suspicious individuals sniffing around the beck, but more often than not it all came to nothing. I decided on this occasion as was usually the case to go and investigate just in case, I gathered all my necessities which took me longer than usual due to my recent sick leave, in fact it was my first day back at work. I approached long dub from the wood on the east side leaving my vehicle up at the top of Broxton Park. The wood was knee deep in brambles and I only had shorts on, so some care was needed. It took me a while to get a decent view of the pool and it was about 15.00 when finally I raised my binnocs. My legs were smarting and scratched to hell as I scanned the pool, the view that greeted me made my whole body stiffen. Walking through and across the middle of long dub was a man carrying two large fish, he wore shorts and a t-shirt and had one fish held in each hand with fingers through the gill chambers. I watched as he hid them in the grass on the right bank before returning in the same direction. I left immediately to return to my car, where I phoned the Police at Brockley and as ever got a promise of swift help. I then drove round to Stanwick Bridge and waited. Less than ten minutes went by before PC Dave Martin landed up, Dave was what they now class as a wildlife and countryside Officer and we had already worked together a few times. Billy Ferguson also landed up, so the three of us set off on foot carefully down the lane to long dub. I was still suffering balance problems at the time so I approached with some trepidation; nevertheless we got to the wall overlooking the pool from the road undetected.

A quick assessment of the situation determined three men in total including one still in the water wearing a face mask; a second man was on the rocks above the waterfall and the third on the far bank. The man in the face mask dived right under the falls in the white water, which was only possible due to low flows. I gestured to Dave Martin indicating we move in fairly sharpish, he nodded as did Billy. Together we dashed down to the beck,

"Water Bailiff, come out please"

The man on the far bank began walking away, but Dave Martin soon reeled him in, the guy in the mask obviously dropped something in the water before coming out. He was very large, ugly and not a pretty sight, the final man was also in the pool at this point and inviting Billy to come in and get him. Finally we got three dripping wet poachers lined up on the road. Swift checks by the Police revealed they were from Egremont up the west coast, or the "Wild West" as we referred to it. A Large Police van swiftly came and transported them off to the nick in Brockley, while we remained to find the fish. With surprising difficulty I discovered five salmon hidden in the grass complete with Gaff marks, which prompted me to suggest that maybe the Police scuba diving unit might like some practice. Two hours later after an exhaustive effort one of the Police divers located a shiny gaff under the falls, holding it triumphantly aloft. Traffic cops had also located a vehicle down at Broxton Hall that checked out to the crew now in custody. I made a decision there and then to seize the vehicle, but obviously I needed the keys. We all left the scene to regroup back at the Police station, where our prisoners were booked and processed before I broke the news about the car. The big guy went apeshit to say the least, so I was thankful he was locked up at that point. I went with Billy to bring home the green Mondeo left by the gang, it is a strange feeling driving somebody else's vehicle in such a situation as that, but by 18.30 the car was locked up and out of sight at Bridge House depot. A week later I was given the news that Roger Mcbane had ordered the car to be returned, needless to say I wasn't happy and I was on the phone to Roger all ready to blow my top. Roger explained that the vehicle was registered to the girlfriend of the big guy therefore we had no legal grounds to keep hold of it. The only thing I insisted upon was, that I personally wouldn't hand it back, so Jean Slater got the unenviable task herself. By all accounts this proved rather intimidating even though Frank Bell acted as bodyguard.

The trial at Barrow later in the backend was straightforward enough, despite several adjournments that had wasted everyone's time. This was due to the defendants indicating they would plead not guilty, only to then change the plea to guilty on the day of the trial. This practice was quite common amongst poachers purely as a buggeration factor on their part. It did them few favours fortunately because each man was fined £300 each plus £100 cost as well. That was a great result even though they hissed and spat at me on leaving the court, I just hope I never bump into them ever again.

Johnny Jones was made up of course and still gives me tip offs to this day and I still call in for a brew and Tunnock.

38

THE FINAL FURLONG

My career as a Fisheries Officer is nearing the end as I head towards calling it a day at 60, I once had ideas of retiring at 55 but of course this was wishful thinking on my part. I still enjoy the job immensely despite being surrounded by hungry younger colleagues of which some are obviously keener than others, but that's human nature I suppose. I can remember back in the seventies analysing several of the over fifty employees and peers who moaned and groaned about life in general. I can recollect Hank as a typical example, always looking for an easy ride and totally cynical about company policy or expectations. I always told myself that I would never become like that, but I guess that's life and it creeps up on you. The exception to this mindset was poor old Joe Marwood who was as keen on his last day as he had been on his first, perhaps it was old fashioned moral values that lasted longer. Joe was a fine example to anyone keen to do a job well and to also enjoy it.

Cliff Woof's Father poached before him and was still just about around when I first started, when his own eldest son also poached it was hardly a surprise, but when Cliffs own son Jamie arrived on the scene it was not in circumstances anyone expected. I received a telephone call from Jean Slater that presented me with a bit of a dilemma,

"Jack I've had Queen Mary's School on the phone wanting placements for a weeks work experience, can you help?"

I didn't react well to the proposal, mainly due to past experiences when I had taken on some right Muppets. I never considered taking kids into areas of possible poaching as a good idea any way. I didn't want to be too cynical however, so reluctantly put my name forward. Jean said she would relay my acceptance back to the school. The next day she was back on the phone,

"Jack its Cliff Woofs lad Jamie!"

I nearly crashed the car,

"What? Oh no, hang on a minute, I can't can I?"

Jean giggled mischievously down the phone,

"Well who knows he may be perfectly okay, surely everyone should be given a chance Jack, come on for Christ's sake"

So it was, Jamie Woof was allotted a week with Fisheries, which went very well as it turned out. Jamie was an affable lad of fifteen going on twelve, but despite his childish ways he was also well clued up on hunting and fishing. Jamie and I had a mutual love of dogs and he never shut up about taking his Lurcher lamping at night for rabbits and hares. Jamie never shut up at all in fact, so I got a useful insight of what living with a real poachers family was really like. I began to bond with Jamie finding him surprisingly intelligent and keen. By the end of the week I had almost convinced myself he would make a Becky himself one day. I set a precedent with Jamie by taking him into our world, showing him the tricks of our trade, even into the confines of Croftgill and the Office, a line that no poachers or their relatives had ever crossed ever before. Jamie was also a keen Angler regularly seen on Brockley town stretch, which all led me to believe I had helped to guide him down a straight path and making me feel good in the process.

During 2001 the Environment Agency had another bash at performing the only activity it does consistently, which was to reorganise and change things. The process this time was affectionately called B.R.I.T.E, which stands for better regulation in the environment, I believe there was also ULTRA BRITE, I can't say for sure what that meant, but maybe "Usually Likes To Run Away! "Who knows? Once again due to a sterling effort by Roger Mcbane Fisheries remained in tact despite the inevitable reductions in funding.

My team was amalgamated with South west Cumbria and Jean Slater very wisely bailed out to a job in Policy and process. The writing was very much on the wall, the vacant team leader's job she left behind was one I felt I should try for, but deep down I wasn't confident, what with all the young talent around bursting with qualifications. My time for progression had been and gone as I soon found out, a young whiz kid got the post complete with his corporate head on his corporate shoulders. In fact after a dodgy start before his sense of humour was located he was a pain in the arse. To his credit though he learned very quickly and made an excellent team leader before moving on in his quest to rule the world.

Further cuts to funding have put more pressure on Fisheries resulting in several early retirements which I have also been offered recently, so I'm off to grab the proverbial carrot at the end of the equally proverbial stick.

In the summer of 2005 Jamie Woof was caught by Billy Ferguson lamping the river at Stoneybase pool, this inevitably proved to be the start of his career in poaching, drugs and crime… unlike the Agency some things never change.

****

The persons described in this book are based partly on real characters of different name, but are not definitive descriptions of act ual personalities and their actions although based on factual events they do not in anyway truly reflect known individual's actions. Some place names have been changed to facilitate the storyline.